Joyce Grenfell was born Joyce Phipps, daughter of the youngest of the beautiful American Langhorne sisters, of whom the most celebrated was Nancy, Lady Astor.

Her girlhood, spent on the fringes of the famous Cliveden set among such men as George Bernard Shaw and Noel Coward, spanned the twenties, but it was not until 1938, at a dinner party, that she gave an impromptu imitation of a Women's Institute speaker and discovered her genius for dramatic monologue.

Also by Joyce Grenfell in Futura:

Joyce Grenfell
Katharine Moore

AN INVISIBLE
FRIENDSHIP

An exchange of letters 1957–1979

Futura

A Futura Book

First published in Great Britain in 1981 by
Macmillan London Limited, London and Basingstoke

First Futura edition 1982
Reprinted 1988, 1990, 1991

ISBN 0 7088 4904 0

Typeset by Rowland Phototypesetting Ltd
Bury St Edmunds, Suffolk
Printed and bound in Great Britain by
BPCC Hazell Books
Aylesbury, Bucks, England
Member of BPCC Ltd.

Futura Publications
A Division of
Macdonald & Co (Publishers) Ltd
165 Great Dover Street
London SE1 4YA

A member of Maxwell Macmillan Publishing Corporation

Introduction

In 1957 I heard Joyce Grenfell quote a verse by Professor Walter Raleigh in a radio programme:

> 'I wish I loved the Human Race;
> I wish I loved its silly face;
> I wish I liked the way it walks;
> I wish I liked the way it talks;
> And when I'm introduced to one
> I wish I thought *What jolly fun!*'

She commented: 'I do not know who this Professor Raleigh was, but he must have been rather a miserable misanthrope.'

Remembering him as a much-loved lecturer and tutor at Oxford, I could not quite bear this, so I ventured to write to her and enclosed two other poems of his of a very different nature. By return I received a characteristic reply, and this was the beginning of a pen friendship of twenty-two years. We agreed long ago not to meet, we liked it better that way. She has referred to this friendship in the second volume of her autobiography: 'I have a pen-friend whom I have never seen . . . We share a taste for reading, the eternal pleasure of seasons, music, sounds and sights, and for people who pleasantly surprise us by their diversity. We seem to agree in some fundamental ideas and are interested in each other's lives.' For myself, her letters, growing in length and intimacy, were a great treat. They are such good letters and cover such a considerable stretch of years that I feel I would like to share with others this record of an unusual kind of friendship, which perhaps also may add something more to the appreciation of a singularly generous and lovable personality.

A year ago Joyce sent back to me a packet of some of my own letters 'for my grandchildren'. I certainly did not originally intend to publish any of these, but a friendship is a reciprocal affair, and so I have been persuaded to include those of my letters that are available as providing an interchange of references and comments, thus making the book a more complete record of this invisible friendship.

K.M.

1957

5 February   *Flat 8, Elm Park Gardens, Chelsea, S.W.10*

Dear Mrs Moore,

It was so nice of you to write as you did, and I love *both* the
Raleigh poems. I'd no idea. I love him from now on.

I expect you are right about 'I wish I loved the Human
Race' being written in an off moment. I suspect, too, he was
justifiably pleased with the pleasant flow of the first line
even if the 'wish' was never a sincere one!

Again thank you for writing. I am gratefully yours

Joyce Grenfell

30 October   *Hill House, Seal Hollow Road, Sevenoaks, Kent*

Dear Joyce Grenfell,

I wrote to you some time ago about Professor Walter
Raleigh and sent you a copy of some of his poems and had a
very nice reply from you. That is by way of placing me.

Now I just want to say 'thank you'. I was at Hammer-
smith for your show last week and enjoyed you more than
ever. For one thing there was more of you – I spared the
dancers from the programme very happily. Then, I consider you were quite at your best. Shirley's Girl Friend
excelled herself, and of the other sketches I especially liked
'Committee', 'Counter-wise', 'Songs my Mother Taught
me' and 'Boat Train', all very different and all quite satisfying and delightful – the last, something more. I also
appreciated the *truth* of the song 'Time' (I am now in the

third stage of the song!). I do think though that the present moment of the old contains all the past as well, which is as vividly present *as* the present and makes it marvellously rich, 'Thank the Lord'.

Anyway the whole entertainment was *real* entertainment and took me out of a rather trying present and even more trying probable immediate future, giving me two hours' pure pleasure and a good deal of retrospective enjoyment as well.

I do think critics today are often lacking in a sense of enjoyment. They seem to want everyone to be angry or cynical or analytical or just plain miserable. Entertainment is relegated to the silly and insipid musical or to thrillers. That is why you are so refreshing. Thank you again.

Your sincerely

Katherine Moore (Mrs H. Moore)

P.S. There was a wonderful number on Enid Blyton (not by that name) in your last show. I can't remember what it is called and fear it isn't recorded on the long-playing record of 'Joyce Grenfell Requests the Pleasure'. I suppose there isn't a recording of it in existence?

31 October   *Elm Park Gardens*

Dear Mrs Moore,

How nice of you to write. Thank you very much. I'm so glad you liked 'Time', for it is one of my favourites. I agree with you about 'now' containing the past, for of course there is *only* 'now' and that holds the past, present and future. In fact no time – or only eternity. I always find it strange that people are afraid of the thought of eternity. Why should it be awful? Why not perfection? It is, clearly, a spiritual state, and as such has no conflicts – for I take it that harmony is the rule and harmony is never dull. It is simply a human supposition that peace would be all ease and nullity. I have an idea peace is gloriously un-dull but cannot be perceived by the *human* mind, only by the spiritual awareness of the Divine Mind.

8

But I'm out of my depth!

I'm afraid the 'Writer of Children's Books' *isn't* recorded. I'm not very keen on making records of monologues if I am still using them. They seem to go round and round and wear themselves out that way. I still do that one in my repertoire when I tour.

Again thank you so very much for all your kind remarks.

Yours sincerely,

Joyce Grenfell

5 November   *Hill House*

Dear Joyce Grenfell,

I can't resist writing to you again, but *please* don't think you have to answer. It is just that I want to go on with the conversation about time and eternity instead of doing other things. I so nearly brought eternity into my first letter and then thought 'better not perhaps'; and then you said more or less what had been in my mind.

I think people make the mistake of thinking of eternity in terms of quantity – endless time, instead of quality – perfect time, and that's why they fear it. Because eternity is perfect time it is timeless, as it is fulfilled and whole – in short, as you say, perfection and overflowing with peace or harmony or divine energy (however one tries to express the inexpressible) in a way we can't apprehend, though we *do* experience 'bright shoots of everlastingness' here and now. I suppose the timelessness one feels in great art is one of the hallmarks of its greatness; and, to get back to your old lady, the timeless moment of old age is another 'shadow of eternity'. Of course one is immediately out of one's depth when one begins to think about such a subject, but how dreadful it would be to have to keep in one's depth.

I do hope you have enjoyed your season as much as your audiences, I can think of no nicer wish for you. Of course I see your point about the records. I hope there will be a recording of 'A Miscellany' one day, including 'Time'.

My husband and I have just acquired a record player and

9

are glorying in it and are slowly collecting records. Our last was Dennis Brain playing Mozart's Horn Concerto. There is plenty of eternity there.

Yours sincerely

Katharine Moore

29 December   *Elm Park Gardens*

Dear Mrs Moore,

Thank you for your Christmas card and for your second letter – I've wanted to write to you ever since it came but there was always a pile of duty letters and I never got down to pleasure ones till now. (That doesn't read grammatically but you will know what I mean.)

I did like what you said about eternity being quality and not quantity – 'perfect time'. I was asked to do a four-minute talk on Woman's Hour for Christmas Eve about what makes me laugh, cry and think, and in it I found myself saying that about eternity, in reference to crying at the sight of happiness. It seems to me *that* is a foretaste of eternity – or a *present* taste, of course.

During the last week of November I recorded a long-playing record for H.M.V., and 'Time' is on it. I believe it is coming out late in January.

We had a quiet and lovely Christmas in the country with cousins of mine and their two nice children. It was a warm house; it was possible to sit and sew; we discussed such things as time and progress and laughed a good deal as we went. It was a refreshing two days.

Now I'm sorting out and preparing to go away to Canada and America. Last time when I had a long tour to do I discovered the wonder of staying still and letting the journey go round me! I'm out of practice but I'll get in to it again. I don't like leaving home; still, returning is good. And I have a nice brother and his wife with two really fascinating children of three and a half and one and a half, so I have lots to look forward to. But I'll miss the spring here.

Not till late May can I get back. I hope you have a good 1958 and I send you wishes for it.

All good wishes, Yours sincerely,

Joyce Grenfell

31 December   *Hill House*

Dear Joyce Grenfell,

Your letter this morning was such an unexpected pleasure that I must write and thank you for it and send you my very warm wishes for 1958 and for your tour in Canada and America. I know it is a tiresome habit to reply by return, but I can't resist it sometimes. If I wait the ardour cools. Besides I want to catch the New Year and you, and I don't know when you start. Besides, again, it is not as if I expected or even wished for a reply this time. Also it happens to be my youngest and nicest grandchild's third birthday today, *and* I've just heard that, instead of going into hospital next Monday for an unpleasant and protracted operation (the third for the same trouble) it is being deferred because I have been so much better for the past month. So I am happy and must celebrate, which I shall do by writing to you. It gives me such a marvellous feeling of wealth (of time) not to be going into hospital that I can afford to write unnecessary letters with the Christmas thank-you post still half done. Life is so entrancingly unexpected, and it is so odd to be carrying on a correspondence with you about eternity! I have learned some more about it, I think, since I have been having bouts of acute pain coming quite suddenly and knocking me out of active life for the time being. There has been a revelation about the quality of ordinary everyday experiences, that these ordinary moments, too, can become glorious. Also I think I have learned how everything exists in its own right and its essence can't be changed. I mean one would imagine pain and loss would spoil what has been, but it can't, because glory, once having existed, can't be 'unglorified' – there is eternity cropping up again. Aren't paradoxes interesting? In a sense the insecurity caused by pain and illness have taught me a new sort of security, just as you have learned the art of staying still in your crowded and journeying life.

I am glad you had a restful Christmas. I enjoyed mine, because I felt well and able to cope with a largish family party, though Easter is my favourite festival.

I am sorry you will be away for so long. I had hoped perhaps I might see you in the audience at *Idomeneo* done by the Impresario Society at St Pancras Town Hall in March. I saw you there at the *Clemency of Titus* last year. I enjoy these productions especially because so much true devotion to opera goes into producing them.

Thank you for your Christmas Eve broadcast – a great refreshment. Thank you too for telling me about your record. I shall get it.

I really ought to stop now. Goodbye. May you have nice peaceful 'still' journeys, perfect audiences and a lovely time with your brother and his family, and come safely back to us in May, for your debtors here can't do without you.

Yours sincerely

Katharine Moore

1958

Dear Mrs Moore,

    Do you know Thomas Traherne's poems? What I've seen
I find *wonderful*. From something you said in your letter
about essence made me think at once of this poem.

> My naked simple Life was I;
> That Act so strongly shin'd
> Upon the Earth, the Sea, and the Sky,
> It was Substance of the Mind;
>   The Sence itself was I.
> I felt no Dross nor Matter in my Soul,
> No Brims nor Borders such as in a Bowl
> We see: My Essence was *Capacity*.
>
> *That* felt all things;
> The thought that springs
> Therefrom's its Self; it hath no other Wings
> To spread abroad, nor Eyes to see,
>   No pair of hands to feel,
>   Nor knees to kneel:
> But being Simple, like the Deity,
>   In its own Centre is a sphere,
> Not shut up here, but ev'rywhere.
>
>   Thomas Traherne

    I came upon it a few years ago in a Faber anthology called
The Testament of Immortality, and it has been a constant light
in my life ever since. I subscribe to all it says. More and
more do I get the sense of Man containing the Universe.

Not, you will note, 'man', but 'Man' – the idea of God.

Yes, 'everything exists within its own right'. I feel that too. It takes practice to go on knowing that, doesn't it, even though one has been vouchsafed glorious glimpses. But the fact is those glorious glimpses *are* eternity, going on now. In fact the miracle is the norm, and that's an exciting thing to realise. I'm very fond of I John 3, verses 1–3 (but *specially* verse 2).

May I wish you very well?

Unless you happen to feel about it as I do I suppose it could be maddening to be told 'All is well'' with so much evidence to the contrary before our very eyes. But not I think before the eyes of God. All is well *there*, and that's where it matters and where we have to look. Where we *are*, in fact.

Goodness! I do go on.

Tonight I sing 'Time' on T.V. in the 'Off the Record' programme, and I must assemble a dress, shoes, music and my voice.

I like letters by return. Here's one for you.

All wishes to you for now 'andcetera' as Shirley's Girl Friend says.

Joyce Grenfell

1959

Dear Mrs Moore,

I did enjoy your letter. Thank you so much. I have waited to answer it until I had some space to do it for pleasure, and here I am with an hour to sit down in between lunch and going to hear Elisabeth Schwarzkopf sing Handel and Wolf.

I love the account of your grandchildren. We never had any children. It was a sadness when we were young, then one got used to it, now I am almost grateful, for there have been so many compensations. Our particular companionship over and above love, and that as well; the need to canalise the various little talents that I'd played with as a child, etc., etc. I must say I would like to have *grand*children. They are the best idea of all, for one is just removed enough in all ways to enjoy them and appreciate them too. My brother's children are young enough to be my grandchildren, and so I do have that fun, but alas, with all that Atlantic between us most of the time. Sally is four and a half, and Lang is two and a quarter. Both are shining blondes; she is quicksilver and an actress, he is a double-bass and a thinker. When asked to 'Sit still, my sweetiepie' at the hairdressers, he said he wasn't a sweetiepie. To keep him interested, he was asked what, if not a sweetiepie, he was then? There was a long pause, and then in his basso profundo he said, 'I'm a tiger'. He was a bookworm at six months and sat cross-legged in his cot humming to himself and concentrating on the pictures in his rag-books.

I wonder if your niece is going to be at the University of Michigan at Madison? I played there last March and liked it very much. Set by a lake with big trees. The lake was frozen over and students walked across it wearing coloured sweaters and jackets turning the grey scene into a Brueghel. *Lovely* hall to work in, and I was impressed by the steadiness and clearness of the young men and girls I talked to.

It was there that I suddenly felt the very essence of America. I'm more than half American by blood, my mother was a Virginian, and my English father's mother came from Rhode Island – by way of Dundee, where her father came from. In Virginia one is still linked, strongly, to England. In California I felt the melting-pot still busily at work. But in Michigan I felt it has amalgamated and all that was best in intention has in fact happened. It was a sober, upright, civilised place with the strength of both the old country – countr*ies* I suppose – and the new fused into something entirely and clearly American. And no sense of rush. Of course it is *largely* an agricultural community – whole State I mean – so they know about seasons and have patience. And the horizons are so enormous and the skies so high. A good place to get into proportion in.

We are off to South Africa on the 29th. My husband goes annually on copper business. He is a director of a smallish mine in North Transvaal. Now happily there is a concession in Southern Rhodesia, so we don't have to be in the difficult union all the time. It is so warming to find our flag waving at us as one crosses the great grey green and greasy Limpopo going from North Transvaal to Southern Rhodesia! Back in early March. Then I *may* fly out to the United States to do a film. Not certain. But I fly to Australia late in June to do a twelve-week season in Sydney.

The past year has been a lovely *restful* one after a four-month tour of Canada and the United States.

I've been writing. Also doing bits and pieces of radio, T.V., some talks – including the Literary Society at Eton, which alarmed me at first but turned out most enjoyably. A few money-raisers and a *lot* of quiet life, bedroom-slippered, by our own hearth.

I like that Herbert you sent me.

Now it's time for Schwarzkopf.

Again thank you for writing.

With good wishes, yours sincerely,

Joyce Grenfell

Dear Joyce Grenfell,

Your letter tempts me to write once more before you go out of the country again, but *please* don't think you have to answer, as I know how busy you must be.

It was delightful to hear something of your doings and your life and I was so pleased to get your letter and glad to have such a favourable picture of Michigan. Perhaps one day I shall now see it for myself.

About children, I am not sure that it isn't much better for women with special gifts to have none – they are such a *constant* preoccupation. For myself, I am jack of all trades, and I fear, a master of none. Never mind, life has been extraordinarily rich. Our family has been a rather complicated C. M. Yonge-ish one. (I think perhaps you are not quite old enough to have been brought up on C.M.Y.?) By the time I was twenty-five I had five children to cope with, three little step-daughters and mixed twins of my own. Then, a good while later a small Austrian Jewish refugee boy for a time, and ten years ago a D.P. orphaned baby from Germany, became an adopted grandson, living with us. But the two most lovable, cleverest and best of our family, my second step-daughter and my son, are gone from us and this life in time, one in 1944 and the other in 1947. It is often so that the best and rarest and most fitted for life go first, when we seem to need them so, but I try to have faith that they are needed elsewhere and that they are having now 'life more abundantly'.

If you are not overcrowded with anthologies I wondered if you would care for one that I was privileged to have a part in compiling some years ago.* It was *such* a joy to do, only

* *A Treasury of the Kingdom.*

now we keep on finding bits to put in. Perhaps we may be allowed by the Oxford University Press to bring out a second enlarged edition. I am also sending with it a little children's story written *ages* ago and illustrated by my daughter then eleven. I thought possibly your niece and nephew might enjoy it. These two books are just a very small token of gratitude for all the pleasure you have given and are giving me.

My main job, apart from family though, has been teaching, which I tremendously enjoy. I have been lucky enough to have a good girls' grammar school near and started teaching there during the war full time, then had a year off and then went back part time till about eighteen months ago when ill health and family combined made me resign. But I am still lucky enough to be able to keep in touch with lots of old pupils and to sneak back and give a lesson when I feel like it, and to do the odd bit of University Entrance coaching, etc.

I *did* like the bit in your letter about American and Africa. I envy you getting about the world so. But I have been to the Naga Hills (North of India) and to Greece – the two most beautiful places that one could imagine. The worst of it is that one's capacity for roughing it on journeys and one's income both decrease at the same time. However we now go without a car in order to save up for holidays, which we both adore. My husband, a metallurgist before he retired, was Director of the British Non-ferrous Research Association, so he is not wholly unconnected with copper!

It annoys me not to be able to see you on T.V., but if we had one I should read less, talk less, write less, listen to music less, sew less – all of which I wish to do *more* of, so I must just lay in a stock of records.

Goodbye – I am afraid this letter is rather disjointed, but it has had to be written in odd snatches, and I want to get it off before you disappear overseas again. I hope you will have a lovely time in South Africa with plenty of sun. How I love sun – and space. As E. M. Forster so rightly and tragically said the other day in his broadcast, England is too crowded now for any feelings of peace and space – only sometimes on a winter's day of rare frost and sun, when the cold has sent the tourists and the cars and the aeroplanes to sleep, the old magic of the English countryside is recaptured again. Such a day was last Friday, when I walked for miles by the river between Abingdon and Oxford, and the swans came crowding to be fed, and all the trees were bright silver against a deep blue sky. On such a day one doesn't want to be anywhere but England.

Goodbye again, and thank you again.

Katharine Moore

24 January   *Elm Park Gardens*

Dear Mrs Moore,

How nice of you. I've been dipping into the anthology already and it *looks full of treasures*. Thank you so *very* much for sending it to me. And for *Moog*. That looks fun, and I'll read it, too.

I love being given books so it has been a lovely surprise. Thank you *very* much.

We saw *My Fair Lady* today. It is charming. But not as wonderfully exciting as *West Side Story*. *That* is a most extraordinary experience. It's a fascinating theatrical event. Don't be put off by the violent theme – after all, the original *Romeo and Juliet* was violent too. It has *great* beauty and horror. I've seen it four times. I hope to see it again.

No time to write properly. I'm off to Cambridge tomorrow to do the poetry recital I originally did with John Betjeman in November in London. We begin with Innocence and the World – Blake, Wordsworth, etc., and end with some of John Betjeman's own works. I do some love poems in the middle. And some splendid Hardy pieces. I'd no idea how lively he was. Do you know 'The Pink Frock' and 'The Dolls'?

Again I *do* thank you, and for your letter.

In haste. Yours sincerely,

Joyce Grenfell

Dear Mrs Moore,

Thank you so much for your nice note, and I have put your new address in my little book.

Australia was thrilling, and now it is America again in the middle of January – a huge tour taking me all over the U.S.A. and then across Canada.

Have you read *Cider with Rosie*? I think you might enjoy it. Laurie Lee is a good poet, and now he proves himself a good writer too, but then they are the same thing. I think.

Happy New Year to you.

Yours sincerely,

Joyce Grenfell

1960

Dear Mrs Moore,

Because your card gave me *such* delight I have to write and say so. Thank you.

And while I think of it, I wonder if you have heard a prayer that I came on at a memorial service the other day and which I like so much. I don't know how it began but this is the bit that I memorised and love:

'Death is only an horizon and an horizon is only the limitation of our view.'

I think you will like it.

So glad you found *West Side Story* so enjoyable. I've seen it five times and agree.

Another recommendation. *Edward Marsh* by Christopher Hassall. I have *never* enjoyed a biography more. It's very long and beautifully in focus, and it has a splendid rhythm. Funny, moving and fascinating.

Happy year to you – Yours

Joyce Grenfell

I'm keeping your watch and fob as a marker in my diary for 1960: *So* pretty.

11 October   *Elm Park Gardens*

Dear Mrs Moore,

How nice to hear from you – I didn't know the W. J. de la Mare poem and *I love* it. Thank you *so* much for sending it to me.

es. Your watch fob card is still in my diary and I enjoy it ..ghtly.

The American-Canadian trip was enjoyable and energetic and I got home in May. Then a film (another St Trinians, but I had the fun of playing (?) the recorder in it, and that was enjoyable), and then a busy summer with my brother and his young family from New York.

Now I'm doing a provincial tour of concert dates – this means two or three a week in big halls, and to my surprise it is working well. The Scala week came in the middle of it. I can't resist boasting to you: the final figure to be shared by the Seven Good Reasons is £9,100!* It is an incredible sum, and I'm amazed and delighted and so very grateful. Can you think of anything pleasanter than doing a job you enjoy doing and on top of that making such a fat Christmasy sum for some very good reasons.

I'm off to Birmingham tomorrow and on to Newcastle after that. It goes on till mid-November, but I do get home every now and then, and how one loves to be in one's own pretty turquoise blue and white striped bedroom with white chintz curtains splodged with pretty pink roses from a French print, after the off-cream wrong-red damaskish curtains and sleazy eiderdowns of hotels. How I dislike what are known as warm reds – usually tomato-ish or rust and never clear and gay. Above all I most dislike orange.

But I sleep anywhere I find! So no more complaining.

We've got a beautiful plane tree outside the window here and it is hung with bobbles and tipped with gold.

The parks are a sight with dahlias.

I'm so glad you liked my Musician's Wife. She's hard to do but I'm getting better at her, I think, and I was *much* encouraged by your letter.

Have you read *The Borrowers* by Mary Norton? Meant for the young but that includes most of us. Penguin have it. I'm reading an American book about Agassiz that is very attractive. And I've just finiushed Richard Hoggart's *superb* blue

---

* A week of solo performances at the Scala Theatre, London, in aid of seven charities and entitled *For Seven Good Reasons*.

Penguin *Uses of Literacy*. This is worth a great deal. He's on the Pilkington Committee with me. Interesting man. *That*'s a good job – but a very demanding one. But I'm enjoying it.

Yours gratefully,

Joyce Grenfell

1961

24 January   Elm Park Gardens

Dear Mrs Moore,

How good of you. Thank you so very much. I've sent the cheque on to the Employment Fellowship* and I know they will be so grateful to you. Thank you *very* much indeed. Will you accept this as a receipt? Perhaps I should have told them to send one to you – I still can if you'd like me to?

Thank you, too, for the Vaughan. Lovely. I think that's exactly what angels are. Ideas that call to the soul, or, moments of vision revealing the eternal constant truth.

I've read a good deal of *The Phenomenon of Man* and very much like his conclusions. I intend reading *Le Milieu Divin* too. Such things are very nourishing, aren't they?

I don't know if you have heard of the Pilkington Committee? It's been set up by the Government to look into the future of all radio and T.V. Twelve men two women. I'm very honoured to be on it, and it is a fascinating job. I'm very impressed with our chairman, Sir Harry Pilkington, who makes glass in Lancashire. A man of flawless integrity and wide horizons. As Sir Harry said to us when we first met: 'Well, there's one good thing about us – none of us has an axe to grind.' And it's true. We are all passionate believers in truth.

It's a big assignment. We meet a great deal. So far every two weeks, but soon for two days every ten or twelve days. Homework comes in by every post, and we have to read,

* J. G. broadcast an appeal for the Employment Fellowship on 21 January, 1961.

24

digest and educate ourselves as we go. We've just begun to take evidence, and I came off the night train from Edinburgh this morning after a very long day of doing that up there yesterday.

What are called 'Responsible Bodies' – and individuals – submit written evidence, and we are to see an enormous number of them to hear oral testimony too. Not only about ideas but the people who have them. Prejudices and axes show like petticoats *at once*. Dispassionate seekers for good reason shine like stars. It is all highly confidential. I burst to talk about it and do to Reggie, but he is off to Africa tomorrow on his usual Spring trip, so I'll just have to bubble. We are having a four-week break in meetings in mid-February, and I am flying out there to join him for three weeks *duty* social life, some bird-watching, sun and a nice stretch in the warmth.

All this means I'm not doing much of my own job, but I am trying to do some writing, and that is keeping me fully occupied when I'm not committeeing. No tours this year.

It's good to sit at home for a while.

An American tour may happen later in 1962. And Australia has asked me again.

I've just written a straight monologue called 'Telephone Call' for an Australian actress to do in a review in Sydney. It made her husband cry when she read it, so I was relieved to hear it seems to work. I think I'm a little too old to do it but I dare say I'll try some day.

Again thank you so much for helping the *good* cause. It *really* is.

Yours

Joyce Grenfell

I'm reading Diana Cooper's last memoir. Amusing, shameless and somehow unsatisfactory in spite of skill and a sort of twirling ungay vitality. What is it that is lacking? Any sort of spiritual perception I believe.

I enjoyed Violet Powell's *Five out of Six*. Mark Twain's biography – a life of Agassiz – can't remember its title. Yes I can – *Adventurous Alliance* by Louise Hall Tharp.

If you can you *must* see the Old Vic *Romeo and Juliet*. It is breathtakingly good. They are young unselfconscious lovers – *perfect*. Directed by the Italian Zefferelli. Really worth the effort. And *so* is *A Man for all Seasons*.

7 *February*   *Elm Park Gardens*

My dear Mrs M.

Please forgive me for not having forwarded this [receipt] to you sooner. The Fellowship sent it last week and somehow in the accumulation on my desk it got forgotten. I'm so sorry.

I'm glad you liked the sound of my room. It looks particularly pretty this morning in the clear windy light. I've had a cold and am indulging in bed. Pink and white double tulips are fanning in a cornucopia vase against my turquoise blue and white striped wallpaper. The birds are chirping away – that nice promising noise they make before they sing properly.

I'm reading *Out of Africa* by Isak Dinesen. I wonder why she calls herself that? She is Baroness Blixen, isn't she? That's not much better, but to take a spiky 'Isak' seems curious. I imagine she's quite a complicated creature. This is a lovely book. I saw her on T.V. once. A face drawn with tiny pencil lines, lean as a whippet, fierce, not very lovable but, possibly, loving. I don't know.

This isn't a letter!

It says Thank you, once again.

Yours

                                                                    J.G.

1962

Dear Katharine Moore,

Do you know I've still got your nice Christmas letter in a clip, meaning to write and thank you for it; because I enjoyed it so much. And now, with perfect timing comes your agreeable Holland one to welcome me back from Wolverhampton today. (Civic Hall last night. Quite a challenge to turn it into a congenial place after the joys of the Haymarket. No backing, curtains or proper lighting. But it was a good evening. Warm and friendly people; pin silence for 'Telephone Call' and 'Three Brothers' and 'Time'; lovely roars elsewhere.)

Thank you so much for writing so generously I did enjoy your letter. Thank you.

I do hope your *Magic Flute* was lovely. I too saw it in Salzburg about four years ago, I think. And loved it.

The Haymarket 'season' was really wonderful. Far the most enjoyable I've ever done, partly because it's such a heavenly theatre, partly because I felt a new steadiness, and then, of course, because of the remarkable audiences at *every* performance. Much to be grateful for.

Glasgow tomorrow followed by Harrogate, Huddersfield, Brighton, Manchester and Cheltenham. Then it's Easter, and then after two important Pilkington meetings Reggie and I plan to go to Avignon for ten days until another Pilkington meeting calls me back. Have you been there? We might get to the Camargue and could see birds. May ought to be pretty, and warm, D.V. I shall take a sketch book.

(I'm *so* bad, but it is a lovely indulgence, and I find great pleasure in it.)

Do you know Laurence Whistler's poetry? A neglected poet, I think. His is the kind of poetry I understand but an increasing melancholy and lack of joy – or rather only joy in what is past, makes me sad for him. He married a beautiful young actress, Jill Furse, and she died just after their second child was born. He still, ten or twelve year later, writes of her, longs for her, seeks signs of her. But he married her enchanting younger sister and they have two children, so one reels from the feelings she must get when he goes on writing of his lost love so passionately and so yearningly. All this is in his newest book, just given to me.*
To be *so* sensitive for himself and surely, insensitive to Theresa, seems inconsistent. But poets have their own rules. Sometimes he writes with great beauty, I think. He was a great friend of W. J. de la Mare, and I met him there. Do you know his glass engraving? Exquisite.

He also told W. J. the splendid story *he* told me and which I put in a Woman's Hour programme recently among things that make me laugh.

An elderly woman was much troubled by constipation and paid long fruitless visits. Finally persuaded, she saw a doctor who was kind and understanding and who said to her:

'Do you take anything?'

'Only my knitting.'

I hope you enjoy this as I do.

The new Mary Renault is nothing like as good as either *The King Must Die* or *The Last of the Wine*. I *rather* enjoyed parts of *George* by Emlyn Williams. But most of all, lately, I've liked *The White Nile* by Alan Moorehead. And a novel called *To Kill a Mockingbird* by Harper Lee. I believe you would like this. American, Southern, but not depraved for a change! In fact dry and crisp and charming.

I must just tell you a favourite 'fan' story. A small boy of nine was heard saying ecstatically to his father at the end of a

* *Audible Silence* (1961).

matinee at the Haymarket last week: 'It's even better than *Puss in Boots*.' A real compliment.

Thank you so much for writing, yours

Joyce G.

Do you like the *New Bible*? I do. *Particularly* John.

Dear Katharine Moore,

Such a good letter from you, and it was only the Call of Duty – just what I can't now remember – that prevented me answering it at once. Thank you very much. I want to comment on several things.

I think I'm an un-political animal in that I don't like or believe in any of them. I've voted all three in my time. A natural rebel – a natural left-ish feeling – but the dealings I've had with actual Labour members and the slipperiness has put me off badly. And their cowardly totally political vote-catching attitude over the Pilkington Report did disgust me, I must say. Because I know a lot of them were on its side, but courage and honesty were lacking, I fear. I'd *like* to be a Liberal if I didn't think it was a waste of a vote. I know and like several Tories, but I don't like the Carlton Club type, and I strongly disapprove of the ones who are Tory for the wrong reason – social, big business – and not because they *really* believe it is the best way to get things done for the rest of us. Some, unpropelled by motives of 'have' or 'have-not' or keeping the Status Quo, do have my respect as honest men. But, oh dear, there's not much to choose between any of them *politically* – all are out for themselves and *against* someone else. Roll on the day when we all really care for each other! For *everyone*.

I have a young (23) Australian poet friend here who is starving in Tufnell Park N.7 – or was till he got a job feeding facts into a computer at University College, London. He is what is known as far out, against everything like respect, sanctity, Royalty and wealth. It is so touching to see him

29

talking about a system of barter, *everyone* to be paid exactly the same sum, be he a scientific giant or charlady, pop-novelist, doctor, chorus girl or chairmender, railwayman or tycoon! His eyes shine. But the fact is, when I question him really closely what is revealed is a latent resentment against those who 'have'. A wish to take the seniors down a peg or two, just as one longed to at school. He says he doesn't believe in anything much but, again, when pressed, believes in Good, in love and in brotherhood of man. Gently I said: Then you do believe in God for these are attributes of God. It seems he hadn't thought of this.

Yes, Coventry. Simon Phipps, Industrial Chaplain to the Cathedral, is my first cousin, and I've been watching it grow in yearly visits. In January I did a money-raiser for it at the Belgrade Theatre and as a result was sent a ticket for the dedication service. Reggie, my husband, got one in the ruins-stand and saw all the processions, so we went together but sat separately. Visually wonderful. I love the John Piper lemon-yellow copes. And the grey cassocks. I'm not wholly happy about the Graham Sutherland, but I love the colour of it. Best, for me, is the Piper window. And Simon's quite bare Industrial Chapel. I like *very* bare churches. I'm not very much for ceremony and ritual – except visually. Spiritually it doesn't speak to me at all. 'Because God is I am' is what I feel and am grateful for. I like total simplicity of surroundings to recognise and be gratefully humble and joyfully grateful about it.

Our holiday in Provence is a pale sunny memory. It was lovely. Lots of birds. Bee-eaters, hoopoes, goldfinches, etc., good food, walks in vineyard country exploring Arles, Nîmes and the Camargue. Ponies – white – the black virgin at Les Saintes Maries de la Mer crypt chapel. Only she's worn white by pious gypsy fingers except for a few black shadows around her nose and eyes. I'm afraid she's a disappointment in her art satin and cracked pearls, but the idea of her is romantic. Better not actually see her!

A week at Aldeburgh in June for the festival was very nourishing. Birds by day, Britten, etc., by night. Weather smiling and a full moon over the sea most nights. In August five days at Stratford seeing four plays and playing tennis in the mornings.

It's been a luxurious year for holidays – now, on Thursday 27, we sail in the *Queen Mary* for New York. My brother, his pretty wife and Sally, nine, and Lang, six, are waiting for us. We go for an eight-day trip up to Vermont to see the foliage with old friends and then have two weeks in New York with the family. I'm supposed to be doing a T.V., but Ed Sullivan is 'sick', so they say, and no one quite knows if the programme is on or off . . . Never mind. It will be a lovely change, and I'm glad it isn't longer. New York is fine for ten days. Just possible for two weeks, and then it is awful. Unless you are working when it can be thrilling.

I've re-read Margaret Kennedy's *A Long Time Ago* and enjoyed it. Re-read some E. M. Forster, too. *Lovely*. I've been re-writing a T.V. play, but it isn't right. Stephen Potter and I wrote and recorded 'How *Not* to Listen' for the Third Programme on 10 November to celebrate the fortieth anniversary of B.B.C. sound. I get home on 5 November I think, but as it isn't *sure* because of possible T.V., etc. we pre-recorded it last week. Do you ever listen? I do. I like it best. As a child I know says: 'I see it much better on radio than on T.V.'

Do write again. Yours

Joyce Grenfell

1963

Dear Katharine Moore,

May I ask you a question? Did you send me a handkerchief at Christmas? On a list of presents received I put your name and on the floor among the tissue papers I found an exquisite handkerchief. I feel K.M. and hanky go together, but I may be wrong? I may have meant your name to be on the cardlist I sometimes compile, but if I did then who gave me the handkerchief?

You see the problem and, please, will forgive the chaotic confusion? May I say thank you, anyway, for the lovely Christopher Smart poem, 'Stupendous Stranger'. What a joy. And 'mosaic thorn'. It's so *exact*, it makes you gasp with pleasure.

Thank you, too, for the handkerchief? And, yes, a very belated thank you for 'The Defence of Images'.* It's masterly and moving. *Thank you.* I, in turn, have something of William Penn's which being of your persuasion you may very likely know. It, and the Henry Vaughan on the back page were part of a memorial service for an old friend of ours just before Christmas. Both are discoveries to me.

I loved your account of trying to hear our 'How' programme. It was done again on New Year's Eve and I meant to 'postcard' you but quite forgot.

My autumn, or anyway the five weeks before Christmas, was spent in making a thirty-minute film, for T.V. about Christmas. I talked to old and young about their views, trying not to influence them in any way, so that we got their

---

* From Maximus of Tyre's *Dissertations*. It is the first item in *The Spirit of Tolerance*.

real ideas on the subject. I'd hoped that some of the truth of Christmas might emerge, and it did. It's good to know what a lot of Christmas has rubbed off on to those who aren't particularly Christian. It was a very small programme. Indeed I called it 'A Small Corner of Christmas', and it was quiet, but I liked it. and so did a lot of people who wrote and spoke and telephoned. I began it with a four-year-old with a thin neck and rather a worried face saying very loud and clear in purest Islington:

'Look at that bright light!'

This was the opening of a Nativity play being rehearsed in a Nursery School I knew about. We finished the programme with a repetition of this shot. It made the comment perfectly. In between came much of the nursery school; and then there were old people in a workshop for the Elderly in Hackney, some lovely, some gay, all glad about the children or the occasion. One splendid lady, Mrs Bailey, eighty-ish without teeth was going to be 'on me own – upstairs'll be out – I'll be solo'. I remarked that she seemed cheerful.

'You gotter be, aincher?' she said, and roared with laughter.

I visited a girl I know married to a writer-actor, and her three children contributed to the programme. In answer to 'Have you any special plans for Christmas?' her nine-year-old Christopher said, quite unprompted, 'Oh yes, we're having a bring and buy sale for Oxfam' and went on to explain to me what Oxfam was! He also said that when he and Dominic (7) went to doors selling Oxfam Christmas tags only one door bought any, but when they went out with the Guy in November they got *lots* and *lots* of money – he didn't know why.

It was very endearing and pointed. We finished on Clemence Dane, an old friend. She was warm and wise and reminiscent, and we did it before a log fire in her studio-living room, and it came over very well, I think. And, before this visit, we went to our tiny local Post Office toyshop and talked to the nice Welsh couple who run it.

Christmas was good here, very mixed company and all ages. I love all the preparing, don't you? Gold paper stars spun off cotton threads, red velvet ribbon (now in its fifth year) hung round a rather ornate gold (carved wood) mirror. Red candles everywhere – holly – and of course cards from floor to ceiling stuck in the bookshelves like a brilliant wallpaper. The usual foods, crackers, children, carols, games, competitions and a *lot* of washing up. But we enjoyed it very much.

Our Vermont 'foliage trip' was lovely. The colour is astonishing, and those toy villages with white clapboard houses and the churches were so restoring. One can believe *only* ordered lives are possible in such places! I felt very close to Emily Dickinson and Louisa M. Alcott while in New England.

The big project this year is a return trip to Australia in July. Before this I hope to do some writing. We plan a bird–music ten days at Aldeburgh in June and a small escape to Cumberland in May with luck. Avignon would be *perfect* late September–October, I'm told.

I wish this was more legible and that I had more time to pen write as prettily as you do. Your hand sits so lightly on the page and is very pleasing.

I hardly dare mention it but I've begun to write a little poetry again after years of not doing so. It's no good, but it gives me a sense of joy.

May 1963 be good for you in discovery and in peace.

Yours sincerely

Joyce Grenfell

Please forgive me about the carelessness over the handkerchief. Was it yours?

10 January   *Riverside House, Shoreham, Sevenoaks, Kent*

Oh dear! I wish the handkerchief had been from me, but it *wasn't*, though I should love to give you any number of them if you wanted them. Still, I haven't given you even one, and now you will be worried to know whom you haven't thanked and I have got a letter undeserved, or at least almost undeserved. I am so glad you liked 'The Defence of Images' and the 'Stupendous Stranger'. Thank you so much for your enclosures. I did know them and love them, but I like very much to know that you love them too.

I am consumed with activity. I think I should like to be a Victorian grandmother for a change. To lie on a sofa nicely protected from the cold with a respectful loving circle of grandchildren, willing, nay eager, to fetch and carry for dear grandmamma – How restful! And I don't believe they were Ivy Compton-Burnett characters either. My own Victorian grandmother was a dear, though she did lie on a sofa sometimes. By the way, did you read that *lovely* Paul Jennings 'The Holly and the Ivy' on I. Compton-Burnett's Christmas present catalogues?

I *should* like to have seen your Christmas T.V. film and was interested and amused at your account of it. These *are* the occasions when I want T.V. But I did manage to hear the 'How Now' programme again in peace at my own fireside and enjoyed it thoroughly. We also so much enjoyed the two Ruth Draper broadcastings.

I am going this Saturday to *Lear*, and almost dreading it as well as longing for it.

I like to hear of your plans for 1963. I am just now very busy on a book on 'Tolerance' for Gollancz. It is intriguing but difficult and involves a lot of reading, and it has got to be done by May which is rather a nightmare because one can never give *enough* time to it. I haven't been able to spare more than snippets in the Christmas holidays. Of course the bitter weather makes much more work. I spend ages providing food for the birds. I enjoyed last winter's snow, but this has seemed cruel and caused so much suffering. It has been very grey and desolate here, and I long to see something green again. Still, the children have enjoyed it, and there was one lovely vision of distant golden hills lit up by slanting sun rays, the foreground all dark.

I am glad about the poetry, if you ever felt you could let me see some, I should like to so much.

It is nice of you to like my handwriting – I always feel it is spoilt by doing too much of it. This time I've lost my pen so am using a biro, which I don't like!

I do wish you a *lovely* year ahead, and hope for my sake

and the sake of many many others there will be chances of
hearing and seeing you.

Yours with love

Katharine Moore

My two-and-a-half-year-old American great-niece (at
Michigan) asked for 'a medium-sized reindeer' for Christmas.

12 January   *Elm Park Gardens*

Dear K.M. (may I use your initials? I think this is a good
way of addressing unseen friends, and I will sign J.G.)

May I say how relieved I am about the handkerchief for
the reason that I never use handkerchiefs any more. Tissues
are so much easier. I like to see a pretty fine lawn handkerchief, but mine just get grey in the folds; for if I take one out
it *stays* in my bag and I *use* a tissue. So thank you *very* much
for NOT giving me a handkerchief.

This isn't a real letter, but I wanted to tell you my
thoughts about the anonymous handkerchief.

'Tolerance'. *There*'s a subject. When I was sixteen I went
to school in Paris and wrote home to my father in rage at the
venal French. I said in one letter 'They get my goat'. My Pa
wrote back and said I should be like – who was it, the
Psalmist? Isaiah? – and keep my sheep on a thousand hills.
He was a great man for tolerance. I hold it to be a beautiful
quality, when it is the outcome of love and understanding.
Careless tolerance is almost as bad as intolerance, I think.
The kind that says 'I don't mind' or as Mrs Patrick Campbell is supposed to have said, 'I don't mind what people do
so long as they don't do it in the street and frighten the
horses.'

I think you must *mind*. You must also understand.
Condemnation has no part in *true* behaviour, does it?

It's not such an easy subject to be clear about, is it? I
expect Shakespeare got it right in that sonnet 'Love is not
love which alters when it alteration finds', etc. Tolerance

36

means 'loving in spite of human imperfection', I think. It endures. It *is* love.

If I may, when I have time to find what I'd like you to see, I would love to show you one or two of my pieces. Thank you.

Just back from Bristol where I was on 'Any Questions' last night. This was my first time, and I found it alarming. John Freeman surprised me by having red hair. I thought he was white-headed, and longer. He's pink and thick through. Bronowski is fairly brutal, but saved by a soft Jewish heart. He is small and square and fruity somehow. Gerald Nabarro hides his reality behind a mock county voice, opulence, levantine sparkle and a pair of strange kiss-curl-sided moustaches. But there is something enjoyable at bedrock. Gusto, energy and the-sky-is-the-limit mentality aren't cosy qualities, but one is forced to admire them in one who has so much fun conquering.

The West Country looks *so* lovely in the deep snows. Yesterday afternoon from the train there were miles of unmarked snow with pale blue veined shadows. The trees were rust red! And as we swung into Bath whole rows of houses were on fire in the setting sunlight.

This morning all was edged in rime, but no light to show it off.

At first the programme scared me silent. I had nothing to say about the Coal Board, for instance, but later there was a question about cities and T.V., and a stage one in particular, so I could take part. I liked meeting the company, and we had lots to talk about before and afterwards.

You are at *Lear* as I write, and I know you will be stirred by Paul Scofield and by the Fool, Alec McCowen *and* by Alan Webb as Gloucester.

I don't like all those leather clothes, but the iron sheets and the storm are completely successful, I believe.

I didn't mean to write a letter, but the flesh is weak, and you are so enjoyable to write to. *Don't* answer till you have space – months later if you like.

I hope your pipes don't freeze and your fires burn brightly.

Yours with love,   J.G.

My grandmother was pretty, tiny and wore little black buttoned boots. I've been doing a poem about her for *weeks*. She was reticent and a little forbidding. She didn't lie on sofas but gardened and sat up very straight. Not easy to love.

23 January   *Elm Park Gardens*

Dear K.M.,

You were kind enough to say you would like to see what I'm writing and I enclose 'Winter', 'From the Train' and a piece on 'Candles and Lamps'. I sent 'From the Train' to *Punch*, and they have taken it. I'm probably going to try 'Candles and Lamps' there too.

As you see these are very 'occasional'.

It has been good to feel the stirrings again, and I hope to do a bit better.

I wonder just how frozen you are? We are so fortunate with partial central heating and a paraffin stove and only one tap out of use. So we have baths and are all right for gas – so far – to cook on. We are running a sort of 'meals on wheels' from here for a friend, widowed and mother of five, who is just back from a second time in hospital and whose nineteen-year-old is trying to do the housekeeping *and* be a freelance journalist. They have *no* water in the house and have to use a tap across a garden belonging to a cousin. My housekeeper who is an expansive loving character has embraced the situation and makes large casseroles ready for reheating and they are delivered at intervals.

The idea was to spend January and February trying to write new material, but the Lord has found other uses for my time and quite genuinely I'm very grateful to be free enough to be a bit useful. Ordinarily I'm so booked up any extra is almost impossible.

The birds eat all the bits of fat and crumbs from the window ledge. Those bullying pigeons are very rough and elbow the littler birds out of the way unless I watch and ward.

Yours,

J.G.

WINTER

The sky is white,
The snow is white,
The sun's an apricot above.
The trees are black,
The birds are black,
The seagull and the silver dove.
The sky turns blue
The shadows blue
The sun's a solid orange ball.
West windows blaze
And flare and daze,
Rose light suffuses all.
The sky goes dark,
The snow goes dark,
The evening star is sparkling white.
The frost is hard,
The earth is hard,
There is no mercy in the night.

FROM THE TRAIN

An apricot sun in a silver sky,
A world of white below,
The pillow fields are folded neat
Beneath a weight of snow.

Poor miserable sheep in dishcloth wool
Eat miserable dishcloth hay,
The farmer's miserable dishcloth face
Is clenched-fist small today.

O apricot sun grow melon gold,
Let winter's hold be done,
And man and beast and root stretch out
Beneath a yellow sun.

CANDLES AND LAMPS

When I was a child I dreaded candles
Because their restless double shadows leapt

Upon the pale walls at my grandmother's
In that uneasy spare room where I slept.

The oil-lamp in the drawing-room below
Came hissing in at sunset, and its light
Pulsated like some heavy-breathing thing.
By day I prayed postponement for the night.

Our grandmother was beautiful but cool,
And her small dignity remained austere.
I think she never was surprised by joy.
I think she did not need us very near.

So staying in her house was not the same
As home, and we went down a tone or two
Meandering in the August garden there
Along brick paths not knowing what to do.

So with the dread of candles and the thought
That, upstairs, moths were waiting in the dark,
We were not sorry when our stay was done
And we went home to London and the park.

But we were sorry when she died, because
We were accustomed to her patterned ways;
No loss of life, no threat to all-is-well,
But landscape altered and a chilly day.

The dread of candles left me long ago,
The drama hiss of lamps soon lost its fear,
And as th'emotions of the past withdraw
My grandmother comes nearer year by year.

January   *Riverside House*

Dear J.G. (yes – I like the use of initials – I was always called
by mine at school.)

Thank you so much for your second handkerchief letter.
Handkerchiefs are a sore point with me just now as I am in
bed with one of the most furious colds ever invented. That
is why I am afraid this may be rather a long letter.

Now – this morning, to cheer me up, comes another letter

with your poems. I like the grandmother poem best – it is the most characteristic of you and besides, poems about grandmothers are so much rarer than poems about winter. I feel with this, and the description in your letter, that I can picture your grandmother very well. How much better (I think!) your two last amended lines are to the typed ones.* Isn't it fascinating how it *comes* suddenly. It is strange that I began talking to you of grandmothers while you were writing this. Mine was so gentle and sweet with a soft low voice and a beautiful face. I only remember her as more or less of an invalid. She had had eight children, so she had earned her sofa. She dressed me a doll with three petticoats, nightdresses and caps and long 'drawers' in exquisite tiny stitchery. My granddaughter has it now. My mother adored her, and when she died I remember the sudden 'threat to all-is-well', because I saw my mother cry then for the first time.

This is not to say that I don't like the winter poems too. I think I prefer 'Winter'. I especially like the last line. It is what I have felt so much during this rather terrible month – no mercy. The blizzard on Saturday 19th was really frightening – like King Lear's storm – uncontrolled, bitter, *merciless*. But the fool loves the more.

I can't think how there are any birds left – we have all sorts, but my daughter at the Old Mill House has a wonderful selection of poor water-birds. Starlings and blackbirds are the greediest and most numerous with us.

We are very lucky in having plenty of wood and coal and a small old infinitely precious Aga in the kitchen – there is no gas in the village. Electricity has been low but no actual cuts yet. No burst or frozen pipes.

When I went to *Lear* I asked the programme girl how long it lasted (because of trains). She said, 'For ever'! But for me time simply ceased to exist. I thought Goneril, Regan, Cordelia, Gloucester, Edmund, Cornwall and the Fool could not have been better. They enlarged my imagination of the characters and I shall see *them* henceforth when I read

* The amended copy of the poem has not survived.

the play. Edgar was as good as he could be in an impossibly difficult part – Kent, whom I *love* as a person – was not, for me, good *enough*, and Paul Scofield disappointed me until the last three great appearances – that is to say that, as the redeemed quiet Lear, I thought him wonderful, but earlier he was not royal enough, not uncontrolled enough, not frightening enough. I did not believe in his terrible fear of madness, nor was I convinced by the madness when it came. I thought, though, that the relation between him and the Fool was exquisitely done. The storm scene, I am inclined to agree with Lamb, is un-actable. I liked the decor and dresses and didn't mind that they were all leather. I was enjoying the subtle harmony of colours so much. But *why* did Peter Brook cut Edmund's two last speeches 'Yet Edmund was beloved' and 'Some good I mean to do'? The omission at once diminishes him into mere stock Renaissance villain instead of the much more complicated character Shakespeare meant. I think any cuts that alter *character* inexcusable. But what a play!

Thank you for nice story about Mrs Patrick Campbell and tolerance. I want to use a bit of Richard Hoggart's on the wrong kind of tolerance. I don't know whether I explained that the book is a sort of anthology with notes to illustrate the nature of tolerance. I liked the bit about your father. I find it easy to be tolerant of people as individuals that I *know* or have met, and difficult to practise tolerance towards masses and groups. I feel very intolerant at the moment to someone who has written to the press to say it is sentimental to feed birds when so many people are suffering – as if one could feed people on 'Swoop' or bits of fat, or as if there isn't enough compassion to go round and it has to be rationed. In my experience the people who feed the birds are the same people who care about their fellow-humans.

I enjoyed you on 'The Critics' and even more your description of your fellow-members. You were good about criticism – in other words I agreed with every word you said. Especially do I feel, with you, that critics today often just use their function as a show off for their own mostly irrelevant ideas. They seldom seem to have studied their subject. I don't believe Kenneth Tynan has ever *read* any Shakespeare, or perhaps the trouble is he hasn't been taught it by me. Not long ago Yehudi Menuhin was speaking on the B.B.C. about music critics. He read some of G.B.S. and said how very good it was, and it struck me then that (in spite of being *Shaw*) it was so much more objective and informed and *solid* than criticism today. I say, 'in spite of being Shaw', meaning that he was the last person you would think of as humble or self-effacing, and yet in his criticism he *was* self-forgetful with his eye always on the subject.

Oh dear! I've just heard that my daughter is now all frozen up and having to break the ice and fetch water from the stream. There hasn't even been an apricot sun for the last two days. I *am* sorry about your poor family. Thank goodness they've got you. A friend has just rung up from Fulham to say they are without water, coal or gas – only a small electric fire. I think the Government should organise emergency delivery of small quantities of coal, as the coal merchants won't deliver less than fifteen hundredweight, which is impossible for tiny flats or old people living in one room. But it is easy to lie in bed and say what is to be done. I really must *not* go on to another page – excuse writing and probably spelling which tends to go to pieces when I have a temperature, etc; but it has been nice to chat to you in an unhurried fashion. I do *very* much like the poems. THANK YOU and love.

K.M.

15 August   *Aherlow House, Glen of Aherlow, Co. Tipperary*

Dear J.G.

I wonder in what part of the world you are at the moment. We are having a holiday in Ireland, not at Arles after all, as plans wouldn't fit in. Do you know Ireland? Being in this remote spot is like putting the clock back to my childhood. We jog along country lanes in a pony cart pulled by a fat grey pony called Flicker, and from this house there is not a sound of a machine to be heard – nothing but wind in the trees and a bird or two and distant trotting feet as the horses cart the hay or bring great milk cans on tiny carts from the farms. The lights on the mountains are constantly changing, and there is a scent of hay and pine trees. I know one gets this sort of peace still in out of the way places in other countries, but this is *almost* English, and the peace is that of the *English* countryside of fifty years ago. Besides the pony trap, we bicycle on empty roads and the cottage people give us tea and pile our plates with home-made bread and butter and cake, and afterwards: 'Sure, I wouldn't be charging you a halfpenny for that, I was just having a cup myself and all' they say.

This all sounds idyllic, and I know there is another side to the picture, unemployment in the towns, and the cottages and farms are poor by English standards, but there is no denying that the people mostly look happy and are *very* friendly.

This house is right up in the mountains – we are lucky to be here. We have music in the evenings, for there is a good cellist staying here and two German boys who have brought their recorders with them. There is also a good library of Irish books, and I know much more about early Gaelic culture and history than I did.

I like so much the comments and poems written by the copyist monks of the eighth and ninth centuries, in the margins of their manuscripts – 'Pleasant is the glint of the sun today upon these margins, because it flickers so' (written on the top of a page of commentary on the Psalms) 'I send my little dripping pen increasingly over an assemblage of books of great beauty, to enrich the possessions of men of art – whence my hand is weary of writing.' . . .

1964

Dear J.G.,

I shall indulge myself today by writing to you. It is an indulgence for I think you are the only person I write to for *pure fun* – also of course I hope to get a letter back, as you did promise me one about your travels on your lovely Japanese baby Christmas card.

What an interesting life you have! I envy you – yet when I think about it my life is *full* of interest too. I have started teaching again – one day a week. I haven't really the time for it, and I think they ought to have someone younger, but as I am nearer seventy than sixty I am flattered that they still want me and at the children asking me to go on next year, which I don't think I shall. I am teaching Blake and Jane Austen (how shocked and amused, respectively, they would be to find themselves set for examinations!). However we try to forget the examination part completely. I find it interesting that this lot are more tuned to Blake than Jane Austen. They are too romantic for Jane Austen (except for a few) and don't really understand her belief that restraint creates beauty. The only one that likes 'Sense' better than 'sensibility' is one brought up in a community of free love, etc. But Blake's social conscience appeals to them *and* his beliefs. After all 'The Divine Image' is very much on the lines of *Honest to God*.

After my last lesson one of them came up to me and said, 'Do you know, Mrs Moore, it has all begun to happen to me.' I said, 'What has?' 'The change over from Innocence to Experience. I feel it is all about *me* that Blake is talking.' I had to run for my bus so couldn't continue the conversation then.

I finished my book on Tolerance, and Gollancz has faithfully promised to write the Introduction and bring it out in 1964, and if he doesn't my faith in man will be destroyed for ever. Now I am trying to write a book on 'The Maiden Aunt in Fact and Fiction'. I have done six chapters and Chatto likes it and wants me to go on. Do you know of any *unpleasant* Maiden Aunts? I can only think of Saki's in fact, there are several good ones in fiction.

I have had the grandchildren pretty often while my daughter has been working this Christmas. Katie (aged eight) is very fond of filling notebooks with poems and stories. One that I found began as follows: 'Robert lived in a plain London House. He was a good boy on the *whole*, but on the *half*, no one could call him exactly angelic. His sister Maria was brisk, firm and practical but very agreeable to him. He liked to make balloons. When he was at work on a balloon he did not care a fig for anything.'

So the time rushes by faster and faster. If only one's energies matched one's interests. Of course there are all the public happenings which I should like to discuss with you but it would take too long. In spite of the horror of Kennedy's assassination and of South Africa and of the rising population rate and the violence and sex press and films I feel more hopeful about the world than this time last year.

I have got a young nephew doing voluntary service under Father Huddleston and he sends home letters full of interest.

Have you written any more poems lately? or any new serious sketches for the stage? I always want to go to the East again and should also like to see New Zealand. D. H. Lawrence made me feel I *had* been to Australia.

Goodbye – may 1964 be just as happy and full of interest for you as 1963.

K.M.

My dear K.M.,

You have made me feel self-indulgent, too, with your good letter and I'm luxuriating even further by using a huge piece of paper. It is a dark morning, and I must fit two cotton frocks and buy some anemones for the flower table, but we are out to lunch so no need to think about food. The quotation from Katie's story has given me one of those moments of real nourishment and I thank you for it. Could you better 'Maria was brisk, firm and practical but very agreeable to him'? (Has she read Jane yet?) And after that perfect picture of Maria we learn that Robert liked to make balloons and while he was at work on a balloon he didn't care a fig for anything. What an economic pen. Is Katie as nice as she sounds? Her future seems assured because with a mind like that she can do anything.

While we are on the subject of the young I must report on a romance I had staying on a sheep station in Victoria. It is like an oversized Cumberland with rolling green hills and rivers and occasional forests. Simon is four and the grandson of our hosts. He has salmon pink hair and pale freckles and is the only child of two devoted people who waited a long time for him and go on hoping they will manage another some day. He's very bright and reflective. His new accomplishment, while we were there, was hopping. His voice is like wood-wind with a light Australian overtone and I·found it entrancing.

'Would you like to see me hop?'

'Very much.'

It took a lot of energy and he paused at the far end of the room with one leg still held up.

'Would you like to see me hop back?'

'Yes, please.'

The return journey was just as laboured.

'Would you like to see me hop again?'

'Er – well – a little later.'

He's been told you must always think of *other* people, so all his own wishes are put in that form. 'Would you like to sing me a song?' He always spoke to Reggie about 'your mother' – me! 'Would you like to see what your mother is doing now?' So they came into our room where I was writing letters, and he wondered if I wouldn't prefer to come and see the little blue wrens' nest in the garden?

We found Australia even lovelier this time. It has a real mystique (is that how it's spelt?). I think you sense its oldness more than anywhere else in the world. You can find real silence, for one thing, and those miles on miles of bush full of strange flowering shrubs and coloured birds are quite unlike anywhere else. The changes in the cities since we were there in 1959 are astonishing and all for the better. The European influences are useful, because they've improved food and living conditions and the looks of people and rooms. Last time I was there the shops were so dull and so shoddy, no taste at all. Now the shop-windows are inventively dressed, as good as New York or Woollands here (I think the best in London). Women are more simply dressed; not so much of sparkling 'jewellery'. It is as if the place has found its own character and believed in it. I know it's a mixture of cultures but it's turning into its own amalgam – if that's the word I want. Do you think it is because it is so far away that it is able to develop its own painting and poetry so strongly, whereas Canada has the U.S. breathing down its neck and is producing *nothing* of interest? Australia is tough and often unsympathetic, and I'm sure I'd be terribly homesick for London if I lived there now. But if I was young and still had friends to make, to grow up with, I think it would be a good place to be.

'Culture' is only just beginning, but when you know where to look it's got plenty of small centres. The young are internationally minded and very uncommitted to anything as far as I could see – as they are here. But idealists exist.

Being so underpopulated the talented feel they must pit their strength against world standards so leave home to do it, and at the moment this is a serious drain on the country. But I suspect it will change soon and become a two-way traffic as more and more people visit Australia and enjoy it.

New Zealand is much duller. It's very pretty – if you like Scotland, Switzerland, Norway. But give me the unique Australia. In New Zealand they are so kind and hospitable, and yet one feels the lack of any real sap. It is the Welfare State in full practice and the trades unions are so strong that *no* foreigners are allowed in in case employment might become competitive. They have a real chip on their shoulders about Australia. Jealousy, I suppose. From the theatre point of view they are as good as anywhere. Very responsive and warm. But it's *so* small, so peaceful and so parochial that after the first balm of such a contrast to our home life, it palls. Wellington was *far* too like Scotland for me – the dark rock, grey water, gorse-bushy kind of Scotland that fills me with gloom. Auckland is attractive, and very varied country lies all round it. There are oceans on both sides; one has low flat marshes and beaches, and five miles away across the narrow strip are beaches made of *black* sand that sparkles in a dazzling way, black cliffs and tropical forests. Best of all I liked Christchurch on the Canterbury plain. It's a university town with all the leisure in the world, you feel. A good tempo, pretty layout with willows all along the Avon river that winds through the town, lots of green spaces and very many attractive and intelligent people including nice Ngaio Marsh who is an uncrowned queen, very modest, very genuine with her time and talents, and much loved.

We were taken to see a colony of black swans nesting on the edge of a vast lake separated from the sea by a narrow bar of beach, so the water is brackish. We went early one spring morning, and the whole scene was a pale Chinese water-colour. Pale milk green lake, pale milk blue sky and on the far horizon the Southern Alps covered in snow. In the foreground were hundreds and *hundreds* of beautiful black swans with cherry red beaks. They wear white feathers under their wings, and when they fly the effect is startling and lovely.

There is the best natural history museum in Christchurch I've ever seen anywhere – superb showing of birds. They've invented a new way of mounting them, using plastic for legs and beaks so they can put the birds in natural, moving

49

positions and the result is a very lively set of cases filled with local birds and the huge alarming petrels that live in the far South. I saw tiny blue penguins about twelve inches high when I was on a black beach near Auckland. But compared to Australia New Zealand is very under-birded. The introduced species from here flourish as never before. Thousands of goldfinches, common as sparrows; thousands of blackbirds singing in English accents. Nice for the homesick expatriate but less interesting to birding visitors.

I started from here in July and flew to Hong Kong where I did one big concert in the splendid new City Hall. It's like the Festival Hall in feeling but not as big. Both there and in Singapore they now have first-class concert-sized Steinways and keep them in air-conditioned rooms *all* the time and only move them into the big auditoriums when air conditioning is on there, so they are able to keep them in real trim. It's made the whole difference to artistes, and now all the big Russian ones play there on their way to Australia and New Zealand – Europeans too. I thought Hong Kong most attractive, and one of the reasons is that in spite of appalling housing conditions all the Chinese look so happy and are so *pleasant*. Perhaps it means little, but the minute you land on the air-strip there are friendly smiles and welcoming hands. It's rather like Ireland in that way. You feel they are out to please, and this makes one start relaxed. I had the choice of shopping – *the* local sport because of low prices – or a sail and swim in a junk for my free day. Of course I chose the sail and swim. This junk was wide and comfortable and had three full-sized dunlopillo mattresses under a striped awning. The *silver*-toothed 'captain' pulled up a splendid patchwork sail, and we moved in a stately way over aquamarine water to anchor off a tiny island with a yellow crescent of sand and a little temple with the sea goddess in it. She was cross-eyed and dumpy *à la* Queen Victoria, and the temple was full of paper flowers and empty coke bottles, but the beach was pleasing. In and out of the water all day, a sea of silk with emerald green shadows. I was with American friends, and they produced iced shrimp salad and coffee, and we slept it all off under the stripes. A good day.

The concert was a sell-out and went happily. Next day to Singapore, and I found it oppressive and claustrophobic and uneasy. *Very* hot and damp. The air conditioning in my room though was *so* fierce I had to sleep with my head in a bed jacket. The town is very crowded, and the mixture of races is complete. I longed to have time to draw Sikhs, Malays, Chinese, etc., etc., and oh, so many children everywhere, so pretty, so pleasing and so poor.

The audience was mixed, too, lots of Chinese, and they seemed to love it. We were put on (we being Bill Blezard, who plays for me, and me) by the local Music Society, and I was in the charge of a very lethargic smiling Chinese woman who stood by whenever there was a case to lift or a dress to hang up and never for an instant offered a hand. I became amused about this, but as it got hotter and hotter and every chore seemed more of an effort, I also became a little tetchy, but I hope it didn't show.

Then by night in a big spacious Qantas plane, where I sat next to young Oistrakh on his way to play there, to Australia. Dawn came up, we had iced orange juice, and I got tidy to arrive; for I'd been warned there would be press. Indeed – yes. T.V. cameras and a conference with eight correspondents, and some with tape recorders. It was 7.30 a.m. The next two days were dedicated to promoting the tour ahead and I found it quite hard to say the same things in as many different ways as I could to all the various journalists. I'd made real friends in Sydney four years ago and they were at the airport to meet me. 7.30 a.m.! *Kind.*

(Heavens, this is turning into a book. I wonder if you've got so far?) I had a flat while I was in Sydney. It was right on the harbour, second floor up, with a huge window wall and a view of the bridge on my left and the water all around, and the opposite shore sparkling with little lights at night. Ferry boats link the coasts of the suburbs, and they scuttle by endlessly. I made a pleasing discovery. At night they look like mouth organs. The programme in the theatre was substantially the one I'd done at the Haymarket the year before. It went well. Indeed I broke the record for the Theatre Royal and did it on a mid-week matinée! They'd never had so many *standers* ever before – they were everywhere.

I managed several birding expeditions by getting up early and setting off at eight, back by two in order to stick to my very strict working regime of rest from two-thirty onwards and no social life at all. (Suits me!) In Melbourne I met a young naturalist, the local Peter Scott, who makes nature films and broadcasts a lot, and he took me to Sherbrooke Forest to see lyre birds. My luck was in, and after five minutes we came on a young male in full plumage doing his dance – displaying his great tail and singing his head off while he did it. It's a rare sight and many birders have watched and waited in vain for years, to see it. And there it was, early this cold spring morning after rain, and the ground was rich dark bitter chocolate mud, and the cold was sharp and clean. It's a very prehistoric bird, full of legends and mystery, and I had five minutes of its wonder from within *twenty feet*. Perfect view. It sings most excitingly, a Joan Sutherland sound; round, clear and powerful. It's a mimic and sings everyone else's songs too. When it dances it does a sort of three-beat drumming and makes an actual pattern in sound and in choreography. The same day we drove on to Healesville Sanctuary and saw a duck-billed platypus. His bill and hands are made of finest french kid glove material. He's *warm* to the touch. Birds of all sizes and colours are there in huge aviaries, and because the living is good all the wild parrots and finches come there too.

Page three and it's high time I stopped, but I haven't begun yet to tell you that Reggie flew out in mid-September to join me at the end of the Melbourne visit, and we went together to New Zealand for my three weeks' work there. His sister is married to Bernard Fergusson, who is now Governor-General, so we stayed in spacious comfort at Government House while I played Wellington. Laura went there straight from a small house on the west coast of Ayrshire where she had very little 'help' and no gardener. The contrast was alarming at first, but she's highly intelligent, loves people and is, they all say, the best Governess-General they've ever had. It's a wearing life. Endless small concerns, for New Zealand is *so* tiny – but she actively enjoys Flower Shows and Women's Institutes and Ladies' Chorals and Infant Welfares, so she's perfect for the job. Takes real interest. He is a writer, as you may know, and his appointment is romantic because his father and both his grandfathers were Governors-General before him. He too loves the job. Isn't it interesting that anyone could? Success is becoming, and they are both glowing in the nicest way.

After the tour ended, October 5th, we zoomed off back to Australia, had five days with friends who live on the water in Sydney and have a tennis court. It was a bank holiday weekend and we did nothing but play tennis and sit and talk. They are a pair of good people with four nice grown-up children and a lot of money, but they are conscious of responsibility and very quietly by stealth they do a great deal of good in constructive ways. (Responsibility is a subject, isn't it. No one wants it now, but it's vital to life. Did I ask you before if you'd read John Wain's article in last May's *Encounter* about 'Our Situation' in which he surveyed Great Britain and came out with a plea for responsibility? His paragraph about satire was so good. He said that a new class had found a voice and discovered what fun it was to stand on the side-lines and barrack. He went on to say that the young intellectuals – That-was-the-Week types – were putting it about that to mock the man at the wheel was another form of steering. Which of course it isn't. And he asked for some one with courage to come out and be *positive* about something for a nice change. To take responsibility.)

Queensland for two lovely weeks of absolute quiet with dear friends who live in a house on stilts and run cattle, Santa Gertrudis strain; heavy satiny-auburn beasts of gentleness and quality. The garden was bursting into flower – October's spring there – and nests were building, and the vine that covers the lower half, the stilts in fact, was covered in a white jasmine that scented the air. We slept, we walked, we talked, I sewed for Christmas, I sketched a little. We went to the Picnic Races, a very small affair but gala, and the ladies were so well turned out, home-made largely, and so fresh and pretty that I enjoyed it in spite of not much liking races and horses. (I like looking at horses in fields. Once in North Africa in the war a blizzard came down. The car wouldn't go. We sat there, the girl who played for me and I, with a defeated French driver, miles from anywhere in unearthly silence. Suddenly – a thundering – and about ten wild Arab ponies, white, brown and black, galloped across the road out of the blizzard. It was so beautiful. A frieze. A moment of poetry. It took our breath away.)

We birded *daily*. One evening, we were near the coast staying at their seaside bolt-hole two hundred and fifty miles away. We saw a kangaroo with her young joey eating grass beside her. They both froze. Then she must have given him the high sign, for he jumped into her pouch but left his tail hanging out.

After this a week in Victoria, where we met and loved Simon, then four days near Perth with an old school friend and her ornithologist husband. Reggie and the birding husband had a wonderful time in the woods. More nesting. I saw lovely things too.

And then Reggie flew off to South Africa via the Cocos Islands and Mauritius, and I flew in the opposite direction for California via Fiji and Honolulu. There I made a film called *The Americanisation of Emily*. *Very* controversial. Bitter and savage, about false standards of heroism – anti-war, etc., etc. It was a good small part and I think the script is good. Paddy Chayefsky. But it's rough, too.

And here I am – *pro tem*. But I have to go with Reggie to South Africa in February. I'm also seeing the Institute of Race Relations there and have said I'd do five performances for them next year. It's the *only* organisation I know of that is (*a*) practical and (*b*) permitted which is concerned with race relations. When I'm here it all seems *so* clear-cut. When I'm there face to face with the problem it's all much more difficult. I can't breathe in Johannesburg. Horrible place. But up country where we are, miles off, there are no troubles and it is a *beautiful* country.

I've been writing a little. Some poems. If I have time I'll send them later. I'm re-writing a T.V. play; have done a Shirley's Girl Friend for the Aldeburgh Festival in June –

Britten has asked me to do a performance. Isn't that a compliment?

Now it's 11 a.m., and I've got to go and get those anemones and fit the cottons for Messina (Transvaal).

What an indulgence this has been, and I haven't begun on books. Diana Athill's *Instead of a Letter* is good. Have you heard this, said to be by an Indian philosopher:

'Life is a bridge. Use it but don't build on it.'

I like this. Please write again.

This has been a very one-sided conversation. I envy you teaching. Have you read *An Experiment in Education* by Sybil Marshall? (Cambridge University Press.) I thought it excellent.

Later. I hope you don't feel bulldozed by such a long letter. *It wasn't meant to be*. There are so many things I meant to write about, and all you've got is a travelogue. I want to lend you an address made by Jim Darling, ex-headmaster of Geelong Grammar School and now head of Australian broadcasting. I liked it and thought you might too. We've been to the Old Vic this afternoon to see *The Recruiting Officer*. It was *very* enjoyable. The cottons fit comfortably. The anemones divided into colours look glorious under a lamp's light on my flower table in various small jugs and a mug, and some yellow chrysanthemums, small, are a sharp pleasure in a blue Bristol jug. If there was ever a self-indulgent correspondent, this is she!

Yours affectionately,

J.G.

P.S. Now it is later still, and I've just been rereading Jim's address as I wanted to be sure it was of interest to you. I think it is; although it isn't anything very new. But the fact that he is now an Australian, was talking to a lot of surgeons at the time, and is himself head of the A.B.C. makes it interesting to me. I have never met a complete man who wasn't religious. That is to say one who believes in something powerful outside himself. Not necessarily a churchgoer. But a believer.

I know what I wanted to tell you and that's why I've

begun on another page. While I was in America, early November, I had a letter from a close friend of ours telling me his wife was dying. The day I got home I telephoned, and two days later went down to Sussex to see her in hospital. She was always a person of enormous courage. Very English. Reticent, loyal, witty, warm and *brave*. She was slight and rather precise in looks, but as time went on she became more and more compassionate and loving, and it showed in her rather quiet face. You couldn't have found anyone more understanding. Her faith was a simple un-analytical one like a child's. A nursery faith; everyone would meet those they love again. Maybe she is right. I don't know. Anyway she believed strongly in spiritual life, and she was the most un-selfed creature I ever knew. (*Not* a spiritualist.)

She was very changed when I saw her, but – and the but is so wonderful – I *knew* as I sat with her that her essence, her true being, was absolutely unchanged, whole and eternal. Her husband and children felt the flame of her being all the time. The nurses, the matron and two doctors wrote to Johnny afterwards and said they had *never* witnessed anything like it before. She was so remarkable in her courage and calm. One doctor said he had learned from her about grace. She died finally after weeks of frailty, but all the time she had periods free from pain in which she laughed and reminisced with Johnny and the children. They are a devoted, friendly family, and they have done *so* much for all their friends by the way this whole thing has been. I felt it had been a real privilege to have seen her. I've known her since I was a child: a family friend, close as a cousin. She was such good company. I know all is well with her and rejoice in all the good times we all had together.

Isn't it odd the way people get sad about happy times in the past just because they are past. I go *on* enjoying them. Do you? Being a Quaker you will know William Penn's writings. Do you know the thing he wrote about death? It begins:

'They that love beyond the world cannot be separated by it.'

If you don't know it I'll copy it out for you.

I've come to think that the qualities we love in people *are* the undying be-ing. We may think it's the way they speak, the shape of their nose, their laugh – but it is the essence of them reflected in qualities and these are spiritual *only* and forever real.

Now I'm finished and here is a small poem I began last year and finished a week or so ago. It comes as a belated New Year wish to you.

J.G.

What eye beholds the Spring?
No retina or lens
With signals to the brain
Could compass such a thing.

If on this earth we see
The green immensity
And hear the music's ring
Where can the real Spring be?

From time to time the mind
Sees more than mortal range,
The universe made plain,
A seeing for the blind.

It is the eye of Mind
That sees and hears and knows
The law that holds intact
The man, the star, the rose.

I'm not in a hurry for the speech, so read it at your leisure. Thank you so much for your letter. I enjoyed it very much, and you see what it sparked off!

J.G.

Dear J.G.

I wish I could think of anything I could do for you in return for the enormous pleasure your letters give me – and especially for this last one. But of course I can't. I should think, like Beatrice, 'A star danced when *you* were born' – for you give such pleasure to thousands – I am *so* glad about your success *everywhere* and about your invitation for the Aldeburgh Festival – how I wish I could go, but perhaps it may be broadcast.

That you should find time to write such letters to me! Well, words fail me, though they don't quite, or I wouldn't be writing this. You couldn't expect me not to write again after such a letter. You write so well and so vividly that I can see what you tell me about, and the lovely pictures come back to me in the watches of the night – the black swans by the milk green lake and the frieze of wild horses and the lyre-bird (how *thrilling* that must have been!) Have you read D. H. Lawrence's *Kangaroo*? I haven't for *years*, but his descriptions of the Australian bush have remained in my mind and match yours. I understand what you feel about the difference between Australia and New Zealand, but I must say Canterbury sounds most attractive. The *space* in both and the underpopulation must be lovely. I *would* like to hear and see multitudes of birds again. It is terrible – the depletion of birds in England in my lifetime, and I get horribly depressed at the contraction and disappearance of wild life everywhere. Pierre de Chardin says in his letters that at first he felt very sad at this, but as he sees it as a necessary step in evolution he has learnt to accept it in faith. I can't feel like this because, I suppose, I'm not convinced that it *is* a step in evolution.

Your letter is so full of nice people too, from little hopping Simon to the Governor-General of New Zealand. Talking of Simon makes me want to talk about Katie again. No, she hasn't read Jane Austen yet – eight is a bit too young, don't you think? – but I often think how she will revel in her later on, and I can't help seeing a resemblance in 'her economic pen' and in her early developed rather ironic humour. I can't resist sending you a poem of hers, though I don't really think poetry is her line, because it shows her character so clearly. Her brother is very different, dreamy, *very* musical, *very* unpractical and something of a mystic. But they are great friends and never quarrel as witness the following conversation:

D. 'I boast about Katie at school, you know.'

Me to K. 'Do you boast about Daniel?'

K. 'No, but I wouldn't have any other brother!'

He looks like his character too. It is curious how some people's looks fit their essences and some are like irrelevant possessions passed down from forebears but not fitting – like the wrong sort of house. I think voices are often more characteristic than faces, which is one reason why I prefer listening to T.V.

This brings me to what you say about the spiritual essence of people and to your friend. Thank you for telling me about her. It is lovely to hear of such people –

> They are indeed our Pillar-Fires
> Seen as we go;
> They are that City's Shining Spires
> We travell to.

It may be 'a nursery faith' that we shall meet again those we love – but if one has experienced love as *the* reality of this life surely it is not too much to believe that love cannot be mocked by death – that, as Penn says, 'Death cannot kill what never dies. Nor can spirits ever be divided that love and live in the same Divine Principle.' And if we love, we must love *persons* and so, to mean anything, personality must continue (just as it seems to me the Godhead if it is Divine Love must *contain* personality). Yes – I utterly agree that the spiritual essence of people is what we love, but it is such a miracle that this is *different* in each person. Yes – I also agree of course about the past, though sometimes, while enjoying and treasuring the happy times one can at the same time be overcome with longing for the people who are no longer here. Perhaps some people can't face that.

Some, too, seem to think that because the past is over it is no longer real, or not as real as the present. As a matter of fact, of course, it is never over.

I have read Darling's address with much interest – I am sure that it is encouraging that so many are *aware* of the dangers of specialisation and departmentalism, but it *is* a problem and it seems to be getting worse. For many years we gave a prize to the two big local Grammar Schools here, in memory of my son (who was a 'whole' person if ever there was one) for an essay or original piece of work done by one of the Science VIth on something entirely outside his own subject. We had some *very* good and varied work submitted, but gradually the quality and quantity deteriorated, until about two years ago we discontinued it on the advice of both heads who gave as a reason – more pressure of competition in VIth and more social life and more T.V. The last two of course *can* have their own widening effect. As to the Faith which Darling speaks of as essential, of course I agree again, and I believe this age may reshape the expression of that Faith to its own satisfaction and get back a right feeling about responsibility.

Books. Yes – *An Experiment in Education* – fascinating. I'm immersed in late eighteenth century and early nineteenth century at present, because I'm doing Lady Caroline Fox as one of my Aunts and I'm a great addict at getting lost in a period. Also reading a new Penguin *The Church and the Age of Reason* by G. R. Cragg – very interesting.

If I went on trying to answer your letter properly I'd never stop, but don't think I wasn't interested in the things I have *not* commented on. Another lovely thing was that it came just as I retired to bed with a devastating cold – I had just been nursing my husband who crawled down as I crawled up.

I *do* envy you sun in February in South Africa. Aren't anemones a joy this time of the year. A sweet old village woman (family lived here for generations) brought me a bunch on Christmas Eve, which I only threw away last week and my daughter brought me some more yesterday. I liked your spring poem *so* much – the best of those I've seen yet. I think what 'the mind sees' 'from time to time' are 'bright shoots of everlastingness'.

I *must* stop. I don't NEED or WISH for an answer to this but I fear I must ask you to post me back the children's photographs as I haven't other copies of these. I ought not to trouble you with them but you will forgive a fond and foolish grandmother and just send them *without* bothering to write again.

Bless you. Yours affectionately

K.M.

18 January   *Elm Park Gardens*

My dear K.M.,

If I don't write now I doubt if I'll write for a week, as next week is full of American friends and meetings, etc. What a good answer you wrote to me. Thank you *so* much for all of it. I like knowing what Katie looks like; and Daniel too. Herewith in your *thoughtfully* provided stamped envelope. I think Beauty by Katie aged eight is *remarkable*. I love the mountain as a 'great heap of dirt'. It's all so free and exuberant; an unlimited pen as well as an economic one! Thank you very much for writing it out for me.

On Thursday I heard the following as I passed by an elderly woman – granny? – talking to a small girl of about three. Subject unknown. Granny spoke with confidence:

'Now you won't lose it, will you?'

Small girl with equal confidence: 'Yes'.

It made me smile happily all the way down the street. Was the child being honest or in fact so conditioned to saying an agreeable 'yes' that she wasn't thinking?

Do you know Virginia Graham's poem about 'Aunts'? Not maiden, I'm afraid, but general aunts.

We are going to see *Tom Jones* this afternoon and are lunching on top of the Hilton first. I disapprove of the

Hilton, but I want to see the view, and it's a pretty day for it.

Again *thank you* for your good letter and details.

Yours gratefully,

J.G.

Dear J.G.,

It was nice to hear you last night on 'Frankly Speaking', though I don't think it told me anything I didn't know before, except that your mother was interested in education and that you were interested in Christian Science. For though we have talked about religion I don't think this particular aspect has ever cropped up. I know very little about it, myself – only I think their places of meeting always look very attractive from the outside.

I couldn't help comparing what you said about the relationship between yourself and your audience with what I feel (in less degree of course) when teaching a receptive and appreciative class. There is the same two-way effect. Also the same *variety*. For instance, this year I have two divisions (about twenty-two in each) for the same subject, so that my lesson is supposed to be repeated. But it never is. The reception is always toally different, and so I can understand how you too never give the same performance twice. When you gave the 'provocative eyes' illustration to show how the audience's laugh differed from your expectation, didn't you perhaps forget that *you* knew what was coming, but that the full delicious humour of the whole was dependent on the *contrast* of the provocative eyes thrill and noticing the sleeve going into the salad? This the audience could only appreciate after hearing the whole, and so the laugh that followed was for *both* bits and for the delighted recognition. 'Yes, that's exactly what *does* happen on these occasions.'

Oh – I do so love the *truth* of your gentle satire. It gives me as much pleasure as Jane Austen's, and is also, of course, of your own age and so has all the more point. I do hope you've had a good time since you wrote last. The months since Christmas have been much too full of illness here. My poor little Katie has had whooping cough, tonsillitis, gastric flu and bronchitis all in a horrid sequence and is not well yet, nor can be till this weather changes. That whole family has been afflicted – in fact when I went round yesterday to do a bit of nursing Daniel (aged eleven) had put a notice up with a red cross on the door and 'The Lord Have Mercy on this House'. Much comfort can be derived from a comparison with the Plague of 1665!

I used to wonder why Scandinavian literature was so pessimistic and dreary, but since we've been having so little sun for the past two years I wonder no longer. All the same I've got some brave little water-lily tulips out in my front garden and lots of daffodils, and inside I've got a pot of freesias and a bright glowing little azalea. I am so glad you like flowers so much. To me, their extraordinarily varied beauty and scent is always a miracle and *certainly* one of the never-failing 'bright shoots of everlastingness'. It is comforting to think that though in the future the true undefiled country in England may dwindle and dwindle people will surely still have flowers, for so many can be grown in such a small space.

Isn't one fearfully lucky to have had a nice mother and a nice husband. I think one owes life a great debt for that.

I must stop. I never meant to write to you at all this afternoon – it just came over me and I did. I hope you are finding time for more poetry and sketching.

Your always appreciative 'pen friend'

K.M.

10 April   *Stanway*

My dear 'Pen Friend',

It was, as usual, good to get your letter. Thank you very much. I write from an attic in an orange sandstone house in the Cotswolds where we have come in order to go to a family wedding in Tewkesbury Abbey tomorrow. The garden is

63

full of new daffodils, more promise than fulfilment and that's how I like them *best*. Green beaks. It's a big house with a huge high hall, ancient and noble, and in spite of logs and radiators not nearly warm enough for my transatlantic tastes, but the sun is still out, and I'm on a sofa in the attic room away from all the arriving kith and kin. My husband's family. All have gardening in their bones, tend to smoke and cough, are an average seventy-eight years old, some deafer than others. I like them, but enough is enough and nothing is worth yelling fff is it? (I am truly compassionate about the deaf. It's the least sympathised with affliction, and it must be so boring never to get the throwaway remarks and sudden little exclamations. By the time you've said: 'I was only saying "How *lovely*" ' the moment is over, gone, lost, and it's impossible to re-flower it). So here I am in sunset light enjoying myself in the luxury of writing to you. The three King Charles spaniels, named Pepys, Charles and Henrietta, have just barked at the sound of wheels on gravel. Another arrival. We are to be ten. At fifty-three I'm the young thing. (Heavens, I'm fifty-four! I never can remember this.) A sister and brother-in-law are here, an aunt and uncle (he is L. E. Jones who wrote those 'Victorian Childhood' or was it 'Boyhood'? 'Edwardian Afternoon' and 'Georgian *Something*'.* He's seventy-nine and good company. Doesn't cough or smoke, nor is he deaf, so that's nice too!). And four more remote relations.

I'm glad you liked the broadcast. I've had some very friendly letters. I'm not one to proseletyse (is that how it's spelt? Perhaps an i rather than a y?) so I don't talk much about my faith. All I will say now is that it isn't as dotty as the world thinks it is – it *couldn't* be and work! It is a disciplined study, and the *freedom* it gives me is the thing I am most grateful for. It answers all my questions, solves all my problems, is the climate in which I live. It requires constant practice, and only recently have I discovered how worth the effort it is. I was brought up in it, but like anything else it had to be discovered all over again when I

* *A Victorian Boyhood, An Edwardian Youth, Georgian Afternoon.*

64

began to *think*; and what I thought it was when I was young is entirely different from what I find it to be now.

Yes, the recreating of 'teaching' must be very like my work in the theatre with an audience. Keeps you fresh.

What a plaguy time you've all had – Kate and Daniel. I hope these shafts of sun are getting through and being useful, at least to the spirits, even if they don't do much actual warming yet.

Yes, flowers. And don't they have personalities and don't they behave differently for different people. A vase of stiff unloved flowers is worse than nothing; a jam-jar of lovingly stuck in primroses, wind-flowers and two violets makes you glow with joy. I have certain horrors. Bronze chrysanths; six 'glads' in a cut-glass vase; *most* orange flowers unless part of a mixture. I've got a friend in Suffolk for whom two roses will spin in an old jug and evoke all the poetry and music of roses you've ever known. She can't do flowers badly. She's a painter.

One of my favourite exercises is to look *into* a small flower like a daisy or a hellebore or white violet. As you say – 'bright shoots of everlastingness'. What *designs*. Shells, too. I like all white flowers, specially when they have green shadows.

Yes, I had a superb father as well as a fascinating mother. He was good, just, funny, wise, handsome and the *best* company to do things with.

Now I've had a bath and feel warmer. It is eight. We always eat early at home because it's so good to get the washing-up over and done with, and anyway we get hungry. A blackbird is making the most lovely wet notes. There is a cedar tree, black against the azalea sky. It's by the church. There's a blue-faced clock on the tower and a delicate weather-vane above it. It is very English and *so* pretty.

I'm doing a little writing. Talks for 'Woman's Hour', a poem of two; half a monologue I can't finish. (I've done a Shirl for Aldeburgh Festival about a music festival. I like it.) Next week I do a money-raiser for family planning in Newcastle, and on the nineteenth an Old People's Welfare one in Nottingham. To Switzerland on the twenty-eighth –

May 3 to do four concerts in and around Geneva. Then May 4 to 17, two three-quarter-hour T.V. programmes of my solo theatre 'show' for B.B.C. Possibly a film after that.

I sketched in the bush in Africa. *Difficult* but absorbing to do. Not frameable but reminders.

I did like your letter – I hope the children are mending properly now.

Yours affectionately,

J.G.

14 September   *Riverside House*

Dear J.G.,

You left out white jasmine, which for me has more magic even than white lilac. But how right you are about flowers and music. All sorts of sounds are magic – bird song especially, and the wind among stretches of sedge – you are right about seasons too – intimations of spring and even summer in hot January sun on brick and the sudden smell of autumn (my favourite season) in wet leaves in an August lane. I have a secret valley, too, not far from yours – it can't be the same, for mine is in Yorkshire. There was one evening there, by a stream 'in that faint light with which the hills are dressed after the sun's remove'.

It was so nice to hear you talking about these 'shoots of everlastingness' yesterday. By the way I came across this in Maria Edgeworth's letters not long ago and thought of you – written when she was in the eighties – 'Slip on, for Time's Time!' said a man, exhorting the railroad omnibus. ' "Slip on, Time's Time!" I have been saying to myself contin-ually; and now I am coming to the last gasp, and Time slips so fast, that Time is not Time – in fact there's no Time.'

I must tell you of a more obvious magic I've been enjoying lately – the magic of a wonderful holiday. A friend gave us some money *only* to be spent on holidays and we've been travelling about Scandinavia – Denmark (which we already knew and loved), Sweden and Finland; from there we crossed over to Leningrad. Do you know Russia? I was unprepared for feeling that I'd stepped back into a Russian

66

novel. I thought things would be too changed, but I never felt that they were essentially so.

We arrived in a Leningrad which *looked* quite unreal. It was evening, and the colour was that of an old print – a gunmetal shining grey, with soft pink clouds and the improbably beautiful great green and white buildings and the gold towers against the flat grey sky and the huge trafficless square – all seemed part of another world. So did our nineteenth-century hotel with a little old peasant woman with an ivory face, peaceful but suffering, who worked the huge ineffectual Victorian lift – our bedroom with its Russian green silk coverlets and dark red walls and the *very* poor plumbing and sanitation.

The most interesting thing I found were the people – often very poor and tired looking, but also vital, childlike and *loving* a joke – the crowds of very good children. I never saw or heard a crying or complaining child. The most exquisite things were the Hermitage and the Summer Residence and the view across the Neva; the most inspiring the service I went to in a ruined church – *crammed* with devotion and with the most lovely singing I have ever heard; the most amazing were the metro stations – each one like Coventry Cathedral. They are better even than the Moscow ones, less ornate and more beautiful.

What I love in Scandinavia is the space and walking for hours in the huge forests with water always near – and inside of people's houses – *so* bright and pretty and clean.

I *do* hope all goes well with you. Have you written any more poetry?

My book on 'Tolerance' comes out soon and I've almost finished 'The Maiden Aunt'. I hope it finds a publisher because I rather like it. Teaching begins again this week. Grandchildren in good form.

With my love

K.M.

It is silly to generalise after such a short visit anywhere, but of course one always does. And to go back to the Russian people again, what I felt was they they were essentially still a religious and spiritual people – a people of dreams. Their metro stations are part of a dream, and that is why they are such an achievement. They are not interested in the ordinary business of living – so the sanitation is bad and there are holes in the roads and the buses come apart. But, oh! how lovely it was to get away from advertisements and to see the buildings properly without all the proportions being spoilt by cars. All the same getting back to Finland was like getting home!

16 September   Elm Park Gardens

Dear K.M.,

It was particularly good to see your writing yesterday. Thank you very much. I'd been thinking about you earlier on and planned to write, but I'm off to Canada tomorrow to do four big concerts, and then we – my husband is going with me, isn't it lovely? – go to New York to see my brother and the children and see friends, so I've been busy in getting ready and hadn't written. Now I ought to be upstairs planning which stage dress goes in which case with which other dress, etc., etc. However, I'll indulge myself in a brief note to thank you so much for your letter about the broadcast. I do wish you'd heard the original, because Sunday's was a cut version and left out the bit about colour and Victoriana, etc., and *words*. I think I may have the thing typed out as a sort of Christmas card, and if I do, please may I send one to you? I think it is very interesting to find that a very simple talk such as this was can communicate with such a *wide* variety of people. I had the most remarkable letters – some quite illiterate but full of appreciation – particularly about wild white violets!

(That seems to be the end of that black pencil pen called a Pentel which is a joy to draw with and comes from Japan.) One letter came from an old lady called Myrtle, seventy-nine, who said she'd been darning her husband's socks as she listened (to the original full-length talk) and that it took her back to pre-1914 days when she used to walk home down the lanes from church with her dear parents and brothers and found the first white violet. (It was in Epsom!) She added: 'All have been taken now. I shed a tear as I listened to your fresh voice . . .' and went on to say they weren't tears of sadness but of happiness remembered.

It's been a lovely summer, hasn't it? We had our week in Cumberland in May. Then ten days at Aldeburgh for the Festival in June. This was very exciting for me as Ben Britten had asked me to do the final Saturday entertainment, and I'd written four new items for the programme. It went most gaily and was the most exciting evening of *all*, I think.

It's been a busy summer, starting with four concerts in Switzerland, early May. Two fifty-minute T.V. programmes taped in late May – and one seen on Channel 2 in August, and the next due September 26 – a film *The Yellow Rolls-Royce* in which I played the down-trodden Southern companion of Ingrid Bergman as a rich and domineering Swedish-American widow. She was very nice to work with; is as she appears to be, straightforward, friendly. Curious attitudes to morals, but somehow simple and basically decent too. It's *not* a great film, but will be good glossy entertainment I suspect.

Quite a lot of writing this year. Some poems. Mostly holy ones. Next year I've been asked to give *the* lecture to a big Technical College in Coventry and haven't any idea what to do it about, but it's certainly a 'challenge', and quite a new sort of area for me, and I'd like to do it well. Perhaps some sort of link between the Arts and Sciences – on the level *I* can understand, that is. In other words: the whole man must include the arts in some form or other or he is deprived of his full inheritance.

Yes, white jasmine. And I have a distant affection for snowdrops. I loved all you told me about Russia. What a *lovely* holiday. I look forward to *Tolerance*. It was one of my father's pet subjects. It must be a loving tolerance, of course, and not a to-hell-with-it one.

I must go and pack. This is really being too self-indulgent. But interrupted self-indulgent. The telephone hasn't stopped ringing since I started this letter, so forgive incoherence and thanks for a very good letter.

With love,

J.G.

Dear J.G.,

Your welcome September letter remained unanswered, because I knew that you were in Canada and New York and that you had a very full programme when you returned. I do hope you had a very successful four concerts and that you enjoyed your family and friends in New York to the full.

This has been a *glorious* Autumn. I have never known a better one – the wooded hills at each side of our valley were great banks of burning colour. I enjoyed every moment of it – my favourite time of the year.

I want to write about so many things. First – I have just finished reading Laurence Whistler's *The Initials in the Heart*. I remember you had written to me about his poems. I thought this book beautiful and triumphant, and it said, though much better than I could ever have expressed it, so many things that I *know* to be true about suffering and bereavement and the assurance, through one's own experience of love, of God as Love. I liked so much all he says about eternity and time and happiness and the descriptions of the country. I remember you said you thought his extreme devotion to Jill might be a bit hard for his second wife to bear, but now I don't think this would be so. She must have realised it before she married him, and somehow that dream at the end of the book when all three were together in perfect happiness and union seemed to explain the inexplicable – how one love and one joy doesn't exclude another, even of this sort.

I am sending you my *Tolerance* book as an early Christmas present and I do hope you will like it. It is really meant to be read consecutively because the arrangement is important, even of individual passages. I would like to know something more about your own Christian Science philosophy. I know so little about it, nothing at all from the inside. I should also love to see some more poetry, especially the holy ones. Have you decided on your subject for the Coventry lecture yet?

I am finding the Reith Lectures exciting – are you? Do you know Sir Leon Bagrit at all? I was very interested to see that he is Chairman of the Friends of Covent Garden. I do like many-sided people. I wish I could understand more about science and that I had been taught by this new method of *starting* one off on mathematical *thinking*. I had a blind spot in my brain as far as maths were concerned, and in this scientific age it makes one feel illiterate. My husband and son both had this width of interest in both the sciences and the arts (by the way I'd like *you* to know that the passage in *Tolerance* on page 84 is about my son).

I am sure we shall have to avoid early specialisation by making our university courses longer – as of course they do in many countries in Europe.

I ought not to write any more – so many jobs waiting to be done, but I don't mind any of them, for they are none of them tiresome. I hope you'll have a *very* nice Christmas and take some time off. I am looking forward very much to the typed copy of your broadcast with the bits in it that were cut from the version that I heard. You promised it to me for a Christmas card you know.

With very heartfelt wishes for Christmas and the year to come. Yours is one of the lives it makes me happy just to think about.

With love

K.M.

[The next letter was written before my letter of 3 December had arrived.]

8 December   *Elm Park Gardens*

My dear K.M.,

Before the rush becomes too intensive I write to send you wishes for Christmas and the New Year. I thought perhaps you might like to see the text of a little broadcast I did for 'Woman's Hour' in August. They gave me the title – 'My Kind of Magic' and left me free to explore it. Later – last week – the Poetry Society had one of their Fridays and gave me the hour to expand this talk in, with illustrations, and that was quite an exercise and *very* good fun (for me). Hard work too.

In fact ever since we got back from Canada and America at the end of October I seem to have been writing various talks and pieces for magazines, etc. Above all looms a real 'challenge' and one I'm rather awed by: an hour's lecture to a college of technical students, engineers, in Coventry in May. It is *the* lecture of their year; gets put into a little pamphlet afterwards, and never has it been given by a woman until now. '*Any* subject' they said, 'except engineering.'

I *think* I'm doing it under the wide umbrella heading of 'Communications'. It's a bit fashionable, but it's also full of interest to me and embraces almost literally everything – eye – ear – heart *and* mind. I've already done a lot, scrapped it, re-done it, re-arranged it. It's indeed a 'challenge', but I'm fascinated by it.

It's been a lovely year. In brief – Africa for February, miles away from trouble, in the loveliest rolling country with birds and beasts and blessed sun. Also six days at the Cape bathing in blue sea. March was full of jobs – opening a theatre in Lancashire, doing concerts, etc. May took us both to Switzerland where I did four shows to crowded houses. Very surprising. Spring and the fields full of flowers. April was rehearsal time for two big T.V. hour-long programmes for B.B.C.2 shown in August-September. The first was repeated on B.B.C.1 in October. So I suppose the second one will eventually appear on B.B.C.1 too. I played in a film *The Yellow Rolls-Royce*, in May–June. Our ten-day break in Cumberland was perfect with bluebells and pied flycatchers and peace.

For me the year's high-spot was Aldeburgh Festival. The greatest honour I've ever had came when Ben Britten asked me to do the 'light' evening on the final Saturday. I wrote special material, and it went happily. In between all these journeys and concerts, I made a new L.P. record, *just* coming out. Then we went to Canada and the U.S.A. The American fall is so breathtakingly vivid and beautiful and never ceases to startle me with its wonder. This was a special year somehow. High blue skies and the blaze of red, pink, orange and yellow trees. We stayed mainly out in Connecticut with an old and congenial friend in a white wooden house, 1740, and as cosy and comfortable as possible.

I have two stories for you. My New York nephew and niece are eight and ten and eager, but not very accurate, seekers after culture. We played general knowledge at Sunday lunch and sought the name of Great Painters. No one was to speak until absolutely sure he had one ready. Lang's arm shot up. He had one (This is such a New York remark): Leonard da Vinski. Sally is much more sophisticated but equally erratic, and her's was 'Piscassio'. She knew she'd got it wrong, though, and said 'No – silly of me – that's a nut.' Department of utter confusion!

In a New York Museum I watched three ladies with one catalogue. One held it and informed the others but she hadn't got her spectacles. 'Oh look' she said, 'they've got a Louise Lautrec.'

One more quote. Lang typed a story on his father's machine at high speed and this immortal line came my way: 'Instead of strangaling her he huged her.'

No more. I hope you have got this far. I'm about to confer with the producer of a gentle half-hour I'm to do for *radio* on Christmas Eve and with another one for 'Five to Ten' on the Light some day.

Later. This is a very egotistical letter. One more item. Last year in November I went to Hollywood and played in a fiercely satiric piece against war; Paddy Chayefsky wrote it. My scenes were interesting to do and though harsh and possibly cruel in their attitude toward making death romantic and heroic, whether it was or not, were not offensive. But friends who've seen the picture *The Americanisation of Emily*, in New York have been very upset *and* offended by it. I haven't seen it and am now apprehensive and wish I hadn't done it. I knew there were crude scenes in it, but hadn't realised they were 'offensive'. A pity.

I hope all goes well with you. How are the grandchildren? Have you read *The Initials in the Heart* by Laurence Whistler? A remarkable book and I was moved by it.

Don't write till you have time. I expect you're very busy. This brings affectionate wishes for Christmas and the New Year, from

J.G.

8 December   *Elm Park Gardens*

My dear K.M.,

I've just come in from posting your letter to you to find yours to me – and the book, which I'm longing to read. Thank you *so* much. I now realise I had told you most of our year's news in an earlier letter. *Forgive me!* Dottiness!

I enclose a little pamphlet put out by the Christian Science church that may help to answer some of your questions. It was done for the Christian Science Pavilion at the World's Fair.

Coming back from a visit to Marks and Spencer and then a singing lesson in St John's Wood, I listened (car radio) to a *very good* talk on religious points of view by someone called Kenneth Barnes, a Quaker and a headmaster. I think it was probably part of schools broadcasting, and if it was it can have done nothing but good for its tolerance and open-minded honesty.

I too have enjoyed the Bagrit lectures. Did I say this in my letter?

I've just had time to look at the letter about your son and it is such a tribute that I feel full of joy for you that you had such a son.

This isn't a real thank you for the book. When I've read the book I will write again.

Meanwhile, how pleasant that we were thinking of each other about the same time.

With love,

J.G.

1965

Dear J.G.,

I said on my card that when the Christmas rush was over I would answer your letters and enclosures properly. My spate of visitors has now dried up; my dear teenage adopted grandson (an orphaned child from a displaced persons camp in Germany, whom we got through the Friends' Relief Service and whom we have had since he was two years old) has now gone back to his farming college and the sounds of the transistor and the motor-bike are silent at last. The other grandchildren have started school, but I don't begin my teaching again till next week, so in this more or less peaceful interim I want to catch up with letters, and especially yours.

I was so pleased to have your magic talk in full and I *do* like it. In one special way I think this sort of magic is stronger than when one is young, for in youth it is so mixed up with personal emotions (like being in love). Now it is 'bright shoots of everlastingness', and that is that.

Thank you too for the Christian Science booklet which I have read with much interest. It has a good deal in common with Quakerism, in being a lay society, for instance, without either a priesthood or a creed. The Friends too believe in spiritual healing though they would not go so far as to say that 'the origin of *all* disease is mental'. I am glad you like Kenneth Barnes. He is a fine man, a science master with a school of his own. He has written a short book which I think you would also like called *The Creative Imagination* (to be still got, I think, at The Friends' Bookshop Euston Road).

He is also one of those Friends who was responsible for a pamphlet called *A Quaker View of Sex* which caused rather an outcry within and without the Society about two years ago.

Thank you for what you said about my son and the letter which I included in *Tolerance*. Yes – it was and *is* a joy – for if there is *any* meaning in existence such a personality as his and all others so cut short must surely be experiencing life more abundantly in another sphere. He always loved life so. I remember once, when he was a small boy, asking him which was his favourite time of the day. He answered immediately, 'Oh the morning, because then I've another long lovely day in front of me.' Yet, when, just after his thirteenth birthday he was knocked down by a van and had a badly fractured leg, arm and head injuries, he asked me how long he would be laid up and I had to tell him, his only comment was, '*Don't* mind so much, Mother, considering how long I've lived and how long I'm going to live, a year out of my life doesn't really matter.'

I loved the stories of your niece and nephew. My daughter is having another child this spring. The other children of course are delighted.

I had a lovely book on The Hermitage collection for Christmas, also Pierre de Chardin's *Future of Man*, of which I only understand about half, but that is well worth while as an antidote to lack of faith.

I also had the most beautiful *white* cyclamen that I have ever beheld – like a flock of white angels – *not* the sentimental kind, but the strong terrifyingly pure ones.

I enjoyed your Christmas broadcasts very much. By the way I listened to you and my granddaughter broadcasting on the same day as her form at school were doing carols and readings in 'Lift Up Your Hearts' on Christmas Eve.

What a wonderful year you had in 1964. I *do* hope 1965 will be as good for you. Goodbye and love and *thanks* for our pen friendship which I *so* much enjoy.

Katharine Moore

My dear K.M.,

Your letter has beaten me to it. Thank you so very much. The reason I haven't written till now is that I have been rationing your *Tolerance* to a few pages a night, and I didn't want to write until I'd savoured every good word *slowly*. It is a *lovely* book. I have already given it to three people and plan to increase the circulation further. I've not only enjoyed it but been moved to new positions through it. It must have been a labour of love; it is full of it. I find it particularly well done when you make the clear distinction between *laisser faire* and tolerance. 'I couldn't care less' is my unfavourite expression of an unappetising attitude; and a very contemporary one. But to care enough to love enough is the way of course.

I loved the unexpected piece of Lady Ottoline Morrell. I've also marked Bishop Tillotson – 'Knowing no man can grow wiser without some change of mind, etc., etc.' And Blake about 'reptiles in the mind'! And of course Traherne – almost best of all. And Marcus Aurelius – 'Man is made of kindness'. Hooray – *yes*. Liked all your de Chardin pieces, particularly p. 57. And Richard Hoggart, p. 71. He is a friend; we were on Pilkington together, and I admire and like him. What a good book he wrote.

I was particularly interested in Stafford-Clarke's piece on love. Carefully uncapitalised, I note! Never mind: Love *is* love and love *is* Love, whether it is always recognised as such or not.

I thank you so much for the book. I have loved it on a first, slow, deeply enjoyed reading of it and I shall keep it near for further enjoyment, nourishment and delight. *Thank you!*

Have you heard of a book called *Self Renewal* by ? Gardener? American. It is about individual self renewal, of course, but also of nations and businesses, and it is most interesting and good. I'm in bed, and when I get up after a luxurious morning of writing while the rains pound the windows I will look it up for you more accurately. I think

Mr Gollancz should do it here if it isn't already being done. He wrote another called *Excellence* that I'm told *is* excellent. All you tell me (and I have read in the letter) of your son is full of wonder. Thank you.

My days have been full of this lecture-talk I'm writing and I *think* I have finished it. It is still too close to me to know if it has any worth. I'll let it set and then reappraise when I'm free of it. I've found a title: 'View from a Small Corner'. The *view* needn't be small no matter how modest the corner!

We had an unexpected delight in seeing Micheál Mac Liammóir in his Irish evening. The Wilde one is good, but the Irish one has fascination in it. He talks about the old Irish heroes, poets, the eighteenth-century writers, the twentieth-century giants (or are they nineteenth? – Wilde – Yeats – Shaw – O'Casey – all born before 1900). He is an unattractive man, froglike and mannered, and yet he has the storyteller's power, and I found myself sitting on the edge with my mouth open while he did a brilliant piece of James Joyce. I do recommend him. One more week at the Queen's, I believe.

Today we are off to see *Camelot* in spite of the notices. People I trust have found worth and pleasure in it and say it looks good too. So on a wet mild Saturday afternoon we are off to the matinee, and I'm looking forward to it. I'm busy writing 'material' for a possible season (three weeks or so) at the end of March. I half want to do it and am half lazy.

I'd like to go on talking to you for hours, but I must go and cook chops and tidy the place up. I have help all the week but not on Saturdays and Sundays, and I'm amazed at the way crumbs come and spread and little bits of unneeded fluff appear!

With love, and I too *very much* enjoy our pen friendship.

J.G.

I love the angel cyclamen.
Self Renewal, The Individual and the Innovative Society, John W. Gardner (Harper & Row, 1963).

Dear J.G.,

You couldn't expect me not to answer such a letter as your last immediately! It was the very nicest kind of appreciation because so discerning and knowledgeable. Of course your way of reading my book is the way I wanted people to read it, and I was much pleased also to read Richard Church's review in *Country Life*, where he says 'I have been browsing in the book at bedtime over several weeks and have found much profit.' I *do* value yours and his approval. Thank you *so* much. Yes – it *was* a labour of love, and I miss it and my 'Aunts' book too. Now I am busy over a queer little thing on *Kipling and the White Man's Burden* commissioned by Faber for a series on contemporary history for VIth forms. It is really on the literary influence upon people's ideas about the Empire and Commonwealth, etc. I shall touch on E. M. Forster and Paton and Joyce Cary too, because I want to, though that was not in the bond. It is interesting but difficult to do well and not really much in my line. Kipling was a most contradictory character and I find everyone disagrees about him.

I wish I could hear or read your lecture. I like the title and the idea behind it. I *do* hope the season comes off at the end of March and I shan't be too bogged down by grandchildren to hear you. I shall make a good effort. By the way your nice flower card (I think we are both a bit mad about flowers), was inscribed 'from your unseen friend' – but of course *you* are *not* unseen by me but I am by you – ha ha! It is rather amusing that I could be quite near to you or see you at a concert or something and you wouldn't know it was me. I like that, it makes me feel invisible, which I always thought would be great fun to be occasionally.

I wonder what you thought of *Camelot*. I want to see the Russian *Hamlet* if I can manage it.

I have heard and seen Micheál Mac Liammóir's *Wilde*. He was wonderful, but I did not altogether like it. I don't quite know why. I'd like to see him in something else. I shall do my best to get hold of *Self Renewal* and look forward to reading it. Thank you for telling me of it. While you were at *Camelot* I was with my husband at the eighteenth-century exhibition of paintings at the Royal Academy – the Mellon Collection – two and a half hours in a lovely elegant world – oh, more than elegant, for the Richard Wilsons and Gainsboroughs were *lovely* – a portrait of Gainsborough's brother and another of his niece, almost the best of his I've ever seen, because I think, as they were his family, he didn't bother about anything but the truth in doing them – also a child's head by Hogarth which had all the bloom and delight and freedom of treatment of a Renoir – amazingly good – and some delightful unknown people.

I love BED, don't you – especially in this weather. I sometimes have breakfast there too and write or read in bliss.

Goodbye and thank you again so very much for liking my book.

With love,

K.M.

P.S. This is an extra in the way of letters and emphatically doesn't need an answer.

I hope you can read this badly-written scrawl – my pen has run out and I'm too lazy to refill and used a ball pen which makes my writing go queer.

22 April   *Hill House*

Dear J.G.,

I thought I shouldn't make your show this time owing to illness and family complications, but I just *did*, almost at the last moment and I did enjoy it so. THANK YOU!

It is difficult to say which of the new numbers I liked the most. I always am greatly interested in the serious ones, and 'Lally Tullett' perhaps would come first on my list for transporting me most *completely* away from the theatre and getting most thoroughly into the characters so that I had to 'come back' from a long way when it was over. 'Eng. Lit.'

was a *lovely* double, subtle, and clever satire. I always warmly welcome a new Shirley and Norm because I want more and more of people I like (which is why I am a book serial addict). 'Opera Interval' made me laugh most, and, of the songs, 'Learn to Loosen'. 'It's Made all the Difference' kept me guessing to the end – I am sure it would be like that. Of the old ones 'Boat Train' always brings a lump to my throat. When the phone goes and I get 'Oh, could you possibly take Katie to the dentist this afternoon? Oh, and *would* it be possible for the children to spend the night with you next Thursday?' etc., etc. and I have hastily to re-arrange my week and feel a passing sense of irritation and frustration I often think of your 'Boat Train' and immediately realise how precious such duties and interruptions are, and take myself in hand. I won't go through any more of the programme, all of which I enjoyed but just to say THANK YOU once again. I was so glad to see enthusiastic reviews in *The Times* and in *Illustrated London News* (which, by the way also gave me a very nice review of *Tolerance* by Richard Church).

The *Observer* is nowadays too often horrid about too many people, but in spite of them *how* grateful one is for cheerful and kind and witty satire like yours, and for a bit of sentiment too. Why will people so often confuse sentiment with sentimentality, two utterly different things? *How did you get on with your address at Coventry?*

The last six weeks have been rather terrific for me in several ways. My daughter had her baby a week after doing the dresses and decor for Phyllis Tate's opera *The Lodger* at the St Pancras Festival. The baby, Sophia Margaret, is very healthy and good.

Heinemanns have accepted my book on 'The Maiden Aunt', though they want me to write one more chapter on an American Aunt with an eye to sales in U.S.A. I have done one – Louisa Alcott.

My grandson Danny is well away on his third opera *Childe Roland* – he is scoring it for three instruments, so it is quite an ambitious work. Unhappily school begins tomorrow.

Easter was lovely – spiritually I always find it life-giving and healing and so much less distracting in its secular observance than Christmas. Goodbye and love and gratitude for your blessed gifts.

Katharine Moore

20 June   *Riverside House*

Dear J.G.,

Being laid up for a day or two, I have listened for the first time for ages to 'Home for the Day' and have *so* enjoyed your talk on 'Escape Routes' this morning, that I feel I must thank you for it. Also I want very much to hear from you again if you should have time for a letter. That is silly, for you never really have time to spare – your letters have always seemed miraculous to me and I know I shouldn't ask for one – 'He who bends to himself a joy Does the winged life destroy.' So take no notice of it, and only write, as I hope you have done in the past, because and when you feel moved to do so.

Chamber music, flowers, birds are all my loves too, only I have never bird-watched properly and professionally. As a child I used to go unforgettable walks with an older naturalist cousin (Barbellion, of *The Journal of a Disappointed Man*, which you may possibly have heard of). He taught me many things. One night a very large spider terrified me by sitting just above my bed. I waited transfixed till I heard this cousin come up to bed and called him in to remove it. He gave me a long talk about spiders and about how idiotic it was for small girls to fear them and left me with the spider still for company. I don't think I was ever afraid of spiders afterwards. I used also to bird-watch with a very keen brother.

Oh, quiet: how one loves it! This village gets noisier and noisier, the motor-bikes are roaring up and down at this moment. We had such a lovely 'escape' at Whitsun to real deep innocent country in Gloucestershire. We lost our way on a walk and met an old russet-cheeked man with a scythe

82

in a deep small valley with a stream and ancient orchards. He told us to take a path through a farm yard – 'An doan't take no notice of the ole farmer – 'e's all for Number One – 'e is – you jus' keep on – a right of way's a right of way and King Charles himself can't stop ye!' We were so delighted with this Caroline countryman and with another farmer we discovered who, when I remarked on the peace of the place, said, 'Yes – there's no noise here but the liddle ole cuckoo hollering away all day long.' It was a magically remote place with a big grey heron and a couple of mallards nesting by the stream which had once worked a great fifteenth-century cloth mill – the ruins of which still remained. *That* farmer was a bit of a poet. 'I like to see the moon push up over the jump of the hill there – you get some queer effects then,' he told us. The whole region, like Cumberland, is a district of small hill farms that don't lend themselves, thank goodness, to these huge heartless scientific fields where they kill off all the birds and wild flowers.

I wonder if you are at the Aldeburgh Festival just now. I have been enjoying some of it over the air.

My youngest granddaughter, now three months, is flourishing.

Here are two children's stories for you – an overheard conversation between my half-American great-niece and nephew:

M (aged 5): 'Were you happy inside Mummy's tummy?'

C (aged 3): – 'Yes, *very* happy and *very* comfortable.'

M: 'Why did you come out then?'

'C: 'To see Dada, of course!'

The second was my Katie, talking to the new baby, and telling her a story – 'Well – we caught the shark and brought it home and we fed it on bread – well, no, not on bread, I'm afraid, Sophie, on fishes. But they were *horrid* fishes, Sophie.' (pause) 'Well, have it your own way then – on bread.'

I've chosen my American Maiden Aunts now and written on one of them. She is a wonderful character – Mary Emerson (Emerson's aunt), the other is Elizabeth Peabody, the sister-in-law of Hawthorne and the original of Henry

James's Miss Birdseye in *The Bostonians*. I expect you know all about them.

I haven't had any food for a day, so forgive this letter wandering along and the first page being rather incoherent. But I shall soon be up again. I love my busy life, but it is nice to have time to write an unnecessary letter to you.

As always my good wishes and affection and gratitude for being yourself. I *did* love your show in March.

Katharine Moore

4 July   *Elm Park Gardens*

My dear K.M,

I hope you are fully recovered now. Thank you so much for writing about 'Escape Routes'. It was a lovely subject and I wrote about the time of our visit to Cumberland, so when I got home I added an absolutely fresh bit while it was all so clear and fresh for me. Oh, what a place!

Last week we were at Aldeburgh for the Festival and as usual combined it with birding and, a return to an earlier love, wild flowering. I've been given both the old clergyman's wonderful flora that Collins has done for 35s. with over 1400 illustrations, mostly in colour, and the Oxford wild flower book. This last is clearer and simpler and with *far* fewer flowers so I use it to look up the *kind* of flower – by illustration – then see what the Latin name is and go back to the clergyman's book for all the extra species. I'm not a bit scientific about it – only know about five families – Rosaceae – Umbelliferae, etc., but I can work it out by using these two books and it is *such* a joy. I identified 127 species in that week. I didn't know there were so many kinds of wild roses. I thought there were three – dog, briar and burnet, but thanks to the new book I found two more! And, on a stony beach in Suffolk called Shingle Street I found a vetch that I didn't know existed and found it turned out to be a rare one. The Yellow Vetch. My plant was so pale it was almost white, but the flower was large and separate, and there was no doubt about it. A great feeling of triumph.

The music was perhaps more wonderful than ever this year. Or does one bring more to it, I wonder? Anyway I found it so rich and so moving. And it was less excitable, more tranquil, thoughtful and, oh me, oh my, I didn't 'arf enjoy it. I love being able to walk up the little hill to the Parish Church or along the road to the Jubilee Hall; I like the walk back in the dark with the sound of the sea turning on a steep stony beach. I like the East Anglian air and the height of the skies in those parts.

On the 24th June a recording of a 'Ten to Eight' I did came over the air (and at 'Ten to Seven' next day). It was one of the 'Private Collections' and I had chosen 'Peace of Mind' as my subject and quoted from Wordworth, Shelley, Psalms and Thomas Traherne with a brief line from Romans last 2 verses. I've *never* had such a reaction to anything I've ever done. Letters go on pouring in and all ask for the script, which is so pleasing because it means the voices I used *really* spoke. I've had them from all over the place and from all ages. A woman of ninety-eight and a mother of small children; a cross man in Edinburgh ticked me off for not mentioning the name of Jesus and sent two pamphlets on the subject of acknowledging Jesus. I wrote back to say that I believed Peace of Mind comes from God and is the very presence of the Christ; but it is interesting that people are so insistent that one must do everything through Jesus. As I see it Jesus was 'the most wonderful man who ever trod the globe' but this is because he gave us the Christ – for ever. I've had no reply from the Scot.

I *loved* your Whitsun holiday and envied you your old man and the farmer's 'no noise but the liddle ole cuckoo hollering away all day long'. In Suffolk we heard the liddle old nightingale hollering away all *day* long, too. *Several* in different places. I'm sure I've told you about the Herefordshire farmer who spoke of spring lambs 'dancing on the edge of night'? This it seems is sunset when the cool of dew tickles their feet and sets them prancing. How one goes back and back to *reality*.

Did I tell you I got asked to do a talk to an off-the-record conference of heads of B.B.C. departments in early June?

About my view of B.B.C since Pilkington. Also, as a pro who knows both sides of the mike and was a radio critic. I stuck my neck out by choosing a subject about which I feel more and more concerned: Values. I think that the distinction between standards and values gets confused today. Standards change with fashion but surely values, being absolute, remain constant. I think the B.B.C. is an offender in this. It is concerned with standards – of production in particular – but less with values – content. And I said so to a group of twenty-five earnest men some of whom I felt were not at all in agreement or who didn't care. But the majority seemed to. One young man in one of those tight little boy Italian suits and dark glasses said he thought my piece smacked of Moral Rearmament! Reeling a little, I assured him he was *miles* off beam, but it shows how words get debased. Because M.R.A. believes in absolute honesty, and therefore its women don't powder their poor pink noses because it is more honest to offend the eye than consider the beholder, the word absolute is now tainted. This young man had been concerned with the film of Muggeridge's lecture tour in the U.S.A. – and I suggested that it was a curious ethic that allowed the B.B.C. to commission a film to be made of Malcolm Muggeridge gulling *innocent* American fools (maybe) into revealing their follies so they could be filmed, and the film brought back here for the arrogant British to laugh at. The point was, I think, generally taken, but the young man went on revealing more and more exactly the attitudes I was trying to pin-point so he served me well and usefully. It was a very interesting and stretching exercise I found.

I do *love* your children's stories – the half-American great-niece and nephew and your Katie and the shark.

I have a slightly more sophisticated one for you. A fifteen-year-old nephew forced by his mother to ask the daughter of his hostess to dance at a Christmas party reported next day: 'You humiliated me, Mum, in front of *every*body!' '*How*?' 'By making me dance with that girl. She's got no front.' The modesty of this statement, in 1965, makes a nice change, doesn't it? I've got to make a speech at a public dinner, the Worshipful Company of Musicians; and do a four-minute bit on why I've chosen Richard Hoggart's *Uses of Literacy* for a radio discussion, so I have no business enjoying myself in sitting here writing to you.

I've written one or two half-poems and hope to work on them some time. 'The Reason for Joy' is one and I'll send it if ever I do finish it. Thinking about hearing new music, seeing new pictures that are perhaps difficult at first, I thought I'd try and put my feelings into a few lines. The Schopenhauer is of course the *best* advice: 'Treat a work of art like a prince – let it speak to you first.' This, roughly, is mine:

> 'Bring with you from the past
> Only what you can carry easily
> Leaving you free to move from place to place,
> Leaving you free to explore, investigate
> And make discovery
> Beyond the bounds of time and space.'

I'm sure it's sound advice, but not easy to follow. Little prejudices jump up and block the way, don't they.

I went to the opening performance of *Moses and Aaron*. It was not enjoyable. I'd like to hear the music some time without the orgy on stage. *Nothing* left to the imagination. The *mess* horrifying – I mean literally. Buckets of stage blood all over everyone. I was very Pollyanna the Glad Girl in *not* being in the chorus, or indeed a member of the stage staff. It really wasn't worth the effort for my money. But I went as a guest!

Do you ever discover little areas of unworthiness in yourself that really surprise you? I'd no idea I could ever be jealous – (*not* of a person because of love, I mean) – but in other circumstances. It has shaken me and made me very humble and I don't think I ever will be again. It was so shocking and I was ashamed as I hadn't been for years. Salutary. This is very private of course, but I believe you will understand and I can't tell my intimates.

With love and write again, please,

J.G.

Dear J.G.,

I always want to answer your letters immediately but restrain myself, and then the weeks fly by. I *did* enjoy it so. You are of course a natural writer and I look forward to possessing a book of yours one day. Did I tell you, by the way, that Heinemann are publishing my 'Aunts' book next year. I am now trying to collect illustrations for it, which is an interesting job.

Yesterday I had my niece and her American husband and the two children here. They are on their way back to the States after a year in Rumania, where Adrian has been lecturing on American literature at the university. They have enjoyed the year immensely and were full of enthusiasm for the Rumanians, who, they said, were the friendliest and most charming people they had ever met – *extremely* generous and helpful. They lived in a block of flats with Rumanians and each block forms a sort of colony with a community life of its own, so they got to know people very well. They found them very free of prejudice. The Russian influence seems to be nil. The Church is supported by the State and still seems to be pretty powerful. I was interested to learn that the majority of Adrian's pupils were women. He found them most intelligent. He lectured in English and French. My great-niece and nephew are now five and three – a most engaging pair.

My husband and I have just had a most peaceful two weeks looking after a house, cat and old retainer in Berkshire. I have known the house well for over fifty years. My friend was born there, and when her parents died turned part of it into a day school to be able to keep it going. The part that isn't a school hasn't changed at all since I knew it first. The chairs in the dining-room are still ranged against the wall, ready still for the maids to come in to family prayers – the bedrooms each have their old-fashioned washstands waiting in vain for the brass ewers which hang in rows by the bathroom and were once carried to the rooms four times a day. It was queer to penetrate behind the green baize door and traverse what seemed miles of passage and kitchen and pantries and servants' halls to do the necessary housework for us two. Everywhere the ghosts of our young, excited, romantic selves giggled behind doors and raced up the backstairs away from the older generation who sat in state and did embroidery and pressed bells and read calf-bound books in the library where now *our* old bodies unbelievably reigned in their stead. I felt less real than the ghosts.

Now there are a few days turmoil at home – then I'm away for a very short time with an old school-friend home from New Zealand after seven years – then another week's turmoil getting our refugee adopted grandson off to Zambia. He has been accepted by Voluntary Service Overseas for a year's work helping young Africans to start Young Farmers' Clubs.

Then, I *hope* we get off to Venice and Siena – oh, dream of beauty. Then, a winter of hard work – some teaching, some writing and a good deal of grandmothering and housework – all very enjoyable, given reasonable health for all the family!

Now – I'm going to comment on your letter. Yes – I've got the Oxford wild flower book and find it very good. I do congratulate you on your 127 different kinds in one week, and especially on your rare vetch. I think Suffolk is particularly good for flowers.

I was very cross and sad that I missed your 'Private Collection'. I think I could have made a good guess at your choice – at least I would have got Wordsworth and Traherne, though I might have said St John instead of the Psalms. I think your answer to the eternal question 'What think you of Christ?' is very close to mine, but words are so misleading when one is dealing with such subjects. Have you ever read Baillie's *God was in Christ* and that queer but compelling man – Werner Pelz?

How I agree with what you say about standards and values. One of the things that worries me most nowadays is that I don't think the young are getting a clear lead any more about values and so the poor things don't believe they exist.

The taint of M.R.A. – or rather the *supposed* taint is much like the taint of enthusiasm in the eighteenth century. It was hurled at *all* liberal thinkers in those days, as M.R.A. seems to be at all upholders of values today. It is one of the chief ways M.R.A. does harm I believe. People are so confused and so *terribly* afraid of being sentimental or traditional or of indulging in wishful thinking or of having any faith at all in case it contains any of the above.

About jealousy – no, I don't think by now I would be surprised at discovering the capacity for *any* of the seven deadly sins in myself! I once thought I wasn't the sort of person ever to suffer from jealousy. Not at all – I had/have to fight it like every other temptation. But I don't think one should mind *feeling* this – indeed one can't help feelings, it is only giving way to them that matters. In a way perhaps it is a good thing to have felt what jealousy could be and to have got it under, rather than never to have felt it, for one can now sympathise and understand. I always think this is what is meant by describing Jesus as one 'who was in all points tempted like as we are, yet without sin'. If it means anything it must surely mean that he had these feelings, but dealt with them at once and completely. Perhaps that is why he said, 'Why callest thou me good – no one is good but God alone.' Anyway I don't think one need feel ashamed of having such feelings if one tries at once to drive them out by their opposites – jealousy, which is self-love, by un-self-love for instance. Isn't it odd how, in the end, everything seems to boil down to 'he that loseth his life shall save it'?

I don't much like the sound of the new *Hamlet* from the critics, though I liked Peter Hall's description of it in last week's *Observer*. My favourite *Hamlet* so far has been Alec Guinness's young one (oh, before the war, I think). I liked his older very intellectual one, too (the one that only ran such a short time) but not so much.

I like your lines about experiencing new art. I think it's *effort* rather than prejudice that stands in *my* way. I so depend on music, for instance for refreshment that it is too much of a temptation to go to what I know will be sheer joy than to learn the difficult language of modern music – one never, as it is, gets to the *end* of the inspiration of, say the late Beethoven Quartets – yet I am sure the effort ought to be made. I get on better with modern art than music I think. I'm ashamed that I didn't even make myself listen to *Moses and Aaron* – let alone see it!

Do *please* send me your poem on 'The Reason for Joy', one day.

Do you know Keats's Letters well? I mind about his death more than almost anyone's, I think.

Goodbye – it is long past the time I should be doing something else.

I do so like your mind and it makes me feel happy to think of you.

Yours, with love

K.M.

Please forgive the muddle and scrawl of these hurried pages.

3 September   *Riverside House*

Dear J.G.,

It *was* nice of you to send me – 'View from a Small Corner' and I have much enjoyed it and so have those to whom I have lent it. You are a great comfort – it is so good to know that your gifts open so many hearts and minds to the seed that you manage to sow so quietly and gaily. I do hope that you will have more and more opportunities for this. I was *very* annoyed I couldn't listen to your 'Woman's Hour' broadcast last week. I was away with my New Zealand friend, and there was no radio, only T.V. This is more and more the case in guesthouses and clubs and always irritates me.

I was pleased to see the quotations from Dr Johnson and Blake on prejudice which I *think* must have come to you *via* my *Tolerance* book (as they occur there both on the same page).

I enjoyed the remarks on Verdi and Wagner, etc. and

must add them to my collection. I have a most useful book called *What They Said at the Time* – reviews – comments, etc., on art, literature, music, politics, medicine, etc. Do you know these two? – a contemporary on Mozart's Quartet in C. 'Music is bound to go to the dogs when such barbarians take it into their heads to compose. Mozart, who does not know D sharp from E flat, must have ears cased with iron.' And on the Leonora No. 3 'All impartial experts and music-lovers have unanimously been of the opinion that never has such incoherent, shrill, confused, ear-shocking music been written. The most cutting dissonances follow each other in really horrible harmony.' They were quoted by the General Manager of the Festival Hall in a letter to *The Times* once.

I would like to write so much about your near end bit – the most fundamental of all – the need for communication, but there is no time just now. The distinction between neighbourliness and togetherness, solitude and loneliness, *very* well worth making. In fact, I did so like it all and *how* I agree with the end.

We are in the throes of getting our adopted grandson off to Zambia for a year's V.S.O. work. He leaves this Sunday. Then we hope to get off to Siena ourselves – oh, bliss! But I did want to send my appreciation and thanks first. Excuse scrawl, my cat will lie across my arms and the paper. He is always more affectionate in really wet weather.

Goodbye and bless you –

K.M.

8 October   *Elm Park Gardens*

My dear K.M.,

At last a small pause to write in and to thank you for two letters – August 23, September 3 – both much appreciated. Did you get to Venice? I fear it may have rained on you? Siena?

You ask if I have read Werner Pelz. I haven't but I heard him do a week of 'Lift up your Hearts', and while I liked some of the things he has seen and delights in, I find him too *busy*. It's so restless, so volatile, darting here and there and somehow the impression I get is of tremendous pressure, and I wasn't attracted. But I dare say his book, read at one's own tempo, may prove far better.

I'm boldly enclosing a copy of the 'Private Collection' you missed. I'm *not* in a hurry, but would eventually like to have it back as I've only got one other, and to my surprise it is *still* being asked for. This is the lending copy. Bit battered.

About values and standards. I agree the young are being deprived of any lead, and it's cowardly of us. Irresponsible too. Lots of them find values for themselves though. How good your adoptee got a V.S.O. job. Not easy to get. I was told by someone working on the selection committee that the key question seemed to be: What would you do to fill the *leisure* hours of your African – Indian – or whatever – young people? The answer almost always reveals the gifts and qualities available in the volunteer.

In your August letter you didn't like the sound of the new young Hamlet. We saw him at Stratford. David Warner. He is rather extraordinary, very tortured and totally contemporary and completely compelling to watch. A remarkable performance, credible, touching, maddening, stupid, nice – all the things in the text. It is a fascinating production and not as ill-spoken as we were led to believe. Marvellously directed, theatrical and exciting. My favourite Hamlet is Paul Scofield about eight or ten years ago. He was so moving and so beautiful in his sad clown way. I was a little in love with this performance.

'The Reason for Joy' isn't a good *poem* although it tries to say what I feel and think – and indeed know.

This rather disjointed letter is being written in spurts. After twenty happy years our dear housekeeper, friend cum sort of nanny cum cook cum carer of our hearts and house, has retired. She married again two years ago and has been travelling two and a half hours a day to and from remote Burnt Oak near Edgware to look after us in S.W.10. Far too far of course. Her husband is years older than she is, seventy-five, and she wants to be with him. I understand, of course, and I'd seen it coming ever since the wedding, at which I was her witness, so I wasn't unprepared. I've been so spoiled all this time, for although I've always done most of the cooking, and, of course, all evening and week-end meals except when we had a party, she actually *thought* for me where stores, window-cleaner, laundry, carpet-shampooing, etc., were concerned. I miss her as a friend, too. She's German, large, expansive, warm, generous, humorous, talks a bit too much at times, but is a *dear* woman and kind friend, and the house is a bit quiet! Her ex-sister-in-law, a very nice nervous Cypriot, has taken over, but is vague and unsure, can't – won't take on any responsibility (so far). She's a good house-carer-for-er, and it's lovely and clean, if a bit disorderly. We know the pictures have been dusted for they hang so strangely. She is totally unvisual and never, repeat never, puts anything back where it comes from, including cushions and milk bottles and steak knives. It is hilarious trying to find them. She's only been here a week, and now remembers where the breakfast cups and cereal bowls live, so I'm full of hope. She's so nice, so diffident, and I can see our job is to love her into confidence and expectancy of good. She's very wary and lonely and sad. Parted from her husband, she's alone in a bed-sit. I think she begins to be happier. (Yes! She's just come in to say goodbye and happy week-end, and I said I hoped she was happy here. 'Oh, yes,' she said, 'I am not so much nervous.' So hope rises. But she is still nervous of 'gadgets', and won't touch the dish-washer, which I find such a useful aid. Says she *likes* washing-up. Perhaps she will come to trust the dish-washer.)

On October 23 I fly to Boston to stay with friends. He is literary editor of the *Christian Science Monitor*, and she was an actress. He was a theatre critic for twelve years. I'm going to talk about doing some articles for them and possibly for *Woman's Day*, rather a good monthly run by the A. and P. grocery chain stores out there. They heard of some of the 'Woman's Hour' talks I'd done, asked to see them and bought two. I redid them for the eye. They are in New York.

The other reason for going is that my husband will be in Africa all November, and I'm not working again till I start rehearsing for two big T.V. solo programmes I'm to tape in December and January. Another reason is to see my brother and the children, stay with a very dear friend in the new house she's just built and moves into on the 18th after selling her own bigger family house when her husband died.

I have something to tell you that amused us very much. My nephew Lang is eight, very gentle and loving and patient. His sister Sally is probably maddening, for she is ten and rather bossy. My brother went in to say good-night to Lang and found this note written to himself on his bedside table.

'Remember to hit Sally in the morning.'

I do love it. Knowing his own gentle way he was determined to remember the rage he must have suddenly felt.

Since the departure of our Mrs Gabe I've been very bogged down by domesticity and haven't had any good spaces to write in. I'd hoped to do a lot this month before I went, but it has somehow evaporated, and I can't help thinking one must put to the task in hand the same care one could give to a piece of writing. A lesson I find hard to learn, but it must *all* be done to the Glory of God. Oh dear! However, *when* I do it without a small sense of resentment I find it is much easier and often quite pleasant. Now that Mrs Agos has taken over I'm getting freer by the day. I haven't read anything for ages except a book about St Paul called *And Walk in Love* that I'm quite liking. Henrietta Buckmaster. This very dull letter comes to thank you for your two enjoyable ones. I'm so glad you felt that lecture said things with which you agreed.

With love from

J.G.

THE REASON FOR JOY

The reason for joy
Must always have been known,
The first awareness of the sun,
Of song, of sudden light
In knowing man is not alone.

The reason for joy
Is that Christ rose again
To show us that man's life is whole,
In spite of what the world's eye sees,
In spite of crucifying pain.

The reason for joy's
Deep satisfying grace
Is that the place we live in is
The only heaven and is *now*,
Including all – including space.

The reason for joy
Is God, our only being.
God is the presence of our Life,
The reason for our certainty
In loving, knowing, seeing.

Joyce Grenfell

16 October *Riverside House*

My dear J.G.,
  It was lovely to have a packet from you to welcome me
home from Italy. Thank you so much. I was very glad to see
your 'Private Collection', which I now return as requested
with much appreciation. I am so pleased you quote from
Shelley, who, I think was a much more profound *thinker*
than most people give him credit for. He is still too often
dismissed as an ineffectual idealist. I always like what he
says about morality so much – I expect you know it – 'The
great secret of morals is love; or *a going out of our nature* . . .

a man to be greatly good, must imagine intensely and comprehensively; he must put himself in the place of another and of many others.'

'The Reason for Joy' is your talk put into a poem, of course. I found it deeply comforting because lately the 'crucifying pain' has been very present in my mind – certain tragedies amongst people known to me (not *very* close), the Indian and Pakistan *hate*, the Rhodesian crisis – Vietnam – even in Italy I was haunted by the little wild birds beating their lives out against the bars of tiny cages. You see so many in Siena and the small hill towns nearby and in the markets. They also shoot the small song birds continually for sport. It seems a trivial thing compared with the suffering of the world, but neither St Francis nor Blake thought it trivial. It is, of course, not conscious cruelty, only ignorance. I don't think there's the slightest hope of stopping the shooting, but if the priests could teach the women that it was cruel to cage wild birds I believe it would have more effect than legislation – so I've written to the Pope about it. I'm also trying to find out if there *is* a Bird Preservation Society in Italy. I know you love birds – do you know of anyone influential who would be likely to be interested at all in trying to get this stopped? I seem to have wandered a long way from your poem, but really it is all connected in my mind, for it is only by dwelling on God – 'the reason for our certainty in loving, knowing, seeing' that one can avoid despair at the world's pain.

Apart from the birds and the traffic Italy was so beautiful. Venice is always for me the city above all other. I *love* its colour and light – the perpetual sound and reflections of water – its freedom from traffic – its secret silent little *campos*. It is also now the only city (except Leningrad, for a short time still) whose buildings can be seen in the right proportions without a hideous clutter of cars frothing round their base. But I think what I got *new* out of this holiday was a wider and deeper appreciation of Sienese painting.

I am *so* sorry about your housekeeper. I know how desperately one can feel this sort of thing. For many years, when I was doing full time teaching and my children were more or less still at home, we had a perfect couple of Yorkshire sisters who lived in a nearby cottage and who worked in shifts for us. Matty did the cooking (including all my bread), and Alice the housework. Matty was like a Duchess – she sailed rather than walked and had a 'presence'. She was always perfectly serene. Alice was like a robin or a russet apple, and was quick and darting, demonstrative and temperamental. They left me when they were both over sixty and retired to Oxfordshire to be near grown-up sons and nephews. Alice is now dead, alas! But Matty I still go and see once a year. But I could write a book about my helps – nearly all *angels*. I do hope your Cypriot gets better and better. You made me laugh about her aptitude for putting things in the wrong places. I have a *sweet* help now (she has worked for me for twelve years already) who has a genius for this. She still finds new places for everyday articles. It can be exasperating when one is in a hurry.

I *love* the story about your nephew. What a wonderful rider to 'Let not the sun go down upon your wrath'!

Because of Italy I've been reading that old rascal Benvenuto Cellini's autobiography again. Also I tried to read Meredith's *Vittoria* but stuck – the background is interesting, but the characters don't come alive, and the style (Meredith *not* at his best) is really frightful.

I hope you'll enjoy your time in America. You'll be going soon – every good wish for your time there. When your T.V. performances come off next year I *must* make a point of seeing them. I can always go and look at a friend's T.V. if I know beforehand.

My newest granddaughter is a great pet – very friendly, gay and cuddly.

Goodbye and thank you so much for a lovely letter, etc. I didn't really expect to hear again from you before Christmas.

Good luck to your writing and love from

K.M.

I notice you quote from *The Testament of Immortality*. I have known this well for years and many bits of it I have read over and over again.

My dear K.M.,

I fly today – D.V. – but already we are delayed one and a half hours because the fog, now gone, has caused a hold-up. So I take the chance of unexpected space to write you a small word to say thank you for your good letter.

I didn't know the Shelley quotation, and like it very much. Thank you.

The birds in Italy. I suppose education is the only hope. Italians are a loving people; look at the way they cherish their young. They are sentimental, too, but that's *easy* and has nothing to do with love. It's narcissistic, isn't it? I distrust it. I love the idea of your letter to the Pope about the caging of little birds. A good idea, and I don't see why it shouldn't start something.

We *may* be going to sail to Africa after Christmas – mid-January, because my cousin-in-law has been ordered a rest and a sea voyage. I'm to accompany her to the North Transvaal. I think my husband may escort us, and if so we hope to sail from Venice and go down the east coast through the Spice Islands.

I don't like being trapped on a boat much and would never choose a cruise, would you? But this one stops a lot, I fancy, and we can get out and walk and look if it isn't too hot. A natural aversion to social obligation keeps me from being a joiner, and one is compelled to join on board ship or be considered snooty. I don't mind being thought stand-offish but I have a sort of awful inner conscience that makes me feel one *ought* to join and contribute. I wonder what the answer is. I suppose if one is absolutely un-planning Anny, un-suspicious, absolutely relaxed and natural, one could either join or not join equally painlessly. As it is I'm inclined to resent being compelled to do things. Dear old ego again. As always.

It will be interesting to see Venice in January. We may get two days there *en route*.

The new housekeeper is being very nice and is a most beautiful cleaner. The initial panic over having to *think* about all the detail has gone and we are under control. 'I even remember bread.' She *likes* washing-up and willingly comes back in an evening if we have people, and will do the clearing and cleaning, so that is a huge help. I quite like cooking when there is time, don't you?

I don't seem to have read anything much for so long and I get quite *hungry* for it. I've got Gavin Maxwell's autobiography for the plane and a novel by Lady Snow – Pamela – what is it – Hansford something – *Johnson*. I met and liked her.

Don't you get exasperated about Rhodesia and wonder why a sensible compromise hasn't been suggested such as: one man *who can read* one vote? Why not? It makes sense to me. When I'm out there and see the tragic inadequacy of the average African who is mentally still in the trees I feel with the whites, many of whom are genuinely concerned to *lead on* Africans but not throw them into chaos, which is what one-man-one-vote must mean at the moment. When I'm here I forget the facts and think of the whole thing far too emotionally. Freedom is only possible from within a rule and the only way is through discipline. It may be 'our' fault that the Africans are so backward, but it isn't too late to start *something* to help them.

I must get up now and try to decide – fur hat or felt? Fur is much prettier, more dashing and becoming but weighty. Felt is dull and light. *Difficult* decision!

I hope to be home November 22.

I hate going away because of partings. If only Reggie was going too – I mean going with me. That's always all right.

Love and again thank you for a lovely letter.

J.G.

1966

My dear K.M.,

Today is like the day Thomas Hardy described in his poem *The Darkling Thrush*; at least in the country. 'Spectre-gray' frost and 'the weakening eye of day' lost in a desolate sky. Roughly that's how it is in London. I'm consoled by the charm of the bobble fringe, now sooty black, on the plane tree outside my window. Last year we decided to 'do' my top room, where I have the piano, a huge metal office desk, and the tape recorder, and it has become the nicest room in the house. I love it up here. It's got an attic feeling, and the roof slants. Sitting at the desk I can only see the top of the plane tree, sky and a distant view of that skyscraper somewhere near Earls Court and supposed by me to have something to do with the Admiralty? Two years ago I put a wallpaper up here designed with small coral coloured roses among a lot of little greenery-yallery leaves, light and dark. Very all-over-ish, and it is, I later learned, an early American pattern. Now I've got a seaweed green carpet and three built-in cupboards painted white with white Formica tops in which I keep all my music, scripts and accumulated letters and papers. The rocking chair I used to do 'Lally Tullett' in last year at the Queen's has come home to live after being used for my B.B.C. T.V. last month. There's a coral-red linen-covered armchair, and a sour green smaller chair with wood arms, and the place is cosy – in the flattering sense – remote, quiet and a most welcoming 'hidey-hole'. I'm here as much as possible, but it hasn't been possible much, so that is why I haven't said thank you for the thrush and his poem. I'm glad you, too, like the robin. I think he must have been *the* success of the R.S.P.B. because I had three sent to me, and I dispatched *many*.

Thank you for the poem. How good Hardy is when he is observing. I like the little dramas too, bathos and all, but his real poetry comes out in observation of nature, I think.

Yes, America was *lovely*. Sun every day except about three in three and a half weeks. I caught the end of the colour, and it was exciting and a delight. Only five or six days in New York, and I've outgrown the glamour of cities. It is most beautiful at a distance, and I stayed in a cousin's fifteenth-floor apartment with a view west over Central Park that was breathtaking at night. But the sheer pace and discomfort of the winds and rough pavement and the crowds and the ugliness at ground level made me glad to get out to the country. Three long weekends with my brother in the country and lots of mid-week bits in Connecticut with my widowed friend in her newly-built house on the edge of a little river and a little wood. Quite a *lot* of wood, but all of it little. Spindly trees. Birds, though, of *many* kinds and I showed her how to put up bird-feeders as they call them and got her interested.

When I got home it was time to start Christmasing, and I was plunged into rehearsing for two forty-five-minute T.V. programmes for B.B.C.2. One went out on December 30 and the next is due on January 25 should you be able to get B.B.C.2. I taped the second one last week, and now at last I'm catching up with pleasure letters and some sewing and beginning to work on some pieces for United States magazines.

We had a good peaceful Christmas. Four friends for lunch on the day, two of them elderly, and then five more of one family who are going through a trying time with a very ancient difficult old mother and grandmother who is cross and demanding and who has lost her son in Canada. We had the daughter and husband and the widowed daughter-in-law and the granddaughter and a friend of theirs here for coffee and a view of the Queen on television.

My husband drove the elderlies home about four, and I

got the plates, etc., into the dish-washing machine and was grateful for it as I am *daily*. We had more friends on Sunday and on Boxing Day, but only in twos and threes, so it was very pleasant and we enjoyed it.

Now I'm preparing to go with him out to South Africa again and perhaps to Rhodesia. The whole situation is so *sad*, and I think so unnecessary. I don't know Smith and I quite see *why* he feels it is far too soon for one-man-one-vote, but to have taken U.D.I. strikes me as the most idiotic thing for anyone to have done. His defence is that he could get no co-operation from Africans in any progressive way because they would not bother to try and work multi-racially because they were sure Great Britain would give them one man one vote any day. No one would invest in Rhodesia while the situation was so unsettled (but of course even less so now). Knowing the country and the people, I understand a *little* more *how* frustrating it has been and how very fearful the white Rhodesians are with Ghana, Nigeria, Zambia, Malawi, etc., as examples of what happens when independence is granted – it becomes dictatorship and a police state. (I know everyone says Rhodesia is now a police state, but if it really was would the man (Brind was he called?) who had letters in yesterday's *Sunday Telegraph* and I *think Sunday Times*, have written as he did and expect to go on living in Rhodesia unmolested?)

It is very difficult to see any of it very clearly from here. Emotion is roused; the venal greed of White Africans, and Rhodesians, looms in a light as evil as that that shines on Captain Hook in Peter Pan. The ones I know are fairly liberal, quiet, hard-working farmers who look after their African employees properly with understanding and who further their education. The Africans are still childlike for the most part in the best meaning of the term: needing care, simple in attitude, happy and contented. Whether it is *right* to go on being as simple as that *is* the question, I know. We must all be brought forward to discontent, I suppose; and without God that seems to be the general lot.

I blame Smith harshly for this folly. But I think this bringing of Rhodesia – or anywhere else – to its knees has a pretty disagreeable smell about it. I can't help feeling we are being blackmailed by Black Africa into it all, and the dangers are terrifying. I wish I thought Wilson, clever as he is, ever thought anything *right* through. I wish I thought he really *cared* about people and not only party people. I wish I thought he had any sort of historic perspective and was of larger heart than he appears to be. And I wish he hadn't gone to Lagos, although I think it is a very brave thing to do. We'll all know more about this in a day or two.

We fly off on January 26 and I'll be back about February 22.

I've got a spring concert tour all over the place, and we hope to keep most of May and June free before we go out to Australia and New Zealand again at the end of June for quite a strenuous season of shows there.

I hope to do some writing out in South Africa and we are in a very quiet part of the country, rolling hills and sky and a pool to dip into when the sun moves its fiercest rays off it. I was looking at cotton things today and realise *all* must have the hems turned up. Dammit.

Have you read any Martin Buber? I saw a brief film of him on 'Meeting Point' last night and I *loved* him on sight. *I and Thou is* difficult, but full of interest, I think.

May you be happy and make discoveries in 1966 –
Love from

J.G.

13 January   *Riverside House*

My dear J.G.,

A lovely unexpected New Year's letter to cheer me in this bleak hard weather. Yes, just like Hardy's 'turn of the century' January. I've been cooking extra potatoes for the birds (recommended by the R.S.P.B.) and they seem to enjoy it. I wish the thrushes didn't have to *listen* to every bit of food before they eat it – meanwhile the starlings and blackbirds rush in and devour it under their poor beaks.

What you say about Rhodesia interests me so much because on the whole I hear more of the anti-White side of the problem. I see at the best only a long and painful adjustment, at worst one just doesn't allow oneself to think what may happen. I *do* agree that the majority of Africans are simply not ready for responsibility yet. How seldom though in history is any people ready for this – the pace in revolution is always forced on them by their leaders and of course there is always a heritage of bitterness which can be played on. I simply don't know about Wilson. I think he was sincere in doing all he could to avert the rupture and he is in an exceedingly difficult position. I *hope* he'll show wisdom as well as cleverness and integrity as well as strength. I *am* so sorry about Shastri's death – men of integrity in high places are of *such* value, and I think he was one.

I like so much to read your descriptions of your rooms. I am getting to know them one by one. I feel tempted to describe my home a bit. It is rather a shabby but dear little house (1774) with very well-proportioned rooms. Across the road is the stream (a nuisance in the summer as a focus for noisy fisherboys and rowdies of all kinds, but I should miss it if it were not there). Beyond are two old apple trees, one still covered with pale green apples, a pleasure to the birds. The sitting-room, where I am writing, has two long windows, underneath which, and running the whole width of the room, are two low bookshelves (white shelves). I think you might like the fireplace (we had it put in). It has whitewashed bricks, and inset are five old blue and white Dutch tiles. I was charmed to learn in Holland how to tell the approximate date of Dutch tiles by the kind of squiggly patterns at the corners, and three of these (horses) are quite early. I brought them home from a first visit to Holland forty years ago. Above, at the moment (for I constantly change this) is a very gay Mexican painted candlestick – all yellows, pinks, blues and reds and a wonderful dark green with two absurd little purple birds sitting on it. There is also an old red glass jug full of anemones, and at the other end a tall lemon-coloured glass bottle and a dark blue glass goblet full of jasmine from the garden. Nearby is my favourite calender, I wonder if you know these? We have had these for years. They are called 'Musica' and they have a fresh picture of some musical subject from every possible country and of every period for each fortnight. One never knows what is coming next. Above, is a small original water-colour by Samuel Palmer of a mill and a cloud. It is nice to have a Samuel Palmer in his own village, though I fear it doesn't belong to his best period! It was left me by a dear friend whose father was Keeper of the Prints at the V. & A. long ago.

That is quite enough description for you, I am sure. It is just what I can see from where I write. By the way, once we owned five family rocking chairs. That was too much of a good thing, so I gave three away. That brings me to 'Lally Tullett', so *very* much appreciated by two friends of mine. Alas, we don't get B.B.C. 2 in Shoreham, and anyway we haven't got a T.V., though I can always see it at neighbours' houses (but *not* B.B.C.2). I often wonder if we ought to get it. My husband doesn't want it a bit, and I feel I haven't time *now* for all I want to do and to read. Yet it feels a bit like keeping a window shut when it might be open. I often want to *hear* some of the T.V. programmes, but not particularly to see them. We listen a good deal. Last week to a good slice of *Back to Methuselah*, but there comes a point when to hear one *word* more of Shaw's makes me want to shriek. Especially in *Back to Methuselah*. He goes on and on and on. All the same (like the stream), I wouldn't be without him.

I wrestled with Martin Buber's *Thou and I* some years ago, and he is on my shelves waiting for another go – such a good mind-stretching book.

Have you come across *The True Wilderness* by H. A. Williams? It is a stimulating statement of some aspects of the new theology, only people are so apt to think that a fresh view of Truth (or a little bit of Truth) cancels out what has been believed before. It seems to me that each age discovers (or rediscovers) that aspect of Truth which is most necessary for them, but that the Truth is big enough to include all that is valuable in what has gone before. So that I won't give up my 'God out there' – even if it is now necessary to stress 'the God within'. One needn't be emphasised at the expense of the other.

I meant to have sent you and others this New Year's poem which I liked, but of course lost it at the crucial moment. However it turned up again, so here it is, rather late. It comes with my love and every possible good wish for your South African trip and also for your work in Australia and New Zealand later in the year. I love to think of you and the pleasure you give. Also I do hope you'll have a good *writing* year. Life for me is full of interest, but a good many anxieties as to the health of my family. They do far too much through a heroic sort of optimism that I fear is not always justified.

16 January

Oh dear, since I started this letter comes the news about Nigeria – strengthening Ian Smith's hand – it all sounds such chaos.

I *don't* want or expect an answer to this for a long time. I shall think of you off to the sun at the end of this month.

Love

K.M.

5 November | *Beverly Hills, California, U.S.A.*
(off to stay with my brother in
New York for two weeks)

My dear K.M.,
Your good letter has caught up with me here. I'm on my way home from Australia and New Zealand where I did a *very* happy thirteen-week tour of my 'show' and where my husband went with me for the first time. I mean it, his first tour; we've both been to Australia and New Zealand before and love both – particularly Australia. He just took time off

from his job to go with me, and of course it made the whole difference to my enjoyment. He is to do with copper, and it is the sort of job he can go away from. He says he won't retire, but will progressively do less, and this strikes me as a very fortunate business to be in, and I am *grateful*.

Thank you so much for your letter. Your account of the German holiday was so pleasing. I saw it, quickly; the light and the Rip Van Winkle feeling. And the bicycling time in Oxford. Sorry I can't give the 'Aunts' for Christmas. I look forward to it for Easter! 'Family Fortunes'. That's a good subject. Reggie and I were married in 1929 on £750 a year and we lived in a six-bedroom house with three resident maids! *Not* for long, I may say, but that is how we began. It seems to impossible that we must have dreamed it – but we didn't.

The books I have enjoyed most are *Illustrious Friends* by Sheila Birkenhead – from Keats to Ruskin with fascinating letters and diaries and excellent editing. *The Road to Gundajai* by Graham McInnes? (Angela Thirkell's son) and two other books about Australia *Journey Among Men* – can't remember who wrote it, but Drysdale did the charming drawings. And Lady Casey's *Australian Story*, an autobiographical essay on her childhood in Edwardian Melbourne.

We left England on July 6, and had two nights in Bangkok in tremendous heat seeing the emerald Buddha and getting up at first light to go and see the water market – little canoe-like boats coming in from the country, along khaki-coloured canals, laden with fruit and vegetables. They gather about three miles from the city, and sightseeing launches add to the confusion under the heavy foliage. It is a pretty sight, and the Thai people are pretty to see. They are so beautifully made, tiny with exquisite hands and ready smiles. I think two nights was about right for the city, but I would love to go up to Cambodia and see the country one day. After this we flew by Japanese airline to Singapore and had a three-hour wait in the big new airport loud with crowds of Sikh families seeing each other off. A *lot* to look at as we sank back in deep airport sofas, and a great deal to hear above the piped-in music. Now you can fly direct from Singapore to Perth, and we got there at 2 a.m. on a lovely starry night. Winter there, but not as we know it. It rained a good deal, but when the sun came out its power was glorious. Perth is growing as you watch. A pleasing place sitting on the Swan River. An overgrown university town, but not for long. The money is pouring in with the mineral developments up north, and Perth is an exciting place today. Here I did five performances, and it all went with a gay swing. After this Canberra, over to New Zealand to Christchurch, Wellington, Auckland, back to Australia, Adelaide and finally three weeks in Melbourne and three in Sydney.

This was my third visit, and we now have many real friends and are really fond of them. Australians have a capacity for *real* friendship, and I love them for it. They are generous and friendly in all the obvious ways, but beyond that they honour you with acceptance into their everyday lives. You are allowed to become part of it in a natural and dear way. Reggie and I are very interested in birds, and we have several birder friends in both New Zealand and Australia, and they took us out on lovely picnics even though it was winter and *very* cold, but one could find windless corners and build a fire.

Sydney is my favourite city, because it is so beautiful and many of our closest friends are there. We had a waterside flat with a sensational view of the harbour for three weeks, and it was good to have a kitchen again, and we enjoyed every minute of it. I finished the job in early October, we had two weeks' heat, one spent in Queensland miles from anywhere. No time to tell you how beautiful it was; the silence, the peace. I made some useful discoveries of a religious nature during this tour: one is the fact that you can only get out of a person (or an audience) *that which is already there*. And since man is the image and likeness of God, he must contain *all*, and with this possibility acknowledged there is no limitation to relationships, understanding and potential. Maybe it is obvious, but I have only recently *proved* it. I will draw the veil over Southern California . . . dear people, though. I'll be home end of November. This brings you affection from J.G. Wish I had time to write more. Lots to talk about.

Love

J.G.

11 December   Riverside House

Dear J.G.,

Thank you for your delightful card, full of life and gaiety and humour. I hope it sells well for the youth club. Thank you too for a very good letter (November 5th). I meant to have left more time to answer it, but as usual Christmas has come with a rush and I can't chat as long as I would like.

I am so glad you had such a lovely tour with your husband. About 'Family Fortunes' – yes, hasn't our world changed since the twenties. *We* were married in 1922 on an income of about £1000 but although we had five children by 1924 (three steps) we managed to live in a seven-bedroomed house (in Blackheath) with a huge basement kitchen, and we had two resident maids and one daily and someone who came in and did mending, and a gardener. The cook drank, and I was terrified of her. My knees used to knock together as I descended the basement stairs to her domain 'to give orders'. But we got rid of her after a few months. I was dreadfully inexperienced.

I'm doing a paper for the C. M. Yonge Society – on 'C. M. Yonge and Education', and I'm intrigued at her huge gallery of governesses, none of them repeats. The best of them by the way get *really* very well paid.

I enjoyed the letters and bits of diaries in *Illustrious Friends* and have also *much* enjoyed Harold Nicolson's *Journals* and Berenson's last journal *Sunset and Twilight*. Now am re-living India, brought back vividly by Rumer Godden's autobiography of her childhood – also re-reading Browning's *The Ring and the Book*.

I always *love* your descriptions of your travels. You make me want to travel in New Zealand and Australia, but I think it will have to be vicariously.

About man being made in the image of God – yes, I can see how excitingly it hitches on to 'You can only get out of a person *that which is already there*'. If only one could realise that potential. If not possible in this life (because of its terrible deprivations) surely in another? Do you know Blake's illustrations to Virgil in the basement of the Tate? Miraculous.

Goodbye – love and blessings for 1967.

K.M.

1967

My dear K.M.,

I was glad to see your excellent letter in the *Listener** and agreed with you, all the way. Visually, it was a beautiful piece of Victoriana, wasn't it? The sun through the leaves; the sounds of insects; and the yawning languor of the afternoon. (My Pa once said that Cromwell Road was in space what Sunday afternoon was in time. Now, alas, no longer. This was in the days when Cromwell Road was unfrequented and went on for ever.)

Today my husband flew out to South Africa on his usual spring visit, and I never like his going. But isn't it good to feel like this after thirty-seven years. We are both grateful for this. Nothing is as much fun when we are apart, even though our tasks are different. It is the fact of being able to tell each other what we've done; to be able to sit in silent companionship and speak a word or two without context but perfectly understood. A *lot* to be grateful for. He has the nicest nature in the world.

Yesterday we walked for one and a half hours in the mild sun and saw clusters of crocuses out in Cheyne Walk front gardens. Reggie gave me a new camera for Christmas and it takes good *views*. My Brownies down the years have done well for faces and groups but failed over distances. But the new one is a beauty, and we took some bits of London, on Boxing Day, to see what it would do, and there are lovely

---

* Upon Jonathan Miller's television production of *Alice in Wonderland*.

shots of Chelsea streets and bare winter trees standing out of sage green grass. We took further views yesterday – Royal Hospital, Swan Walk and St Leonard's Terrace, where I lived as a child and where, later, we had our first married house. I think views need people, so we snapped each other to give a period touch, and I managed to include a very contemporary blonde in a trouser suit as she walked down Swan Walk.

I am trying to write some new pieces for my programmes. There is to be a tour around England starting on Easter Monday and I want to add new items. And Ben Britten has asked me to give a performance at Aldeburgh for the Festival in June, so I'm trying to do something for that occasion, too. I find I get more serious, but I have got one dear silly old nanny type, from Bucks, who *seems* to be growing quite well. I'm very fond of her.

Last week I read an autobiography of one Lady Abercon-way, and it made me feel quite contaminated. *So* badly written and so conceited that one began to rejoice over the shameless boastings. I'd heard it was an (unconsciously) funny book so when I was asked to a Foyle's lunch to honour it and the author I accepted. But then I read it, and the atmosphere it invoked was so unpleasant and *evil*, that I wrote and said that after all I couldn't come. I don't think I'm just being prissy. I think it has an element of hell in it. Can't analyse it. She boldly uses four-letter words, but that isn't my complaint. I felt it was false, untrue and so heavily loaded with egotism that it became nauseating rather than funny.

I enjoyed *Two Flamboyant Fathers* and, in small doses, Arthur Pollard's book about Mrs Gaskell's writings. I haven't read enough Mrs Gaskell to get the full flavour of his book, but as a critical essay and assessment of her period I thought it interesting.

We have been watching *The Forsyte Saga* on B.B.C.2, and think it excellently well done. So much so that it has sent us back to the books. Reggie went off today with the first three volumes in Penguin for the journey – and the quiet evenings in the heat of African summer. It is 106°

where he is going and only a week ago 110°. There is air-conditioning in the bedroom, and it is a help to cool the place down, but I don't like sleeping in it. Makes you feel so dry and the noise is a nuisance.

To go back to Alice. She has always been one of my blanks because I found the book frightening. I was very matter of fact and *hated* fairy tales and magic. I wanted books about real people doing real things, so I could identify with them. Talking rabbits and cats were not for me, and I really disliked the size changing in Alice. It felt like a temperature felt – a sort of unstable affair of shapes. Now I see the point of it and like the jokes, but it isn't a book I feel warm about.

We had a lovely unexpected family reunion here when my brother and wife and two children came here for four days on the way back from Switzerland where an affluent cousin had brought them for Christmas. I had twenty-five kith and kin in this flat for a buffet supper, provided seats for all and the kind of food you can eat with a fork or fingers, and it was a happy success. All ages including a cousin's three-year-old child who got under the feet of the ten to fourteen group I'd sent up to my workroom where they could play records and games and eat their heaped-up plates. After being ejected once he climbed upstairs again, only to rejoin us below saying in all truth 'I'm crying again'. A nice child with a scarlet face and royal blue tights. He ate only cheese. Lots of it.

I hope you are well and happy, and the book is growing. When can we get it? It is the 'Aunts' one, isn't it?

There's a lovely production of *Love for Love* at the Old Vic. I very much liked a French film called *Un Homme et une Femme*, but the critics were very snooty yesterday. I think it has real feeling and real understanding of relationships. It also looks good. But the critics are not to be trusted.

Love,

J.G.

My dear J.G.,

It was *very* nice and unexpected to have your letter last week. Thank you so much for it. I hope the first horrid blank of missing your husband is passed by now, but I'm so glad you do miss him! You describe so well the *comfort* of having a nice husband – that effortless exchange of experience in talk and in silence. Mine has been my ANCHOR in life for nearly forty-five years. We are very different in temperament, but share values and a good many tastes. He has taught me much about music, and I have taught him something about literature (he knew a lot before) and we are always about neck and neck over pictures and architecture.

But he has science too, where I can't meet him at all. Psalm 15, plus a great sense of humour, describes him.

I do *hope* I hear your new pieces one day. I wish I'd seen your T.V. programme at Christmas – it's one of the times when I *would* like to have it. But there aren't many, and I am afraid of having less time for talking, reading and doing embroidery while listening to music, which is how I like best to spend my evenings. Also we can't get B.B.C.2 in Shoreham – also the best programmes are mostly so late. I would like to see *The Forsyte Saga* (an enjoyed but not a favourite book) especially Eric Porter as Soames.

We saw *Alice* at the Vicarage – the poor Vicar hated the hymn tunes. Yes, I did like the background and would like to have seen it larger. I am glad you approved of my letter. It wasn't directed against Jonathan Miller so much as the remarks of the critics. I do dislike this fashion of reading something sinister or miserable into things and people. It may have been a healthy reaction against sentimentality once, but it has gone too far, and we've had enough of it. I also did think Alice herself very unpleasant. Again – it isn't a book I *love*, though I think I always thought it funny and it was as the dormouse at the age of seven in a family production that I had my first much-enjoyed taste of acting – but I have always liked *Through the Looking Glass much* better because of charming characters like the White Queen and the White Knight. I hope Jonathan Miller keeps off that. I never cared for the ordinary Andrew Lang *Fairy Books* much – once could always tell what was going to happen, and the people were not real. Princes and Princesses bored me very much, but I did like books in which magic happened to real people with whom, as you say, one could identify oneself. I loved E. Nesbit's *Amulet*, for instance, and always hoped it might happen to me. But I'm not really a 'romantic' at heart. I prefer Jane Austen to Charlotte Brontë, Dr Johnson to Bryon, Mozart to Wagner, etc., etc.

How horrid about Lady Aberconway. I'm glad you didn't go. All I know about her is that she was Courtauld's mistress and therefore possesses some most lovely French Impressionist paintings, which we saw once when we went over her London house with the Georgian Group or the National Art Collection people – I forget which – and which I coveted horribly. It is exasperating that people like that should command adulation and Foyle's lunches and so forth.

I want to read Mrs Gaskell's *Letters*, if I can get hold of it. She is a person I like very much. Just now I am dwelling in the Ancient World – just finishing Freya Stark's *Rome on the Euphrates* – a bit too much campaigning for me, but lovely bits. Here is one from an early Greek father which I wish I'd been able to include in my *Tolerance*.

'*Diversity*, which God hath made a common attribute of the nature of men . . . Bethink you that the Author of the universe rejoices in this diversity and has made the mode of men's worship depend on the will of each. This is a law against which no confiscation, no crucifixion, no death at the stake has ever yet availed: you may hate and kill the body . . . but the mind will escape you taking with it freedom of thought.' Themistius.

Then I am in the middle of Mary Renault's *The Mask of Apollo*, in which the life of an actor in Plato's time is described so vividly that you can hardly believe she hasn't been one. I wonder if you have read this? One classical scholar friend of mine says it is all authentic, and another turns up her nose at it. I don't suppose either of them knows really, but I find it fascinating.

My Aunts book called *Cordial Relations* (Heinemann's title – not *mine*) comes out very soon now, and Mary Stocks is talking about it on 'Woman's Hour' on February 13th. I'm much enjoying, at present, writing a paper for the Charlotte M. Yonge Society on 'Education and C. M. Yonge'. When I've finished this I must get on with my little social history book. I'm a *hopeless* jack of all trades. But I wish I got more time for writing – soon the garden will be screaming at me for attention every time I look at it.

Hasn't the weather been marvellous? There's been a charm of goldfinches in the river meadows all last month. I've seen them almost every time I've walked along the footpath to my daughter's.

What a nice party yours sounded! I love the description of the cheese-eating infant.

I would so like to see that French film, but don't suppose I shall – depends on how long it runs. February is very full, and I can't do as much as I always want to do.

Goodbye and thank you again. Your letters are *such* a pleasure and I so often think of you as a person with joy.

Yours with love

K.M.

About fairy tales again – I always liked, and still do, the nonsense ones like *Alice* and *The Rose and the Ring*, and for the rest, the ones that had real flesh and blood characters in unusual situations (as Coleridge aimed at in 'The Ancient Mariner') or else the reality must be implicit somehow in the fantasy like George Macdonald's or Tolkien. I'm afraid I must confess too to a weakness for talking animals from Beatrix Potter onwards – probably perhaps because animals were a great comfort to me as a rather lonely youngest.

Giants and dwarfs and the stock fairy-tale people never appealed. I have a friend [Dr K. M. Briggs] who is a great authority on folklore, but a little of this goes a very long way with me.

My dear K.M.,

It has taken me till *now* to have time to read your lovely 'Aunts' book. I bought it when it came out but was determined to read it gently, in quiet places and at *last* I've had the space and the place. It is a lovely book, and I do thank you for it. It is so timely. Soon there won't be any who actually knew any maiden aunts. (Reggie's sister is one – 65 now. After endless good works with girls' clubs in a miserable part of the East End she has become the link between families and the haven for nieces and nephews in transit. She is fulfilled; her little house in Berkshire in full use. She also has a battered little house in London at the end of its lease and there suitcases are left, children dumped between dentist and the train and she loves it and is rewarded by affection and, best of all, being *needed*. And used.)

Mustn't H. Martineau have been tiresome! Oh those large overwhelming do-gooders. I used to see them in droves at receptions given by my aunt Nancy Astor at 4 St James' Square where the Arts Council now lives. I was there to help, and guests were given little identification badges to wear bearing their names and their interests. I've never forgotten a huge battleship woman in grey lace who was surrounded by the curious. I was one of them and soon spotted the reason. On her badge was written: 'Miss So and So. Unmarried mothers'.

Maiden aunts contributed enormously in their time, and of course they are still needed badly, but economics don't allow their existence any more. I suppose some modern grandmothers now do their jobs?

We are here for the festival. I did a programme near the beginning, and ever since have been free to enjoy this enchanting country and little Aldeburgh and the music. Our idea of the perfect holiday. We go birding by day – or Reggie birds sometimes and I paint (*badly* but very enjoyably), and then there are good things to hear in the evening. And it is casual in tempo here and the music of enormous quality – or I should say *high* quality, shouldn't I?

Briefly this year has been busy and flown swiftly so far. I spent all February and half March writing new material for my current programme. I seem to be doing things a little differently; the pieces are more like short stories told in character I think. I write slowly now and with more care, I expect. Anyway I've only done two new longish ones and two short and two songs.

From the end of March till late May I was on tour doing my programmes up and down the country. Encouraging to find I was sold out almost everywhere; it was the best tour I've done, and the audiences included lots of young. This *is* pleasing.

After Aldeburgh we'll be in London till we go to America in late September to see my brother and family. Then when Reggie goes to Africa I do an interesting new thing: a combined lecture and 'concert' tour to colleges. The idea is to talk to the Drama Groups the first day; to discuss and answer questions. Then, next day, do the programme. Eight weeks of this widely spaced, so it should be enjoyable.

And you? What are you writing? I drove through Sevenoaks on the way to some south coast concert and wondered just where Shoreham is – then I saw a signpost and wished for an affectionate wave of the hand.

I think your book is a beauty, full of warmth and humour and you do write so – *well*. Wish I could put it more richly. The point is it reads to naturally and easily, but is full of depth, understanding and quality. Thank you.

Yours affectionately,

J.G.

P.S. I've also *just* read Rebecca West's *The Birds Fall Down*. Have you read it? An astonishing achievement, I think; and it's that modern rarity, a novel on the big scale. I'm quite haunted by it. How does she know so much about Russia and Russians? William Plomer read some of his poems here the other morning, and there was an unpublished one called 'A Bavarian Church' that I found most telling and streets ahead of the rest of his pieces. I don't much like his funny ones, but some on South Africa, deeply felt, and this church one were the real thing.

Tonight we see Ben Britten's *Fiery Furnace* again. I loved it last year and look forward to Orford Church at dusk. Hope there are nightingales as we arrive there. There often are.

I did a song for Ben Britten in celebration of this being the twentieth festival. In the mock-recitative bit at the beginning I say, 'Let us now praise famous men and partly in Italiano sing it – because praise in Italiano is less embarrassing than in Inglese – so raise the voice and sing it:

'*Bene, bene,* molto *bene*–'

It's all a play on his name: B.B., benefactor, he started the Aldeburgh Festival of Music, by the Suffolk sea etc.

> How benevolent is the setting
> Suffolk winds benignly blow
> Benefitting all who come here
> And to concerts go-o-o-ho, etc.

There's a good deal more, but you get the idea. Bill Blezard set it to very good swing music. A nice twist. Mr B. was pleased.

J.

20 *June*   *Riverside House*

Dear J.G.,

Your letter gave me a great deal of pleasure. First, many congratulations on the lovely success of your tour. I do wish I could have managed to hear you. I had hopes of Tunbridge Wells, but after all it turned out to be impossible. I think your Aldeburgh song for Ben Britten must have been delightful – a neat idea. If you ever make another recording please let me know. One day, anyway, I am determined to hear some of your latest sketches.

Thank you so much for what you say about my 'Aunts' book. I am proud and so pleased that you enjoyed it. Except for *The Times Literary Supplement*, that wanted a Sociological Tome, and the *Observer*, that would have liked a Freudian Study, and the Dublin *Times* which scolded me for not writing more about Ireland, the reviews were very kind (Richard Church in *Country Life* the best) and the book was sold out in May (and is now reprinting). But what pleased me most were the appreciative letters from elderly maiden aunts or from those who cherished memories of these and who had obviously been made happy by the book.

In answer to your question as to what I am writing now, I must sadly confess that the business of living and all my dear family and friends seem to leave too little time to get going on anything much. I know if I were a real writer I'd put writing first, but I never can feel quite justified in this, and as I believe that one *does* do what one really wants to in life I certainly can't complain. But if I ever do make time I'd like to do a proper life of Lady Caroline Fox. I found, when I was doing the sketch of her for 'Aristocratic Aunts' that there was nothing written on her at all, and she seems such an attractive character. I'd have to get permission from the family to research among their records and papers. Meanwhile I must first finish the little sociological book for schools on 'Family Fortunes', 1900 to the present day, which I find difficult to do well. Then I've taken on a bit more teaching (for next term only), and I may have to coach my grandson in O level history, which he wants to do in defiance of his school timetable which can't fit it in with his other subjects. His music is coming along well. The other day he was discussing a great friend of his (aged thirteen) and said, 'Sam gets very distressed about the state of the world. You see, it's difficult for him because he's tone deaf, so music means nothing to him, and so he doesn't understand about perfection. Because, when you've heard some things of Bach and Mozart you *know* that perfection exists – and that makes all the difference.'

I'm so glad he's got that assurance for life.

Yes – Harriet Martineau was tiresome, but also magnificent in her determination not to let plainness and poverty and deafness quell her spirit. I confess I always rather admire do-gooders, even the large ones, and feel guilty about them too. I once went to a concert at 4 St James's Square while it still belonged to your aunt and often drop in there now, not only to exhibitions but to chat to a great friend – Nora Meninsky who works for the Arts Council. Now I shall think of you there and of 'Miss So-and-So. Unmarried Mothers'.

Orford. I am so glad nightingales still sing there. We were there in the mid-thirties, and it was an enchanted place. I remember a summer day. We rowed out to a pebble ridge and bathed naked on a deserted beach and came home at sunset with the castle and church black against the sky.

I'm not sure whether you are doing your tour to colleges in England or U.S.A., but wherever it is I wish you a satisfying and good time over it.

I like some of William Plomer very much, and always feel grateful to him for giving us Kilvert's diaries. Thank you for telling me about Rebecca West's book, which I've added to my library list. At the moment I'm enjoying Bowra's memories (I know his sister and taught his nieces) especially of Gilbert Murray and Yeats. It's not very deep, but he's nice about people.

I must stop – this is written in a hurry – I always feel I could go on to you for ages. Thank you again for liking my book and blessings on you always,

K.M.

15 September   *Riverside House*

Dear J.G.,

I want to share with you thankfulness that the Italian Government have at last passed an act making the slaughter of song birds illegal. I only hope they will be able to enforce it. Perhaps something will be done about caging them now.

At present I 'have a concern' (as Quakers say) about the abominably cruel slaughter of baby seals that goes on at this time. I wrote about it to the papers (in common with others)

last year, but nothing will stop it I fear but reduction in the demand for seal skins. I enclose a letter from *The Times* which seemed to me much to the point. Now, I am not remotely connected with the fashion world, but I wondered if you, with your wide influence and contacts knew of anyone influential who would take this up?

I have felt in touch with you lately through broadcasts and especially liked your last 'Ten to Eight' contribution. I also read your letter about noise with great sympathy – the noise menace from so many sources gets worse and worse, and I mind it almost more than anything!

Your 'Time of my Life' broadcast sent me back to read the diary I kept all through the war. How I loved those National Gallery concerts, and what a healing, cheering and warming experience they were – and such fun!

Life flows on full of joy and sorrow. I lost a sister at the end of July. It was cancer and mercifully short. She was *very* brave, and we had a happy time together three weeks before the end.

We spent August and part of September in Oxford and lived with a T.V. there for the first time. I enjoyed the sport and the documentaries best – the last programme I saw was that brain operation one. I thought I should dislike the display of a private deep emotional experience, but I decided to give it a trial and was spellbound. It left me with an exhilarated sense of the triumph of spirit over matter.

Goodbye. Love and blessings on you.

K.M.

My 'Aunts' book now in its second impression.

17 September   *Elm Park Gardens*

My dear K.M.,

It is always a *delight* to recognise your writing on an envelope. Thank you for your good letter, I *am* sorry about your sister. That old Bishop's lines about 'death is an horizon, and an horizon is only the limitation of our view' sums up what I feel and I expect you do too. There is such a sense of continuity about those who are no longer visible but still *very* whole. My parents continue to contribute qualities somehow, and these are the reality. The qualities I mean. Do you share my view that individuality is the point – not *personality*? The latter can and does go I think, but the richness of individual manifestation endures because it is compounded of qualities. Reality. Spiritual facts.

I didn't know about the Italians' final decision about song birds. Thank God. I share your horror of the baby seal slaughter. My only contacts in the fashion world are non-furry now, but I will always preach the gospel when opportunity arises. I don't know anyone likely to campaign. I wonder if Mary Quant would? As she doesn't, I think, use fur, I rather doubt it? I don't know her. I return the letter in case you want it.

My 'Ten to Eight' produced a great tide of letters very often from *non*-churchgoers who nevertheless long for God – these are the ones that seem most open-minded. But you will, I know, rejoice with me that the letters came from all faiths most generously. I think if only we didn't wear hats labelled Jewish-Quaker-R.C.-Anglican, etc., we could *all* meet far more simply *in the same place*. That's my idea of ecumenical. No declaration of departmental allegiance, just the sharing of discoveries and the mutual rejoicings.

I wonder if you'd like to see a piece I wrote about my mother. Very light but done in affection. May I please *have it back*. It was in the *Christian Science Monitor* on September 2.

Now the rush is on before we go to America. September 28. Reggie only stays till October 10, just to see my brother and family. Then he comes back to repack for his usual autumn visit to Africa. I do a concert tour of colleges all over the United States and two ordinary performances in Toronto. I think I'll have a chance to see Expo for two days in a providential gap between dates. We meet at home again in the last week of November.

It's been a heavenly summer, hasn't it? Weather does make a difference. It can also add poignancy no doubt, just as the blazing spring of 1940 made Dunkirk and all the preceding horror even worse by contrast. 'The Time of My Life' involved a great deal of reading and going through records at the B.B.C. and I found it quite *churning*. It was a *great* time in so many ways. I learned almost everything I had only guessed at from those hospital tours.

How lovely that the 'Aunts' book does so well. Deservedly.

Now I'm off to church, and then we're playing tennis, our passion – in snow-white too! – at Hurlingham where we play every Saturday and Sunday we can. We aren't good but we're eager, and we keep up a dullish standard to *our* pleasure.

I saw the brain operation on T.V. too and was impressed by the couple and their steadfastness. But longed for them to be just a little less inarticulate about their spiritual awareness, simply as a help to others, or perhaps you felt it was made manifest enough?

I do like hearing from you. With love,

J.G.

Are you really beside a river? Which? I passed a signpost to Shoreham this summer and wafted you a wave.

Riverside House

Dear J.G.,

Of course there's a river. Only a tiny one I admit, but still, not uncelebrated in art or verse (by Samuel Palmer). It's the Darenth, tributary of the Medway.

Thank you so much for another treat of a letter and the delightful piece about your mother (enclosed). It comforts me, for I'm an erratic speller myself, and now I need not bother when writing to you. It also reminded me a little of my own mother, *not* the spelling – but the kind of gaiety and warmth and spontaneity. I remember, for instance, the joy of certain sparkling days when she would suddenly say, 'It's *too* lovely weather for school or jobs – let's all go to the sea for the day' and off we would go with sandwiches, etc., for a heavenly stolen holiday. She was *also* a good if not a brilliant mimic, a gift she passed on to her granddaughter, but not, alas, to me. It's obvious where *your* great gift came from. How *lovely* your mother's spelling is, and how she must have entertained you by her improvisations. I often wish so much we had tape records *and* films and even colour photographs of the past.

Thank you also for reminding me of that saying about death being a horizon, and a horizon only the limitation of our view.

> 'What mysteries do lie beyond thy dust
> Could man outlook that mark!'

I think, don't you, that one has to accept the limitation completely – that it's no use trying to imagine what lies beyond the horizon. Sometimes I long *so* to feel that all the incompleteness and frustration and deprivation of lives here will find fulfilment in the mysteries beyond our dust. I *do* feel trust in Love, for if one has experience of this, one must trust it, and that really is enough when one thinks through to it.

About the T.V. brain operation programme, I felt they were very typically and naturally inarticulate, but that their spiritual awareness was implicit. I wished that the clergyman had been less artificial and stereotyped.

I was interested and pleased but not surprised, that you had such a mail after your 'Ten to Eight'. Yes – yes *how* I agree about the true ecumenical movement – to meet, to share, to worship together and not even to *want* people to think alike about the Sacraments or authority, etc. People so often seem to think that difference implies hostile criticism.

I do wish you a very good trip to America with splendid audiences and a nice time with your brother's family and all your friends.

I've got two such ducks of girls to coach this term – alive, intelligent and charmers. But I'm rusty, and it means quite a lot of work to keep up with them – however it's *their* work that matters, and as long as one can inspire that it's all right.

Again every possible good wish to you and your husband
for your travels. I wonder if you will be back by Christmas.
With love

K.M.

1968

31 May   *Elm Park Gardens*

My dear K.M.,

Such a long time since we were in touch, and I write to say
I hope all goes well with you. We are happy, well, busy. It's
been a good year. I wonder when I last wrote? I have a
feeling I reported on the tour I did of colleges and universities in America in October–November last year?

The reason I write is that I wondered if you had happened
to hear the two 'Ten to Eight' broadcasts I did, and if not
whether you would like to see the text, for the B.B.C. sent
me copies. The first one was called 'After Easter' and the
second was one in the series 'The Debt to my Parents'. If
you heard them I won't bore you with copies. The 'After
Easter' one was very interesting, because so difficult to do,
and after a lot of work on it, and prayer too, I let it go off on
its own power, and it seems to have come through, for
between us the B.B.C. and I sent out over 140 copies in
answer to requests. The thing I liked about it was its
impersonal nature – by the time I'd done my bit. The word
is more powerful than any two-edged sword, and when it is
true it works.

We had a lovely time in February–March when I went
with my husband on his usual trip to Africa. This time we
stopped off in Kenya for six days entirely devoted to seeing
birds. Such a luxury. Everything went on wings. The
weather was perfect, the hired car obliged; the nice girl who
'conducted' us seemed to enjoy it as much as we did, and
our tempi matched in all things. And the birds showed
themselves just when and where they were supposed to. We

stayed for two nights in three different places and saw 195 different species in that short six days. We also saw beasts, and I was startled to find that elephants in Tsavo National Park are bright tomato pink! It's the earth that does it. It's like Devonshire and North Carolina in its terracotta rose, and the rivers are dyed by it, and then, after their dips, the elephant give themselves lavish dust-baths in the coloured stuff, so they are indistinguishable from the high ant-hills.

We had some time at the Cape. It isn't like *Africa*, it's like an enlarged and more beautiful Ascot or Wentworth area always against Table Mountain. We saw many very pretty and pleasing early Dutch Colonial farm-houses, all of them shaded by colossal oak trees and often edged with hedges of blue hydrangea and agapanthus. Startlingly *white*-washed – the whole thing is so pretty and satisfying, architecturally.

I had two and a half weeks alone up in the quietness of the North Transvaal and did some work on material for concert tours coming up here in September–November, and next year in Australia again – the fourth time. It was so luxurious to have whole unplanned days quite alone, for Reggie had to be in horrible Johannesburg, while I wrote. He came up at week-ends. I wrote under a grape-covered arbour by the pool from 9 a.m. to 1. Then after outdoor lunch, a little kip and reading before a swim about four. Then more writing. Early bed and reading. And sometimes I gave myself concerts on a very good hi-fi gramophone, mostly Mozart and Haydn quartets, and a little Bach that I found in the cabinet where I'd put them on earlier visits. Very nourishing stuff. I was also working on the texts for the 'Ten to Eight's and for an address I'm to give tomorrow at my old school. And various oddments, such as a T.V. appeal I'm to do next week in aid of the Council for the Preservation of Rural England that goes out on the 16th I *think*. A very Good Cause, I think, don't you? I wrote a much freer text than they have turned the script into. I plan to simplify when we get to doing the actual job . . .

Last week we had a visit to *beautiful* Cumberland, and it was lovely to have a second spring up there. Bluebells just unfurling, primroses still budding, and *oh*, the scents and smell and the unchemicalised water. Very restored, we were. Ice-cold up there, but sun at least half of each day, and I did some painting from the shelter of the car. Last year I discovered that northern oaks begin bright khaki gold. *Do* they down here? I hadn't noticed.

Are you a Jane Austen reader? I'm sure you must be. I've chosen her as 'My Kind of Novelist' for a series 'Woman's Hour' start quite soon, because she is. I've been re-reading *Emma*, *Northanger Abbey*, *Persuasion* – in Africa – and I decided *again* that *Persuasion* is my favourite. Last week on our way south we stayed with friends near Richmond, Yorks, and went to the Georgian Theatre (230 seats and perfect as it was when Mrs Siddons and Kean played there. I go there to do shows most years now) and we saw an adaptation of *Emma*. It was skilfully done, but not very well played. I like/hate Emma, do you? Prig she is and *so* bossy, but she *learns*. Of course the incident where she was rude to Miss Bates was cut. Box Hill, isn't it? But most of the other joys were there. Alas, Mr Woodhouse was too large and too expansive. I see him spare and, though mild, quite powerful.

Since the return to London from Africa I've been working hard at trying to write material. Some has worked. But it is less easy to be silly-funny as one grows more compassionate! I have, in fact, written seven new items in which I have hope. Three others are not as promising. I plod on.

Soon we have the treat of the year – Aldeburgh Festival. We are going for two weeks, and I'm excited already. I must say I do find pleasures grow in intensity instead of diminishing. Do you find this? Flavours are strong. The spring is more incredible. When a piece of music or a poem works it works *deep*. Friends, I mean real friends not casuals, are more important.

I seem to have read very little of interest, except Jane Austen. Harold Nicolson's letters are fascinating in a shallow way. There is something less than admirable, some false values. And what a strange marriage. Most of it on paper I'd say. They went their own strange ways but still seemed to need each other. He's *too* social for me.

News from my American family is good. Sally is thirteen and goes to boarding school in the 'fall'. Lang is eleven and lives for games and speed . . . Not an egghead but quite a hard trier.

Did you see a movie called *Guess Who's Coming to Dinner?* Spencer Tracy, Katharine Hepburn and Sydney Poitier, the black actor. It had some very good, *honest* moments and was so well made. Recommended.

This is too long, forgive me. I always enjoy talking to you on paper.

Love

J.G.

6 *June*   *Riverside House*

My dear J.G.,

How very nice to hear from you again. I have been meaning to write to you for some time. Indeed I began a letter once, but it never got finished. Your letters are a *luxury*, partly because they are so happy and full of such enjoyable things. So many letters are sad or worried in one way or another. I must say you do have a lovely time, but then you know how to enjoy life properly. I am so glad the African trip went so well. I never knew about the pink elephants. I have just been telling my Sophia (aged three) about them as she is rather an authority on elephants. By the way, fancy *you* not knowing about oaks beginning golden. It *is* all oaks, not just Cumberland ones. I think many people miss this because the golden stage only lasts such a short time.

I would *love* to see the scripts of your 'Ten to Eight' talks. I heard the parents one with much pleasure, but missed 'After Easter' and was particularly sorry to do so, so I welcome the chance to read it extremely. I'll make a point of listening to the Rural England appeal on the 16th. *Indeed* I think it a worthwhile cause. I think we have only hitherto supported the National Trust for whom I used to lecture, and the local Kent Society for Social Service which does a bit of rural preservation.

As to your forthcoming Jane Austen talk I am now going to hold forth. She is *certainly* 'my kind of novelist' too, and I know her pretty thoroughly. (She was really my favourite Aunt also – see *Cordial Relations*, my 'Aunts' book.)

I am glad I didn't see that adaptation of *Emma* that you mention, as it would have enraged me. Leaving out the Miss Bates incident at the Box Hill picnic is unforgivable. It is the pivot of the whole book. It brings Emma and Mr Knightley to the point, it reveals Emma fully to herself (and to us) and it also underlines the contrast between Emma and Miss Bates, whose humility results in real wisdom and charity. I could go on about Miss Bates as a character for pages – but mustn't (see, though, in my 'Aunts' book again, a *bit* about her). Then Emma's behaviour afterwards, what honesty, what self-control! Does she lie prostrate on her bed sobbing her heart out and making herself ill and a burden to others, or tearing about in a passion of despair when she believes her love is hopeless, as any of the Brontë heroines would feel bound to do. (See *Villette*.) Not a bit of it. She is ready, composed and outwardly cheerful to meet her father as usual. *How* good she is to her father! Emma's flaws are due to circumstances don't you think? But she is such a generous, honest, strong character I can't help loving her, though Elizabeth Bennett is more delightful, and Anne, in *Persuasion*, is my favourite, but *Emma* is my favourite book as a whole – it is such a perfect work of art. As for Mr Woodhouse being 'large and expansive', it makes me shudder. Actually, I have never seen any production of Jane Austen that didn't make me shudder (except for my own(!) *Pride and Prejudice*, that I produced at school once). The readings on the B.B.C. lately have been horribly *coy*. *Long* ago there was a perfect reading of *Sense and Sensibility* with Mabel Constanduros as Mrs Jennings, I think. By the way, I believe I will send you, if I can find them, some old parodies I once did to amuse my VIth forms. They *may* amuse you. I wonder if you have read *Sense and Sensibility* lately? It is neglected a bit, and I am fond of it. It may appear from the parodies that I don't appreciate Charlotte Brontë or Dickens. This is quite wrong, but parodies always must work from weakness not strength – but I don't love any novels so much as Jane Austen. I once wrote a sequel to *Emma* (what cheek!). It is about Emma's grandchildren. I had in mind the change of opinion, etc., that took place between the Regency and the mid-Victorian age – enormous. It was fun to do and Jane Austen lovers among my friends like it. I *might* send that to you one day, but only if you thought it would appeal to you.

You see what you have brought upon yourself by even mentioning Jane to me. I don't think you ever did before.

Harold Nicolson's letters I liked better than you did. His kindness and tolerance appeal to me, and although I agree that there are certain false values, they seem to me the result of his class and upbringing (like Emma!). It takes a more original mind or a rebel to fight clear of them. He wasn't good at judging character, but unlike Leonard and Virginia Woolf or Lytton Strachey he errs on the generous side here. I like so much his deep and unselfish love for his wife and sons and his respect for their personalities. There is a moving passage about him having missed fame but not caring because he had them.

Yes – my year has had a great deal of happiness and fulfilment still, thank you. I am past my seventieth birthday now, and my husband had his ninetieth in January, and we had a lovely family party of children, grandchildren and our two refugee children (now grown-up) and a cake (made by me) with ninety candles and special odes and music (composed by grandchildren). He is extremely active still (more than I am) and at the moment writing one of the science books for the Nuffield Foundation educational scheme, which amuses me – that they should get a nonagenarian to contribute to the most modern of all series of schoolbooks.

We have just got back from another good holiday in Austria – finishing with a lovely chamber music concert in Salzburg (Mozart and Brahms). We had a short stay in a village in Upper Austria, rather off the map, where the innkeeper's wife welcomed me with a bouquet of carnations, and her delightful crippled and courageous husband watched over every mouthful we took of his far too lavish and excellent cooking. This was embarrassing but charming. There was also the nicest horse show round about the village maypole that I have ever seen. Oh – but the beds were hard!

I was *so* interested in all you tell me about your time at the Cape. I was greatly moved by hearing on the air Sally Trench talk about her experiences with the methylated spirit addicts. She must have a genius for loving, and she seemed to me to be a really Christ-like character. I must read her book, but I should like to know why she wrote it and why she was interviewed. Was it to get money to help them and/or to arouse public sympathy? I am *sure* it wasn't publicity for herself.

I am so pleased your 'After Easter' broadcast made such a wide appeal. The response you have must have been an inspiration – *is* one, in fact, because of that reassurance that the Word works, just as I felt in listening to Sally Trench the tremendous reassurance that redeeming love shines always in the darkness when given a chance.

I must stop. I always feel I can go on and on in writing to you. You will probably be at Aldburgh by now? If so you won't have time to read this anyway. But it will keep. I hope you will enjoy Aldburgh. But of course you will.

My love

K.M.

Excuse scrawl. I can really spell Aldeburgh.

7 *June*   *Elm Park Gardens*

My dear K.M.,

What a lovely letter, and how I long to sit down and answer it at once. Thank you for the parodies which are safely put in my book bag for later reading at Aldeburgh.

I'd forgotten you'd written about Jane Austen in your 'Aunts' book. Of *course*. When I get back I'll reread. And I must read *Sense and Sensibility* again. I haven't, for *years*.

Glad about your Austrian holiday except for the hard beds. I used to stay in an inlicensed hotel in Edinburgh where the beds were *so* hard I was able to iron my dresses on them with a little travelling iron.

I must pack and cope and generally get on with going away.

Love – and thank you for your letter.

J.G.

14 June   *Wentworth Hotel, Aldeburgh, Suffolk*

My dear K.M.,

I loved reading the parodies. Thank you *so* much for letting me see them. I particularly liked the C. Brontë one because I am more familiar with her and Jane Austen than I am with Charles Dickens. I know it's a failure on my part, but I can't seem to 'get on' with Dickens. Your Brontë is *brilliant* – and so enjoyably accurate. Thank you.

We are having a lovely festival. A tearing wind is a nuisance, but there has been lovely sun and the concerts have glowed.

Ben Britten's new church work, *The Prodigal Son*, is a real beauty. Having the Maltings for bigger concerts is a growing joy, and I do love its country feeling as well as its technical perfections.

I must get up and play tennis. Tonight we have Arrau and Ben Britten doing Brahms *Liebeslieder*, and before that lots of Purcell sung by Heather Harper and Janet Baker. A treat in store.

Thank you so much for your good letter. I do like our correspondence.

Love,

J.G.

I saw your *Tolerance* book in a friend's house, and I said: 'I write to the author, who knows what I look like, but I don't know what she looks like, but we are pen friends.'

(Please forgive return of your envelope. The hotel has none to offer.)

My dear J.G.,

Thank you, in the first place, so very much for your Easter broadcast. I like it more than I can say. I had a similar sort of revelation to the one you describe about your mother and spring. It was after my son's death. I could not for some time bear the beauty of the garden or music or anything that he had enjoyed so much. Then I suddenly saw that what he had enjoyed was reality and the expression of it here, in this life in all these things were 'bright shoots of everlastingness' and that neither he nor I would have to say 'goodbye' to 'the real spring'.

Thank you also for your last letter, which gave me such a good vivid taste of Aldeburgh. I see William Mann praised that concert you were looking forward to most highly in yesterday's *Times*. I am particularly fond of Janet Baker's voice. I am looking forward to listening to the concerts broadcast from Aldeburgh this afternoon and evening.

Your letters and the Easter broadcast have helped me through a rather dreary week of a bad throat and temperature which I caught from a granddaughter (though she, I am glad to say, was only bad for two days). It is still obstinately with me, and my daughter isn't well either, and her nurse girl is leaving. If only a Maiden Aunt or two were around! One's bodies *are* such a waste of time – I mean when they fail us, and in summer such things as throats are an outrage.

Another thing to thank you for is your talk on Jane Austen which I enjoyed the other afternoon. I am glad you know Mary Lascelles's book which I think is the best critical study of Jane Austen. Do you also know Elizabeth Jenkins's delightful biography – also much the best?

I hope you will read *Sense and Sensibility* again soon. I think those, such as Charlotte Brontë, who deny Jane Austen the power of feeling or depicting passion must forget Marianne. The intensity of young first love has never been better done, and its repudiation is almost physically painful to read. The fact that Jane Austen didn't approve, makes the power and sympathy of her portrait of Marianne all the more remarkable. Mrs Jennings is one of the best of her comic characters, and personally I'm very fond of Eleanor, though I know many consider her to be a prig. But I think I like prigs. I should like to know some time, which are the values that you think wrong in Jane Austen?

Do you ever read Chaucer? He and Jane Austen have much in common. They enjoy their characters so much – even the unpleasant ones. Thank you for returning the parodies. I am pleased that the *Sense and Sensibility* one amused you. I can't listen to your Appeal tonight as we still don't possess a T.V., but I shall send a small contribution to the bank because I approve so much of the cause – and of you.

I wish children weren't made to grow up quickly nowadays. My grandson (aged fifteen) is doing a project on the works of William Golding: I think they should read adult literature at that age but not, perhaps, of that kind and anyway should not be expected to write a critical account of anything so difficult. I told him not to bother what William Golding meant, and certainly not to trouble his head with what other people have said he meant, but to describe as simply as possible the impact made on *him* by the books. This he is doing at great length.

Do you know it is more than ten years now since we began this pen friendship? It has been *such* a pleasure to me.

I wonder, if I were to see you one day at a concert or just somewhere in London, whether I would resist the temptation to introduce myself. I am pretty sure I'd 'lay low and say nuthin''. Because it is for me a unique relationship and somehow being confined to paper makes it freer.

I am so glad you have had such a lovely festival.

With love

K.M.

My dear J.G.,

It seems a long while since we exchanged letters, actually it was in June, just before you set off for Australia. I do hope you had a wonderful tour *and* holiday, and that things go well with you and yours.

Life has gone on pleasantly and serenely with me (on the whole) which is, after seventy, a real bonus, I feel. We had a good six weeks in Oxford in August and September with the usual great pleasure in congenial friends and occupations, and the summer weather was so lovely. I remember, especially, the glory of college gardens, a very interesting exhibition on Erasmus and his friends, and bicycling in the quiet roads of North Oxford. This is about the only place now in which I *do* bicycle, and there are plenty of other elderly, dowdy, intrepid women with their baskets stuffed with books to keep one company. Bicycling has been a lifelong pleasure since I was about ten, when I inherited my next sister's old bike (I've *never* had a new one) and was allowed to ride to school, having first promised my mother to get off at every corner – a promise which so offended my self-respect that I had to bribe my sister to drop her handkerchief so that any passerby might see that I had a real reason for getting off.

After we came home life became as full as ever. I've again had a class of Oxbridge entrants – this time a group of eight (all scientists or linguists). It has been stimulating as we have dealt with every conceivable subject from the permissive society to space travel. They are, as usual, most responsive, intelligent, grave and touching – hopefully excited by and yet apprehensive of the challenge of life today. I am sure it is harder for them than it was for us. It is good for me – after upholding the open mind to them with ardour – I come home and resolutely turn on some modern music programme that I would normally avoid like the plague.

Besides work at school, I've been trying in my spare time to write a short memoir of my son for private circulation, mainly so that he shan't be just a name to his neighbours and nieces and godchildren.

After twenty-two years I have brought myself to read over all his letters, and it has meant both joy and suffering, but gradually the joy grew. The opposite of joy is not suffering for both can exist together – its real opposite is despondency and despair, I suppose.

Now I have finished this I am rather thinking of a book on some 'Victorian Wives in Fact and Fiction' to match my 'Maiden Aunts' book and to be called *She for God in Him*.

The grandchildren, as usual, take up a good slice of time. They all came to stay in October. The two eldest have now reached the age to enjoy your records and wireless programmes to the full.

I've been reading such a delightful old book lately. It's called *Old Time Folk* and is about New England at the beginning of the nineteenth century. It is by Harriet Beecher Stowe (but is *so* much nicer than *Uncle Tom*). I wonder if you ever came across it in your childhood. It is not at all overpious and has delicious descriptions (almost like Hardy) of the woods and country life in the New England villages of Massachusetts.

Hasn't the weather been exciting this year? First the good summer, then one of the loveliest autumns I remember, and now this sudden dramatic snow and ice and cruel north wind. I've just seen out of my window a red rose blooming in the snow and bright pink clouds above. I've enjoyed the Berlioz exhibition and the Claudes very much lately.

People sometimes complain that letters of – say Jane Austen and Horace Walpole – or even ordinary family letters contain no comments on things of real importance and that they therefore didn't think of these things. Of course they did, but they were too weighty to go into letters, don't you think?

So if I make no mention of space travel, genes, the Springboks, Vietnam, etc., it isn't because I don't think about them.

Always very good wishes and love,

K.M.

My dear K.M.,

A long pause. A busy autumn and 1969 is full of interesting 'challenges' too! I hope all is going well with you and those you love, and I'm sending you a tiny little home-made card to wish you a very happy Christmas and New Year.

1968 has been a good year. In brief: my husband had to have a two-hour operation for varicose veins in both legs at the end of August. He was up walking next day, home on the fifth day, and on the tennis court for an hour and a half on the eighth day. No pain at all. The doctor said to me: I suppose you were praying? I said he supposed right. He said the hospital was astonished, and he congratulated me. I said I thought the credit was due to God! Wasn't it *good*. I don't rush about telling this, so please keep it precious. For it is.

In September I began an eight-week tour up and down this country, and it ended two weeks ago with an eight-performance week at the Yvonne Arnaud Theatre, Guildford. It was a wonderful tour; the best I've ever done on all counts and the new material seems to have worked. Some of this is in a fifty-minute programme I taped last Sunday for Sunday, December 15, B.B.C.2 in *colour*. We have rented a colour set and it is *so* beautiful. It has revolutionised T.V. for us. The travel and nature films are enhanced, and the plays – currently *Resurrection* – earlier *Portrait of a Lady* – seem to have a whole new meaning and quality. It will be wonderful when all T.V. is in colour, for we have the best system now available in the world, and it is startlingly lovely. Takes a little learning how to tune it, for it does fluctuate now and then for no recognisable reason. But I do recommend it.

Next year takes us to Australia again, and before that R.P.G. goes out to Uganda in January with a birding friend, and they are to be escorted by John Williams *the* great East African naturalist. I was asked too. But I'm to be away so much next year – four months in Australia – and I've got various jobs to work on here among which is an 'address or sermon', as the invitation said, to be given in Churchill

College Chapel, Cambridge, in April. Also, a lovely job, I've been asked to read five Beatrix Potter books in 'Jackanory' the 4.45 p.m. children's story time on T.V. That's a real challenge. It's a sacred text and must be allowed to reveal itself. Probably the viewers know every word already, and one daren't change a thing.

There is a lot of problem about, isn't there. But I feel it's a very exciting and hopeful time to be alive. All this ferment isn't for nothing, and there is enough understanding and good around to weather the storms. Do you think so?

This is an egotistical (or is it egoistical?) letter. Please tell me your news. One small anecdote. The three-year-old daughter of not very young parents woke her father at 3 a.m. to ask, 'Daddy, do mice do washing up?' Her father grunted a sleepy 'No-o-oh.' 'Oh good,' she said, 'I must have been dreaming.'

This brings love for Christmas and the Next Year.

J.G.

This has just missed crossing with yours – see last page.

This has just missed crossing with yours – see last page.

<table>
<tr><td>5 December</td><td align="right">Riverside House</td></tr>
</table>

Dear J.G.,

I thought I would like to write a proper letter before Christmas rush descends. I do hope all goes well with you and that you are finding time to *write*.

We had a nice summer, but in September we were rather badly flooded. Do you remember asking if there really was a river here? Alas, our innocent little stream became a broad and raging torrent. It is a horrid experience to be flooded – one feels so helpless – with a fire one can throw sand or water about, but with a flood it all happens at once and there is very little one can do. We did not suffer so much as some, but wading about in ice-cold water trying to salvage beloved books and move furniture by candlelight laid us both low afterwards for a time. We are still not straight, as the floor of one room is all up and the workmen have just deserted us for the time being and the sitting-room carpet (my only good one, which I love dearly) appears to have been lost on the way from the cleaners. They had hundreds to deal with.

However, we came off lightly compared with some, so I am not grumbling. It was the worst flood ever in these parts.

Otherwise I've enjoyed the autumn – I always love October and November. I've had some more coaching to do – such extremely nice girls. I am so lucky to be able to keep in touch with the young like this, and they seem to me to get more delightful every year. I visited my last batch at Oxford in November and found them thrilled with life in just the same way as I was fifty years ago. Not any student revolt there, though I think they are as aware of suffering and injustice in the world as the protest-marchers. Not that I am altogether out of sympathy with these, and I know that Oxford and Cambridge students *are* well off, because there is still relatively good contact there between students and dons. It is the same *everywhere* it seems to me – if you have a satisfactory relationship between people as *persons* (*not* treating or thinking of them as groups, or classes, or nations or races) all is well. Being a *person* and treating others as persons in their own right is really at the heart of living – don't you think – a universal law of health which we depart from at our peril. Only, with vast numbers and the complexity of modern life it becomes sometimes very difficult. Still, though more complex, we can't any longer remain in separate compartments – that's something.

I am plodding on with my book about the history of the Englishwoman. It has got to be finished by February for Batsford, and I have two more chapters to write and about half the illustrations to track down. It is fascinating to do, but the word limit is trying and means terrific selection.

The grandchildren continue to consume much time and provide much interest. Katie (thirteen now) is writing such good poetry, though I says it as shouldn't.

I've mostly been reading old favourites lately. The flood sent me back to *The Mill on the Floss*. How *perfect* all the first part is! I've had to read a lot of social history for 'Women' and feel such admiration for the nineteenth-century pioneers. I tried *Diana of the Crossways* after about fifty years. I used to love Meredith, but I can't read his prose now – far too laboured and his characters so brittle. But his poetry still lovely. It is interesting that he judges himself so correctly – always feeling he was better as a poet, though at the time his poetry was neglected.

When at Oxford in the summer I saw *A Day in the Death of Joe Egg* at the Playhouse, almost unbearable, but well acted and so full of compassion. The audience laughed in all the wrong places (nerves, I think). I also saw, and greatly enjoyed, the Christ Church *Son et Lumière*. Since, I have only been to concert and opera rehearsals. We can't manage evenings in two any more. We still haven't a T.V. I don't regret it except for not seeing you sometimes! Anyway we can't get B.B.C.2 in Shoreham.

I shall make this into a Christmas letter and enclose a card and a seventeenth-century poem by my favourite Vaughan* and lots of love and good wishes for 1969.

Bless you always

K.M.

December 6. I've just listened to a rather distasteful 'Woman's Hour' (usually I enjoy this programme, but one can't expect to always) in order to hear you at the end of it, and what a relief it was when it came! I agree of course about giving and receiving. I'm *not* good at Christmas buying now, being nearly always fighting against time and tiredness, and find crowds and having no car rather disastrous – I tend to give up in despair. Yesterday I went to London to read in the British Museum in the morning (refreshing) and shop in the afternoon (exhausting), and couldn't get any of the books I especially wanted and was cross. I tend too much to *muddle*.

As for receiving – I really don't *want* possessions now, but I *do* like things children have made for me – even if I don't know what to do with them. And I love to be remembered

---

* The poem has not been preserved with the letter, but as I sent it to Joyce again on 13 December 1970 the reader will find the text on pages 187–8.

by my old girls and people I don't usually hear from – friends from abroad, etc. In fact I *like* the much-abused Christmas card, both giving them and receiving them, and I spend ages fitting them to the recipients. What a dreadful idea, by the way, on 'Woman's Hour', that one should renew all one's Christmas decorations every year. Ours are rich with memories, some of them go back nearly fifty years, but I like to get *something* new as a fresh enrichment each year.

P.P.S. I've been twice to the Van Goghs – lovely and moving and exciting.

December 8th. I hadn't posted this when your letter and charming card arrived, so here is yet a third postscript. Thank you so much for them. It is always a delight to get a letter from you full of such joys. How wonderful about your husband's operation. Thank you for telling me. Then the success of the last tour – *many* congratulations. Oh dear! You unsettle me so about T.V., and it is tantalising in the extreme to hear about your fifty-minute programme on December 15th. As I said we can't get B.B.C.2 in Shoreham and I expect it is late, so I won't be able to see it anywhere else at a distance. I would like to have seen *Resurrection* too. I read such a good review of this. And you reading Beatrix Potter – my three-year-old Sophia knows them by heart. Perhaps, in years to come I'll be able to get B.B.C.2 and possibly colour T.V. – by the time I'm eighty.

I *am* sorry you can't go with your husband and John Williams to Uganda, as I know how you would have loved it but if one can't have one thing one gets another. I wish you well for your 'address or sermon' at Cambridge.

Yes, I think this is a most challenging and exciting time and I *do* feel the young, though often silly and undisciplined, are not hard or selfish, and are often splendidly the reverse.

I was moved and impressed by Sally Trench and by two Sunday evening radio programmes on drug addicts not long ago.

It is really time I finished this letter for the third time. I know you'll have a happy and blessed Christmas, and I hope 1969 will be as good for you as the last year has been.

Bless you. Love from,

K.M.

I loved the story of the mice washing up! My experience is that they do if you leave them to it. Mrs Tittlemouse certainly did.

18 December   *Elm Park Gardens*

My dear K.M.,

As always I have loved your good letter, and I thank you so much for the poem. How I do like 'It is Thy star runs page'. Henry Vaughan is a beautiful poet. Thank you. How distressing about the floods. I've always thought that fire would be terrible, and floods nearly as bad and even more demoralising. The smell, the mess . . . I loved your account of going to Oxford. I agree about treating people as people is very important. I like the word 'individual' better than 'person', because for me 'person' has a sort of personal responsibility about it – man on his own, battling – and the individual always seems nearer to being the Image and Likeness of His Maker! I do agree about Meredith; prose, alas, no longer; poetry, still *beautiful*.

Do you know I think 'Woman's Hour' has lost all its taste, all its warmth, all its open-mindedness.

When Joanna Scott-Moncrieff edited it, and later when Monica Sims took over, it was alive, loving and a real *quality* programme. It's shoddy, dim and lacks all love as I now hear it. True, I don't listen any more but *when* I do . . .

Don't miss the Bicentennial show at the Royal Academy. Such treasures. Wonderful Wilsons, little Turners and Constables, beautiful Stubbses and such a rich and enjoyable (on quite another level) Pre-Raphaelite section. Wonderful busts; and sketches in the room on the left; all in all a rich feast.

Yesterday I did the unscripted dialogue with Joseph

McCulloch at St Mary-le-Bow and it was taped by Thames T.V. and shown an hour later complete with the audience being asked how they'd enjoyed it as they came out afterwards into the deluge. It was such a huge assignment, I felt. I kept very quiet and prayed to 'let *that* mind be in me', etc., and when we did it I felt free and easy and not afraid. Whether it was any *good* I don't know. 'They' listened with rapt attention and laughed loudly when they were amused. We made a joyful noise unto the Lord, and it *felt* right. I've had some very warm telephone calls – if you see what I mean. (Sudden visions of hot air coming out of the receiver are a little unnerving.) And the people questioned at the door were *very* generous and said they'd very *much* enjoyed it. So – who knows? I feel that if only one small seed of a good idea comes through and lodges somewhere it's been a good job to do. I felt very grateful for the chance to say a bit about what I like about Christmas. Condensed, I said it was the reminder of the promise of the certainty.

My very young nephew is in love with long words – uses them lavishly and without much sense of their meaning. He said that when he grew up he'd 'hate to have a house that was reluctant of elbow-room'.

We are going to an all-ages party tonight and are half pleased and half not. The lure of home is *very* strong.

With love for Christmas and the New Year to my invisible friend – from

J.G.

21 December

My dear K.M.,

I'm having a sit-down and a letter-writing session while there is a little pause. I'm so glad you liked the programme. I feel all set up by your note. Thank you *so* much. Glad you like 'Eng. Lit. Continued' and 'The Worrier' and 'The Wedding is on Saturday'. I think these are the best, so I'm grateful you liked them. Thank you.

Such a nice note from your friend Mrs Bosanquet and the

lovely Twenty-Third Psalm. How kind of her. I feel I have seen it before but don't know where or when and I'm delighted to have it. I have written to say so even though she said I needn't.

I've had fun making angels for all our visitors on The Day as place-cards. They are gaily coloured and thoroughly pagan with golden yellow wings. They are cut out and stand up. They are all wearing flowered garments, and I've left a space for the name of the person sitting at that place to be written in at the bottom. They are more like butterflies than angels, but very pretty. I like the definition of angel: God's thoughts passing to man; and I know these don't need wings – or garments.

With love and thanks, and may 1969 be a Good Year for you and all of us. Love,

J.G.

This angel looks like *Madame* Butterfly, but the real ones don't.

1969

My dear J.G.,

A good and nice thing to do on New Year's Day – to write to you, and how splendid of *you* to write three times of late to me and how I love to get your letters. I am so glad about your unscripted dialogue with Joseph McCulloch – I wish I could have heard it.

I like your nephew's expression 'reluctant of elbow-room' very much. My great-niece aged eight-plus remarked the other day 'Shakespeare was rather prone to death, wasn't he?'

I'm hoping very much to go to the Royal Academy show next week. Christmas has been busy and a bit exhausting with guests and no help, so I'm glad now to draw breath. I managed to get out to Wrotham on Saturday – a lovely drive right along the Pilgrims' Way in bright winter sunshine with pink and white furrows and grey humps of downs. I was going to see my dear old friends, the Bosanquets, and she showed me your letter with much pleasure. She is such a valiant and alive person and she too lost a most dear and brilliant son.

I am reading Harold Nicolson's last volume. I find it of absorbing interest, though not inspiring. I like very much his honesty, humour and kindness of heart, love of beauty and of his family. I suppose this was really his religion. He was a man incapable of tragedy, I think – yet, having made this generalisation I at once want to qualify it. He takes pride in being an Epicurean and yet he chooses to have been able to witness the Crucifixion above all other events in history.

About belief in an after-life – why is it that so many, including Harold Nicolson, just *because* they want it, feel that this *proves* it can't be true? One should beware of wishful thinking certainly, but I have never understood why wanting a thing should make it fallacious.

Thank God – it doesn't depend on what we think anyway.

Today has been so lovely again – the hills covered with that sort of pink snow (as in a Pissarro winter landscape), and green showing through in the valley, and odd roofs in the village dark glowing red, and the birds chuckling softly because of the thaw. In winter this valley reverts to real country again. ' 'Tis by succession of delight That love supports his reign.'

I *would* like to have seen your angels. I love angels, I've got some Austrian ones and one really lovely *old* Baroque one – about six inches high in dull pink and green with a very graceful pose and a sweet gentle rather homely face. I use her in my home-made crib – put together long before they became universal – the stable built of plain oak building bricks we got a carpenter to make when our children were small, the manger made by my little boy, when he was six. There is also a tiny Russian scarlet-branched candlestick that always stands behind it. We always end Christmas Day by singing carols round it.

I was excited by the moon journey, weren't you? If only the Americans and Russians could land TOGETHER on the moon in 1969 as human beings.

I must get on and write Christmas thank-you letters. Oh – I am also reading a very interesting and unusual book – the tape-recorded records of Gielgud rehearsing Richard Burton in *Hamlet*. Have you come across it?

Goodbye, dear J.G. Thank you enormously for the pleasure you have given me in public and in private in 1968, and blessings on you for 1969. Love from

K.M.

My dear J.G.,

I feel I must write and say how much I enjoyed two T.V. items of yours lately. No, we have not yet got a T.V. but I *can* go into a neighbour when there is anything I particularly want to see (only on B.B.C.1 alas!) So, I managed to see your last Beatrix Potter one and *loved* it. Long ago my daughter wrote a nice article which appeared in *Time and Tide* called 'Crime in Beatrix Potter'. It ended – 'In our household we keep Beatrix Potter and Shakespeare on the same shelf.' They are still there, but now that they have served three generations the precious Beatrix Potters are almost dropping to pieces. Some have been renewed, and we have added some French translations with their deliciously gallicised titles. I wonder which is your favourite? As a child, mine was *Mrs Tiggywinkle*, but *The Tailor of Gloucester* has displaced her.

Then, last Sunday I saw and heard you with the students of the Guildhall School of Music and Drama. *What* a good discussion! Of course you were excellent in your sympathy and clarity and the way you unobtrusively drew them out and yet kept them to the point and got them to clarify their own ideas and convictions. But I was also most cheered and impressed by *them*, by their sincerity, thoughtfulness and altruism. Were they a picked lot, I wonder? They showed so much self-discipline in listening properly to you and to each other, not interrupting or making speeches, no arrogance or dogmatism. They were so unlike some of Muggeridge's discussion groups. I found them poignant. They made me ashamed of my own generation (myself included) who, at that age, were far more self-centred, though at the same time I longed to protect these young creatures and give them some of the gaiety and carefreedom which I enjoyed as a student. I am sure they would rightly scorn such a wish, but the maternal instinct is very strong. What one really longs to give them is confidence and hope. The girl who had been so haunted by the War film went to my heart, but she had obviously come to terms with it. I do feel, however, that *children* should be protected to a certain extent, though I could not help remembering, when this subject was raised, hearing a young drug-addict say that she began to take drugs because as a child she had been too *much* protected, and when she saw a Vietnam film she could not take it. It is a very difficult problem, as some sensitive children might be tempted to withdraw from reality into a fantasy world. The most emotionally insecure children would suffer most. I wonder what you thought of the students. I was really cheered by them.

I am glad February is over. It has been a difficult month with family illnesses coinciding with crisis of work and bad weather. Yesterday I was looking after two ill grandchildren – my daughter's old rambling house is the limit of inconvenience when anyone is ill – the bathroom and lavatory being on the ground floor. Sophie (aged three) announced that she wanted to go to the lavatory. 'Can you manage by yourself?' I ask. 'Yes,' she says. I sit down gratefully, but halfway downstairs she summons me and I go. She greets me with a seraphic smile: 'I *can* do everything for myself,' she says, 'but I didn't want to hurt your feelings, Granny dear.'!

Books. I've just finished Peter Quennell's Life of Pope – very well written and good altogether. How perfect, *to the eye*, England was then. If it only could *now* have the same population and architecture and all modern cons. I've also enjoyed Elizabeth Jenkin's *Honey*. Do you know her very good book on Jane Austen, by the way? Also David Gascoigne and Ruth Pitter's *Collected Poems*. My love and thank you for the broadcasts.

K.M.

I read about your encounter with the South African chauffeur. I wonder very much if you write to him about books. How lovely for him if you do.

My dear K.M.,

My natural inclination is to answer your letters as soon as I've read them, but I know this *can* be tiresome – puts the writer in a position of having to be the next writer. Not that I think either of us feels like that about our correspondence. But this time I got caught up in a real avalanche of letters about that T.V. discussion, and I decided to save up for the pleasure of writing to you *when* I'd answered all the others. They were so generous, so awed by the courtesy of the students to each other. (Why not? It never occurred to me as unusual. They were thoughtful people who had a feeling for other people.)

So glad you saw one of the Beatrix Potters. How I enjoyed reading them! I suppose I'm partial to *Peter Rabbit* because he was the first, and because I got to know it by heart and could *pretend* I was reading it before I could read. I'm very fond of *Mrs Tittlemouse* because I'm a bit of a tidier-upper. And because I used to think the sound of 'Tiddly widdly widdly, Mrs Tittlemouse' the height of wit. I remember rolling about with laughter just repeating 'Tiddly widdly widdly'.

I too was 'cheered and impressed' (your words) by the students on February 23. I think they *are* having a fairly carefree time. They were very gay and unspoilt when we talked before the discussion as a sort of rehearsal for lighting, camera and sound. The Lord really did work well that morning for us all. I rang up the producer the day before and asked what time I'd better get to the Guildhall, and he said the taping would start at 12.15, so if I arrived at 11.30 that would be all right. Something made me ask what time the students were to be there. '10.30.' I said, 'I'll come at 10.30, too.' And so I got there, and we all sat in our places and were told to talk. I suggested that we should not touch on our real topic – censorship, values and standards – and proposed that we talk about comedy. I told them my father used to say that a proof of sense of proportion (which I hold to be a sense of humour) is illustrated by the fact that a big man in a little hat is funny and a little man in a big hat is sad. Did they agree, and why? We had a fine time with this, and they asked what made me laugh, and I returned the question to them, and we talked of timing and pathos, and sound jokes and visual jokes, and wit and slapstick, etc. It was a marvellous hour, and I wish they'd taken it on camera, because it was rich and spontaneous and very *enjoyable*. So when we finally got to 12.15 we had already established a relationship and were all at ease with each other. Wasn't it *good*?

I agree with you about wanting to give the young confidence and hope. Some *sense* it, naturally; those with some faith and/or happy background are aware of both. I thought these young people were intelligent, serious, concerned and ready to discover that there is wonder, and it *is* real, and it *is* true, and it is eternal. They were *attractive*, too.

I loved your three-year-old grandchild not wishing to hurt your feelings by admitting she was independent of help. What a future for such a heart!

I haven't read any of the books you mention but I'm a *big* Ruth Pitter admirer. Have you read *The Davidson Affair*? It's a paperback, and I've lent my copy, so can't look up the author. It is a contemporary view, as if it happened now, of Jerusalem *just* after the Resurrection. *Very* well done. And have you read *The Cross and the Switchblade* by the Rev. David Wilkerson, a very impressive account of a Pentecostal preacher who 'listened' and went to New York to work with young drug addicts – and founded a centre for them? It's ghosted, but the facts are real, and it is a remarkable book. The S.P.C.K. have it I believe.

Glad you read about Nicodemus, the South African African driver. No, we don't correspond. I've only met him twice, but every word of the encounters that I wrote to go with the little 'piece' for the Feed the Mind Campaign is as it happened.

I'm doing a 'Ten to Eight' on Wednesday 12th – about *not* being an official godmother. And on March 25th about 'New Every Morning'.

Tomorrow I take part with many others in a poetry recital

at the Aldwych in aid of National Library Week. I was somewhat unnerved to read in the *Evening Standard* that Bernard Braden, who is organising it, had said the programme is 'not for prudes'. I rang him yesterday to clarify. 'I said it off the top of my head,' he said. 'Don't worry. The roughest poem in the bill is "Jo Anderson, my Jo".' I *hope* he is right. I don't want to find I'm among a lot of uninhibited strippers who decide to read curious free verse in their skins. My choice (we each have four minutes, and the subjects are Love and Hate) are Christina Rossetti, 'Had I but known', Landor, 'The Gift Returned', Sylvia Lynd about Harry and Alice, and Ogden Nash, 'Lucy Lake', which I do in a North Carolina voice. I loved your letter. Hope March is being *much* better for you. Love,

J.G.

Thank you for all you said.

31 March   *Riverside House*

My dear J.G.,

People who were coming to lunch today are *not* coming, and, although I love them, I also love the extra time that is suddenly mine, and I'm going to spend it writing to you. I've got a letter and three broadcast talks to comment on, and I want also to wish you a blessed Easter. Of all Easter poems I like best George Herbert's. I know you love it too, but it gives me pleasure to write it out here *in case* you wouldn't otherwise have looked at it this year!

> 'I got me flowers to strew Thy way,
> I got me boughs of many a tree;
> But Thou wast up by break of day,
> And brought'st Thy sweets along with Thee.
>
> 'Yet though my flowers be lost, they say
> A heart can never come too late;
> Teach it to sign Thy praise this day,
> And then this day my life shall date.'

154

The renewal you talked about in your latest 'Ten to Eight' last week links up with this and with spring, and the lovely thing is that it doesn't matter how old one gets, *this* sort of renewal is possible to the oldest of us, until the greatest spring of all arrives. I think people make too much fuss about death – at least Christians do – but more of this hereafter. I got *The Davidson Affair* on your recommendation and was fascinated by it. It is very well done and the characters so convincingly reconstructed. I especially liked Mary Magdalen, too often thought of as rather droopy and remorseful. I haven't yet tracked down *The Cross and the Switchblade*, but I shall in time.

A gentle, refreshing book of memoirs with a great deal about birds and plants, which I think you would enjoy, is *Over the Hills* by W. Keble Martin aged 92 – a great-nephew of Keble's. His own drawings of plants illustrate it.

I do wonder what the poetry recital at Aldeburgh really was like. I know all yours but Sylvia Lynd's. Your godchild talk I loved so much. I wonder if you get a vast postbag after these 'Ten to Eight's. I am sure they help so many people. If only one could stop people worrying so – of course that gift of *interest* in life outside oneself is so precious. I am very lucky I know so many people who have it. I do think that perhaps good T.V. programmes can help people very often to get this interest. Although I can't see them I am so pleased that Kenneth Clark's talks are so popular or more so than the Forsytes. I am *reading* them with much interest.

I am glad you were on 'Any Questions' last week to calm things down. I can't help wondering what the dinner beforehand was like with Bernard Levin's burning hostility to Enoch Powell in the air. The curious thing is that though their views are so opposed they have certain points in common. They both have inflammable minds. Of course I sympathised with Levin over race feelings (though I often dislike what he says, or rather how he says it), but it is very hard to judge hypocrisy in others. My own suspicion is that Powell may be out for power more than anything else, but he has shown compassion in other ways, and I expect his motives are mixed. But undeniably he has done harm.

I loved your boring baby. How I agree! *Silence and Noise*. I am very bad about this. I mind about it dreadfully. Of course towns have always been noisy, but what I grieve over is the end of peace in the countryside (or in most of it). Planes are to me the worst affliction. Everything else one can escape from, but planes can pursue you *anywhere* and at *any time*, and they are getting worse every year. They are equal to hundreds of Hoovers. I remember the bliss of rediscovering the peace of my childhood again in Ireland five years ago and in Austria three years ago. I mind about noise more than ugliness, and when tired or ill it becomes a torture. Even when well and full of interest I can't *think* while a loud plane is overhead. I am sure you are right, and a built-in peace is the only answer, but I sometimes doubt my power ever to acquire it. I think it is my main trouble about life.

Euthanasia – I do agree with the Chairman that today the prolongation of so-called life needs some control. The mind and not the heart should be the test of death. I had much sympathy with a letter in *The Times* of eighty-year-old Rev. J. Bell Saturday March 29th. I don't think it is pain so much as being kept alive when all sense has gone which really makes people afraid. I should like to have heard more from you about this.

Two more books I have read with interest lately are Kenneth Clark's *Gothic Revival* on architecture re-issued in a Penguin, very amusing and informative, though, as he points out in notes, rather outdated in parts; and Alethea Hayter's *Opium and the Romantic Imagination*. She writes so well, and the subject is topical and historical at the same time. I *do* like Charles Lamb. In Crabb Robinson's *Diaries* he tells how he alluded to Coleridge as 'Poor Coleridge' in Lamb's hearing. Lamb corrected him, not angrily, but as if really pained – 'Call him Coleridge; I hate "poor", as applied to such a man. I can't bear to hear such a man pitied.' I was reminded of this when reading the chapter about Coleridge in Alethea's book. None of those nine-teenth-century writers can be blamed for taking opium. It was prescribed as doctors now prescribe antibiotics, for *everything*.

I must stop or you will be wishing those people had come to lunch.

Oh – I must just say how interested I was in your discussion with the Guildhall students *before* the broadcast. It accounts for the relaxation about the talk itself.

We have discovered that Sophie can read quite well to herself, but she only does it on the sly, as she doesn't want people to stop reading to her. I asked her if she would read something to me in secret as a birthday treat, as I have one coming along. She whispered, 'I will if I have the strength.' She can be very enchanting.

I think of 'the avalanche of letters' you may be encountering now as a result of all your recent broadcastings with awe and misgivings. But although I am adding to them, I know that, as you say, you won't ever feel you've got to write to me. It doesn't matter how long (or how short) the gap is. When they come your letters are always a peculiar joy, and I know they'll come sooner or later as long as they can or should.

Bless you. I'm so glad you are alive

K.M.

Elm Park Gardens

13 April

My dear K.M.

It was *good* to get your letter. Thank you so much, too, for the Herbert poem. I have read it, but I had forgotten it, and it was *lovely* to see it again hand-written in your pretty writing. Thank you. I'm so glad your friends didn't come to lunch on March 31st.

We should be in Cumberland, but on Maundy Thursday Reggie stepped wrongly off his bus at Green Park and wrenched his ankle. We were to have put the car on the night car-ferry train for Perth, had four days near Oban with his sister, and then a week in Cumberland and two nights in Yorkshire on the way home. But we had to cancel all of it. At first I felt very sad, because we'd planned it all so carefully, and Reggie's sister was *so* disappointed. Also I thought two weeks of *not* cooking would be *very* pleasant; and I craved clean air in my nostrils. Reggie had no pain, but was very swollen and bruised and couldn't have managed the long journey, so here we were, and the sun shone and shone and shone. It has all turned out *so* happily. Two of our oldest friends, who were newly-weds when we were, arrived from America for a week, and had we gone away we'd only have seen them once. As it was they were here every day and we had such a good, unhurried time of talking and laughing, and I know all four of us really enjoyed ourselves. So it was a good time.

Reggie is able to hobble about, goes to his office in a cab and can now manage to help carry trays from kitchen to table. He had some discomfort as it began to mend, but he is better now, though very respectful of that foot, and doesn't take risks very much. We are hoping to get ten days up in Cumberland in May, and at least it should be a little warmer. The mean winds are back today, and we drove back this afternoon from thirty-six hours in Herts, and the car swayed as it had yesterday on the way down. I go at a stately forty, gripping the wheel. But even so we were buffeted.

I'm glad you found *The Davidson Affair* fascinating. I did too. It sheds no new light, but it makes it feel very immediate, doesn't it? I have a post friend in Jerusalem just now, and I think it is not an easy place to be. She has Arab and Jewish friends and has been a very good link, a meeting-place; but now this is less and less easy . . .

Yes, I've read Keble Martin, too, and its very artlessness is its charm, because it's so badly written, and yet his dear honesty and sense of wonder come through like sunshine. The *Sunday Times* had a profile of him a year or more ago, and with it there were some charming photographs, one in his cap and gown. I cut it out and pasted it into the flyleaf of the flower book which we keep in the car and use continually in spring and summer.

Department of Slight Confusion. The poetry recital

wasn't at Aldeburgh. It was in aid of National Library Week and happened at the National Theatre (Old Vic). I felt very proud reading on those boards and found I was topping the bill – last on. It was a gay and amusing evening. The Sylvia Lynd poem is in W. J. de la Mare's *Love* anthology – page 420, poem No. 525. It's called 'The Happy Hour'. I'm pretty sure you would like it. In the end I didn't read it, because the time was late, and I felt three poems were enough.

I am *so* glad you enjoyed the two 'Ten to Eight' programmes. The 'Wishes for a Godchild' one drew an enormous response, and I believe it was the biggest mail asking for copies that they have ever had! Because of Kenneth Clark I *wish* you had a coloured television; I *do*.

I believe T.V. can be a huge blessing and a spur to further interest, but one must learn to switch off. We look *quite* a lot but only at chosen items; never just to see what's on.

The 'Any Questions' evening was interesting, challenging, and in the end it was without acrimony except on the air. I travelled back with Bernard Levin and Enoch Powell and felt that my feminine task was to hold a balance. Their hostility was well disguised; both are highly intelligent, musical and literary, so we talked of music and books, of accents and dialects, of foods and holidays. Ten minutes before we arrived at Victoria I asked Enoch Powell if he enjoyed his life, and he burst into flower. He said he was wholly happy in his work; he loved the House of Commons and the drama and arena atmosphere. He was reading Gladstone's letters aloud to his wife every night (they always read aloud to each other, nightly) and he was struck at how history repeats itself. The situations, but in changed forms, are the same.

I could not make up my mind about him. His eye is ice-cold; his mouth is fleshy and too big. *Is* he honest? Is he concerned? Or is he simply a political animal enjoying the battle? I feel he is a dangerous man. I think his speeches are alarming because he *knows* that there are so many prejudiced minds afraid of an era they don't understand, who are behind him, because they think he believes in a return to the *status quo* they knew and felt safe in. I think he's a wrong 'un because of this. Clever, yes. But for what ends?

I prefer uncontrollable Levin, who has a lot of attractive qualities that aren't revealed on the air or on the T.V. He is tiny, looks twenty, must be thirty-seven? *Isn't* sallow as I expected; is pink. He is stupid when he attacks, and often it is planned attack and not just an honest rage, and that I find unpleasant. He is very rude in public, and delightfully courteous offstage.

Noise is a thing I can't do with, but if there is enough of it, it becomes a sort of wall of sound and one can withdraw from it and live apart. What I can't do with is roar of any sort – crowds, Hoovers, jets. And I hate road-drills and being in factories! Perhaps the horror of planes is that we hear them coming, and the noise gets louder and louder and LOUDER and is very frightening. I can't hear the telephone or the news on my little radio when planes go over this flat (if the wind is behind them). I can't decide which wind it is that does it, I think it's the east.

About euthanasia. Did you hear the anaesthetist a while ago doing a 'Ten to Eight'? I thought it so interesting because he said the difference between man and animal is that man has consciousness, and animal only has reflex. (How does he know?) And that when consciousness leaves the body (which is often before the heart stops) he considers death has occurred. I'm sure consciousness is Life. And *it* continues. We don't remember being born; why should we remember dying. We only know we *are*.

Do you see the *Observer*? Today's scientist report on page 1 – and inside – is fascinating. I believe more and more they will discover that matter is illusion. Mind is the only reality, the only substance. I spell it with a big M!

I find it difficult to contribute in a programme like 'Any Questions' on a subject like euthanasia, because it involves *so* much more than killing off a body. As we come to understand more of what man really is I think it will answer the question, for you cannot kill *Life*.

In late June we set off for Australia. (Have I told you all this?) I do a concert in Hong Kong, and we will have five free days, too. Reggie hasn't been there, so it will be fun for him. My tour starts in Adelaide, then Melbourne, then Sydney, Canberra, Tasmania – Hobart – Launceston and finally Brisbane, where it will be summer. Then we'll have two weeks' holiday on a cattle station with dear friends called Joyce.

My oldest childhood friend is Virginia Graham, who is a writer and contributed some very good poems to *Punch* all through the War, and lately does pieces in *Home and Gardens* just for exercise; also the *Christian Science Monitor*. Her husband is young – sixty-one – and has premature senility. It is hideous, but she is fortified by the most lovely sense of what Life really is. She is sunny, serene, funny, gay and wholly selfless. This is an example, if ever I saw one. I *wish*, because of her burden, I wasn't to be away for so long, because although we may not meet all that often, we talk constantly on the telephone, sometimes twice or three times a day. She has a flat in a friend's country house and goes there for week-ends. We've just been there, and I know we can be a bit of a help because at least she has someone to talk to. Also I can take him off for a little drive and let her nap after lunch.

All this is *very* private please.

My brother's daughter Sally, now fourteen but looking seventeen, is going through a *violent*, rebellious stage. Says such wounding things to her mother and father. It is *very* difficult to know why, or to know how to deal with it. Apparently it is not rare today. They love her; have been strict but always *very* generous and loving and are a united family. I believe the only way to help her is to try and see the truth about her. God made her in His image. I also think all they can do is go on being available as calmly, lovingly as possible. It is NOT an easy world to grow up in. But was it *ever*? It's the growing up that is difficult. She's a mammoth egotist and I know *so* well about this. I was too. I think her strength, when canalised, will be for good.

I have written far too much, but you are so easy to talk to.

Happy Birthday whenever it is/was? I found wild white violets yesterday, *lots* of them. I'm talking about spring in

'Woman's Hour' on Tuesday, I *think*, 15th. I took the *Radio Times* to Herts and left it by mistake, so can't be sure.

Much love,

J.G.

19–20 April   *Riverside House*

My dear J.G.,

I want to write again now because I have been thinking so much about your friend Virginia Graham (whose writing I remember liking very much in *Punch*). Such goodness and courage as hers have, I can't help believing, an influence far beyond her immediate circle and circumstances. It helps to swell that 'ocean of light' that swallows up the ocean of darkness. The day-to-day endurance is so much more challenging and harder than a sudden final blow, and it often seems to me to come to those who are especially prepared by the spirit to meet it.

I am, too, so sorry about the temporary trouble and anxiety over your niece. I *do* think it is harder to grow up today for a good many reasons. For one thing we were allowed to remain children for longer. You say Sally looks seventeen. She is probably required, not by her family of course, but by the pressure of contemporary society, to behave as if she were seventeen. I was, in many ways, still a child at fourteen and was expected to behave like one, and by the time I reached seventeen I had that much more sense, so that though I too rebelled then, I was not so lost and muddled as I would have been three years earlier. Also, in a way, the War helped, as the second War helped *my* children to come out of themselves in their teens. I wish *you* were nearer Sally, because you might reach her now where her parents can't. But with all that love round her the trouble *must* only be temporary. I do think that besides a too quick growth forced on them now, the young suffer in a way we didn't (or not so much) from a lack of secure values in the world around them.

What a pity about your husband's ankle, but I'm glad it

wasn't altogether a pity, and I do hope the Cumberland holiday comes off triumphantly in May.

Your letter came in time for me to listen to your spring 'Woman's Hour' talk. I agree about the magic of white violets – always such a treasure trove. But my really favourite spring flower is the cowslip – I think because it was my mother's. We almost shared a birthday and quite shared a birthday picnic often on the South Downs near our home, where cowslips grew *thickly* and larks sang like mad, and there were NO PLANES. Cowslips have the warmest sweetest scent in the world – when I was ill once as a child my mother made me a huge cowslip ball to sniff to take away the pain.

I was *most* interested in your description of Enoch Powell and Bernard Levin. I am afraid you have confirmed me in my suspicions of Enoch Powell as a power-seeker, *not* really sincere even in his racialism, I feel. But he's a nice husband and father I believe, and this will save him from damnation. I hope Gladstone does him some good, but I doubt it.

We had a nice Easter and following week with lots of young about. Our adopted refugee grandson came home *without his girl friend*, for the first time for a year. She providentially got mumps (only slightly). I like her very much, but we enjoy Matthew on his own. Then we had our other long ago Jewish refugee boy (1938) now middle-aged but very boyish still. He is the sort of guest that follows one round discussing God and the Universe and all the arts, while you are trying to wash up and plan meals and cook – very distracting but endearing. Then came a nice great-niece, who is getting married shortly and wanted to talk wedding clothes and about her dear Martin; then my brother, just eighty, but working three days a week as a radiologist still. My brother is always amused at our house – the bathroom, for instance, has three taps marked COLD – the one most clearly marked COLD is the hot one – the fourth tap has no mark at all. I takes a guest to point this out to us. As a matter of fact I like our bathroom. It was originally a bedroom, so there is plenty of room and it is always warm. The bath and basin are large and old-fashioned. I hate the modern cramped ones, as I am tall. Besides these necessaries there is a chair that I remember all my life from my schoolroom, a large chest-of-drawers containing family games, travel diaries, postcards and photos with a little old mirror on top and, as mats, three family samplers. I feel guilty about these, as they ought to be protected by glass or laid away in tissue-paper, but I enjoy them as mats. On the walls looking down in pleasure is a large French poster of a carved Madonna – very debonair and gay and smiling, with an equally cheerful and elegant baby – also two Japanese prints and a lithograph, which I love, done by my daughter of children and ducks in a park, and a French etching of a fisherman and his little girl, given me long long ago by my grandfather – also a dramatic picture of fir trees and a huge moon and black mountains done by my grandson when seven.

Could you imagine a nicer bathroom?

I am *so* cheered that your broadcasts (I mean the 'Ten to Eight' ones) bring such a large and appreciative post. People *do* like good things when given the chance to have them. Oh – that reminds me of Kenneth Clark. Yes – I *would* have liked to have seen his lectures on coloured T.V. I have enjoyed reading them, and I think he has a marvellous power of conveying visual experience in words. But every now and then, off his own subject, he makes some bad blunders. For instance he really shouldn't have quoted *Macbeth* of all people, as an example of Shakespeare's own philosophy. Macbeth, far from proving Shakespeare a cynic, shows just the opposite. His terrible speech 'Tomorrow and tomorrow and tomorrow', etc., expresses the utter disillusion that follows inevitably as the result of having denied the eternal values. Besides, it is always dangerous to quote the characters of a great dramatist as if they were his own sentiments. Also, how could he compare the relation between Michelangelo and Verrocchio to that between Beethoven and Mozart? True, Mozart can be 'light, nimble and elegant' like Verrocchio, but he is so *much* more, and I don't think it correct to talk about 'the *progression* between Mozart and Beethoven' – change is all right, but not the idea of progress. Still, all power to Kenneth Clark's elbow.

I do hope the Australian tour will be a wonderful success. I am sure it will be, and your holiday with your friends too. We are off on May 3rd to our much-loved Salzburg and our other home there.

Oh – thank you for reminding me of that lovely Sylvia Lynd poem. I looked it up and realised I had read it. It is so fresh and the touch so sure – *pure* poetry. I ought not to have forgotten it, for I am very fond of that anthology, and not least because my husband, who gave it to me, wrote out two Shakespeare quotations on the fly leaf: 'I, beyond all limit of what else in the world do love, prize, honour you' and 'Perdition catch my soul, but I do love thee!'

That was nice of him, wasn't it? What Brigid Brophy and others writing on 'marriage' in the *Listener* just now don't seem to realise is that it isn't either romance gone dead, or a useful social contract or a restrictive practice but a creative way of life.

I *must* stop. I have sixty-five illustrations for my Batsford book on 'Women' to write captions for, but I'd like to go on for much longer discussing mind and matter, for instance, and the *Observer* article and all sorts of things. But although I must stop writing I shall go on thinking about your letter and about your friend and her husband and your Sally.

Much love

K.M.

P.S. The quotation I had in mind at the beginning of this letter was George Fox:

'I saw that there was an ocean of darkness and death, but that an infinite ocean of light and love flowed over the ocean of darkness. In *that* I saw the infinite love of God.'

15 May   *West Arms, Llanarmon*

My dear K.M.,

I see that is is nearly a month since your excellent and enjoyable letter was written to me. April 19. Thank you very much for your thoughts on my niece, Sally. And I'm so glad you remember Virginia Graham's verses in *Punch*. She is a 'great' woman. Really.

You talk of how we were allowed to grow up gently. (Do you know Kathleen Raine's poem 'O Spring, grow slowly'?) I wore long brown cotton stockings and a pigtail till I was seventeen and then, overnight, changed to silk and hairpins. *That* was a sudden change, but the fact that we were allowed to stay young for longer made the change happen naturally even though it was a shock.

So glad you liked the little talk about spring on 'Woman's Hour'. I heard it again out of the blue in a repeat last week and was very surprised. I agree about cowslips. That tiny click as you pick them and the hairy pink stem, so crisp, and of course the smell. This year up here in Wales the sorrel flowers are thicker than I've ever seen them, and the steep banks in the lanes are buttoned in by primroses and *big* violets as well. What a moment this is in the year! My favourite time – before the leaves thicken. All the bones are still showing up here, and ash has hardly started.

I love your description of your bathroom. I see it *perfectly*. Also you gave me a first hint about your appearance. You say you hate modern cramped bathrooms 'as I am tall'. Ah! My bathroom in the flat is painted a very bright sharp oak spring green, rather acid, with white trimmings. Reggie has been collecting bird prints of real quality, and there they hang to be absorbed as he is soaking. (I'm a wash-and-get-out girl.) A lovely eighteenth-century spoonbill. A ring-ouzel of the same date, and some rather inferior blue-tits. We've just been given a ruff, and he will join them when the framer finally lets him out. The curtains are blue-and-white checked towelling, and I made them by hand, so they don't hang very well, but they have a white fringe and are cheerful.

Have I told you there is to be another little paperback anthology of 'Ten to Eight' broadcasts? I'm to have two in it. Due in the autumn for Christmas, unless the printers strike. (Mustn't it be boring to have to strike *so* much?)

I hope your Salzburg holiday was lovely. Our little time

up here is being very good. We found the hotel in *The Good Food Guide*. I opened up the page on Wales – the map I mean – and saw where the little dot marked down a hotel, got out the motor atlas and discovered that Llanarmon is at the very end of a B road and in a brown patch, so we knew it was hilly. I rang up Mr Carter, the host, and said, 'Please may I ask you some questions?' And he said in a pleasing Lancs accent, 'Fire away', or words to that effect. 'Is it pretty?' 'We think so.' 'Is it heated?' 'Throughout.' 'Is it *very* quiet?' 'Yes. And we'll put you at the back facing up the valley.' 'Right,' I said liking the feel of Mr Carter and his hotel, 'please may we come from May 11th to the 18th.' It is all he said and more. It's seventeenth-century with solid walls, and you can't hear the neighbours. It is toasting warm, with a good radiator in the bedroom, so the smalls having dripped can dry off properly. Good beds, a pretty cheerful chambermaid with a primrose yellow overall and a genuine desire to make the place comfy, and flowers everywhere in little pots held up by stones. At the moment we've got bluebells on our table, and the next table has primroses. Lots of sitting space with good chairs – a 'lounge' with oak settles and cushions with a big open fire; an upstairs drawing-room with T.V., and a big bar with plenty of deep chairs. So in wet weather there are sitting places other than one's own bed. The hotel sits in the wide part of a small valley facing, across a little 'place', another hotel called 'The Hand'. There are about a dozen little houses, including a post office cum general store with everything in it and a Welsh handicraft gift shoppe. Four roads meet in the 'place', and there are always farmers with or without strange tractor-like vehicles gathered for pleasantries. We have an Australian friend with us who shares our tempo and taste for birds and quiet, and we are having a congenial little break from city life. Reggie and I found a ring-ouzel's nest with young in it and watched the parent birds to-ing and fro-ing down a steep hill and into the nest that is just above a rushing torrent below two small fierce waterfalls. Yesterday Reggie took Elaine up there, while I sat in the car and painted a small yellow farmhouse with a touch of turquoise on the porch set up against a rising green field. Nearby is a beautiful bare, bony ash tree. I made such a mess of it. But I enjoyed the try. May have another go if it fits in.

The weather – oh well, it's Wales. We rise about eight and go where we plan to and just hope. Everyone says you must see the gardens at Bodnant – world famous – vast acres of rhododendrons, set above the Conway estuary, etc., etc. Me, I do not like rhodos . . . However it isn't a day for painting, being pewter-coloured, so we are taking a picnic and going to meander over there on little pencil-marked roads well away, we hope, from traffic. We went over to Dolgelley like that on Tuesday and it was a joy. Only once did we have to back down a lane, and that was because two entire oak trees were being hauled on to a carrier by some infernal machine. The men were apologetic for keeping us waiting and moved it all into a convenient space nearby so we could get by. We met with smiles and waves everywhere. It is refreshingly empty up here. Tiny farms, sheep, views, rivers and little woody hills.

Reggie has a second cousin whose husband has inherited the castle that has been in his family since 1200, and we went to see it yesterday. Chirk. Like a toy with five round towers set in magnificent country – a real border castle. What a ghastly weight to inherit and no money to do it with! Of *course* it's open to the public, but it's a losing game. They live in one of the towers in beautiful strangely shaped rooms 'done' by Pugin. Gothic vaulting and a mistakenly elaborate taste in 'chimney pieces'. Such views from every window. But miles from kitchens, cold, huge. He wants to sell it – or get it taken over for historic reasons and build a little house on the land nearby. But she is for trying to hang on. Courageous? Dotty? I dare say if you have been there as a family since 1200 there is an urge to carry on, but why not do it in a small house nearby?

I'm too selfish to want to struggle with roofs and dry-rot for posterity's sake.

I do love your quotation from George Fox. *Thank you* for it.

Now I must get up and set off for Conway.

We go off on June 29th, and I'm free of lists and chores while I'm up here, but doubtless they'll crowd in on Tuesday when we go home via two nights in Somerset.

I'm on B.B.C.2 on Sunday 18th at 7.25 for *fifty* minutes! In colour, too. Should you chance to see it, the dress is a most lovely apricot colour. I'm going to have it for the show in Australia, too.

On Radio 2 (old Light I think) there is to be a series called 'Beginning with the Bible', and I've just taped a four-minute piece on 'Be still and know that I am God'. I believe it will go out in July – 20th? – at 5 to 10 a.m., all among pop music. They say it is a huge potential audience of house-wives and home bodies and commercial travellers in cars. I had a *good* time working on that *beautiful* text. I think of it *all* the time. It is for every minute, isn't it.

With love,

J.G.

Letter from Sally's mother to say Sally rang up on Mother's Day (a different one from ours I think) and Mary was so relieved and pleased. Isn't that good.

26 June   *Elm Park Gardens*

My dear K.M.,

I much enjoyed your letter reporting on 'the Austrian holiday, thank you for telling me. I love wild tops and orderly bottoms, too – as in Cumberland and Wales, where valleys are busy with man tilling and sheep feeding, and the hills are wild above.

We go on Sunday. As always I'm taking far *too* much – But we go into two seasons while we are away: hot summer in Hong Kong and Queensland and hard winter in the middle. They are having a very *cold* one in Melbourne with fog, and Sydney has it too. Grrrr, so I take lots of wool and tweeds too. But I finish the long tour in Brisbane at the end of September into October, and then have a holiday up there, so it's good to look forward to *some* sun and all that lovely fluffy wattle (mimosa) coming out.

I'm *very* pleased, because my May 18th T.V. on B.B.C.2 had such a good 'appreciation figure' that they decided not to wait till Christmas to repeat it, but are putting it on B.B.C.1 on Tuesday – after the evening showing of the Investiture, very flattering. 9.5. p.m., should you be near a set!

About the Third Programme. I wrote off in protest to the *Sunday Times* who organised a campaign. I've done my best by word of mouth. We can but *hope*. It is one of our very proudest possessions, isn't it? It *must* be saved. And we *must* enforce the payment of licences. WHY NOT? Are we just accepting law-breakers with a shrug? Oh, we do need a bit of tightening up, don't we? I must go to bed. I keep making lists of jobs and ticking them off and then adding more!

We had a most lovely two weeks at Aldeburgh, and the spirit of the festival was really very moving. The news of the fire stunned everyone, but not for long. By *8 a.m.* next morning all those connected with *Idomeneo*, a big production scheduled to play two nights later, and everyone connected with the production had their new orders. People went without sleep. Willing hands wrote out new seat numbers, worked out plans, etc., for Blythburgh Church instead of the lovely Maltings, and only one concert had to be cancelled. It was a miracle. And there was such affection and goodwill abroad. Lovely. The last concert in the Maltings – it was the first of the festival – ended with Schubert's Trout Quintet with Ben Britten and the Amadeus. It was a very great performance, and that great string-coloured barn looked so beautiful and sounded *so* perfect. It will rise again and be better than ever.

Wish I was in bed . . .

I'm so sleepy. Love to you.

Happy summer/autumn.

Joyce

My dear K.M.,

It was particularly good to see your pretty fist on the envelope a few mornings ago, and I thank you so much for a lovely letter.

Yes, it is a long time since we wrote. We were away for five months and a bit, and home is very pleasant to be back in after so much moving around and the packing and unpacking. Also I got sick of the same few clothes, all cleverly chosen in the same honey-beige key so as to fit in with each other. But I had a sky-blue scarf that broke the monotony, and that made it possible. It was *almost* all winter for us. But Hong Kong, the first stop, was so hot, though, that we could hardly bear it; and we both like heat, but not 'humidity'! We just poured and felt limp. Six days there and one concert.

We were lent a heavenly flat high on a mountain with a view of the busy harbour below and China beyond the Kowloon skyline. Air-conditioned, too, so we could sleep, and two smiling Chinese to look after us. I was startled when Gun, the 'boy', asked us if we liked 'Flied Plawns'. It was so like a music-hall joke that I had to restrain myself from saying, 'Yes please, velly much.'

After our summery six days in Hong Kong three beautiful cold crisp winter days in Sydney staying with my dear friends on the edge of the water. Lots of 'promotion' for me – press conferences, T.V., radio, to launch the whole tour. After that Adelaide, two weeks; Melbourne, three weeks; Sydney three weeks; Canberra one week, and over to lovely Tasmania for two weeks and finally Brisbane two weeks. Part of these times was spent in promotion, for every state is completely separate, and word of mouth doesn't seem to cross borders, so we had to re-launch in each new place. The questions were usually; what do you think of the permissive society? Would you appear nude on the stage? What do you think about censorship?

I began to sort out my ideas, so I could put the answers succinctly, and I said I thought we got the society we deserved – all of us. That I wouldn't appear nude on the stage. It was too late! And anyway I'd never found it necessary to strip in order to communicate. And finally I didn't like censorship, although I thought the young had to be protected. That we had to be our own censor and judge out of our own sense of values. I also said that no one *has* to read the dirty books, see the dirty plays, etc. We do our own choosing. I also said I thought it pretty sad to think of the *poverty* of the private lives of those who found it necessary to pay out lots of money to sit in a theatre and look through a keyhole . . .

The most rewarding part of the tour, which was the biggest in all senses of the word of any I've ever done anywhere, was the number of young who came to the shows everywhere. Students poured in and poured back-stage. Some came *again*, and they were so friendly and enthusiastic. They looked very odd as ours do here, but they were attractive and intelligent and full of openness to new ideas. It was my fourth tour out there and the best.

After the hard work, and some of it was nineteen nights in a row, bar Sundays, and I'm no longer used to runs, we had three lovely weeks' holiday, mostly up in Queensland in a wild bit of country 340 miles north-west of Brisbane: cattle country, bush. Rolling hills and rich farms in valleys and miles and miles of bush too. Drought had dried it out to the colour of a biscuit, but while we were there gentle rains fell, and overnight a green fuzz appeared, and birds began to sing again. We had very little *real* summer, though, although four faultless spring days without a cloud in Victoria were *very* lovely. There we were in sheep country, huge rolling rich countryside with mountains up to 3,500 feet, all about the landscape, and they'd had good rains so it was beautifully green.

We both love Australia very much, particularly the country. Cities are so alike these days, and all are too full and there's nowhere to park, but in the country in Australia you can go for mile on mile on mile and never see anyone or a house, and I find it restoring. I love the vast trees in the Victorian hills and the clear rivers and rocks. Tiny wild flowers surprised me – wild wood violets, indigenous and quite like ours. I found it very moving one day when we were *miles* off the map up in New South Wales having a winter picnic on a high piece of country to find chickweed growing and a little Scotch fir tree. Yes, early settlers had had a little stone cottage up there and put in the tree, and I expect the chickweed fell out of a bag of grain.

Sunday: I wonder if you happened to hear 'Ten to Eight' today? It was a hate piece such as I have never heard before, and I am writing to ask *why*? It was a plea for a division: Them and Us. They must be *smashed*. No word of Love, no word of unity. I lay in bed finding it hard to believe my ears and wondering what *is* behind the thinking of the Religious Department at the B.B.C. these days? I'm all for new ideas and freedom, but not hate.

I wish I had more time to write now. Lots to tell you about the giant redwoods north of San Francisco where I stayed for three days on the way home. Then four weeks in and around New York, a visit to Boston, to Greenwich, Connecticut, etc., seeing my brother and family. Poor America. It is *so* bewildered, ashamed, torn and stunned. But it is a *world* condition. When will we recognise that the spiritual is the reality and work from that, the *only* security?

Dear K.M., keep writing please. I'll do better later. I'm very behind-hand with Christmas. We'll be eleven on the day.

I loved hearing about your bicycling. I'd love to see the memoir of your son one day if you will let me. No, I don't know Old Time Folk – sounds pleasing. I do agree about why we don't put much world conditions in private letters. One assumes we all know about them, and unless there is a new view to air it is all far too big to begin on.

This brings you love for Christmas and the New Year.

J.G.

We missed *all* the lovely weather. It was rather a grey winter down under.

1970

[Part of a letter] Please excuse bad writing, but my large cat is humped on my lap and is an unequal writing-desk.

I found this year that because of the postage far more people turned their cards into letters and wrote a lot of news inside, and I like this very much, especially from old pupils. We had a family party here on Christmas night with flute, cello and guitar provided by grandchildren.

Now I'm going back to your letter before last mostly about your five-months tour. I am so glad the young were so appreciative. It is greatly in their favour. But I also find all those I meet so friendly and intelligent and really much more knowledgeable and concerned about the world than we were. Your holiday in Queensland sounds lovely – the sense of space is what I should love. I get a feeling of claustrophobia in Southern England nowadays. It isn't only the big towns which are getting all alike by the way, but the small ones too. I have just listened to a talk about winter holidays when Caudebec in Normandy was mentioned. When I knew it in 1921, it was completely French and remote. It had a chateau in private occupation and one tiny inn where we stayed, with the innkeeper (who was a friend of Belloc's) doing all the cooking and where we used to eat omelettes on the tiny balcony looking over the great silent river. Now there are luxury hotels, a nightclub and a car-ferry that operates every ten minutes.

Yes – I'd love Queensland – at any rate for a holiday.

Do you remember in your letter commenting on a 'Ten to Eight' programme which you described as a hate piece. I did not hear it, but my husband did, and his reaction was just the same as yours. He was both puzzled and horrified, and we very much wonder what reply you had from the B.B.C. about it? I am very depressed at the Third Programme disappearing in April. Oh, this majority rule, and eternal hateful plea of economic necessity! What about spiritual and cultural necessities? And anyway they don't give us a chance to pay for it.

But I was favourably impressed by an interview with Gerald Brooke . . .

27 January   *Riverside House*

My dear J.G.,

I expect you will have had many letters after your Sunday evening broadcast, but I felt I would like to thank you for it. Those Sunday broadcasts are queer – some so very good and helpful (like yours and Gerald Brooke's for instance) and some so trivial, like the interview with the parson who was obsessed with flying saucers! To return to yours – I think from your letters I knew most of it before, but it did make clearer to me your ideas about life after death, with which, of course, I agree and they also gave me a jolt about my own slackness in Bible study, which with me is certainly not regular enough. About prayer for others – I find this such a difficult subject to think logically upon, and yet such a *strong* impulse, that I have given up thinking, and just do it. I know God doesn't need asking, but perhaps a bit of extra love directed towards them may be of use. It's beyond logical argument anyway, as all love is.

Thank you, too, for your Appeal last Sunday for Family Service Unity. I am sending a donation to the F.S.U. address, but I have been interested for some time. One of my old girls – a splendid person – was working for them in Manchester. It is such an exacting and trying job but absorbing.

I am apprehensive about radio broadcasting in the seventies. There was an alarming article in *The Times* last week and many letters. I don't like the trend. I wonder what you are thinking about it all?

Just now my two favourite novels are being broadcast – radio not T.V. – (my third favourite is *Middlemarch*). First, *War and Peace*, which I am enjoying enormously. Hurrah! It's Tuesday, and there will be a fresh instalment! Pierre is especially good and the old Prince Bolkonsky and Maria. But it is *so* well produced altogether.

The second, *Emma*, takes far too great liberties with a perfect text – I could have done it much better (!) – contains one of the worst bits of casting and misreading of a character that I can remember – Mr Woodhouse, enough to make Jane Austen turn in her grave. But I must confess Harriet is a joy and Mr Elton and the Knightleys are good. But *Emma*, which should have been far the easier book to do, is nothing like up to the standard of the *War and Peace* production.

The birds all think it is spring and are singing like mad this morning. I saw two wrens and a kingfisher by the stream. Wrens are much more often seen lately again than a year or so ago.

Have just found a piece of paper on which my youngest grandchild (aged four) has written laboriously, 'MY LIFE IS A BANE, UNLESS I HAVE A PURRPUL VELVIT DRESS.'

So now I must try and procure a bit of purple corduroy velvet I suppose and make a dress for her next birthday. But I wish it wasn't purple, as it will be hard to track down and perhaps a little regal for her years.

You must *not* bother to answer this, because I am sure you have masses of correspondence on hand and it isn't long since I heard from you. Next month I shall be sending you my little 'Woman' book, because I think you may enjoy the pictures anyway, and so you can wait till then. Meanwhile bless you always – and love from

K.M.

My dear K.M.,

Thank you for your generous letter. And a special thanks for 'My life is a *bane* unless I have a purrpul velvit dress!' What a sense of drama, what a passionate heart! I have no taste for purrpul, but if I did it would have to be velvit. Hope you've found some.

Yes, I did have a big mail after the interview. Very warming; particularly those who asked how they could read about my faith and where to go, etc., etc. We have a little booklet that is called *Facts about Christian Science* that is a help for these enquiries. Did I ever show you one? I will if you'd like one; don't bother if you wouldn't. About praying for others. Yes, it is difficult. I think that if one can acknowledge that there is no separation of man from his original Cause – whether man knows it or not – and that, being wholly spiritual, nothing can touch the very essence of his eternal being, this is a helpful way of praying for others. As I think I said when Leslie Smith questioned me, I don't believe prayer is for changing anything that is true; it is for revealing this unchanging perfection and realising its ever presence.

Thank you *so* much for sending something to Family Service Units. I hadn't heard if there was much response. It's *not* an easy one to 'sell' to givers. But they are such marvels, and I hope they will get some help.

About the future of B.B.C. radio. Time alone will tell. I find it so hard to know what *is* going on. It all sounds so plausible when they tell us about it at General Advisory Council meetings, and one is very nearly convinced that all will be well, and we mustn't be afraid . . . *But* unease remains. I think there is a growing tendency to streamline without enough concern for *content*, and one of the problems is that our education or our society isn't throwing up thinkers of *quality*, or so it *seems*. I suppose elderlies like us have always felt this? The signs of the times are reflected in the pop music world, where songs often fade out on records without any resolution. This open-ended, episodic, scrappy sort of living wouldn't satisfy me. But I have a built-in need for form, and I hunger for content, as I know you do. Life is so wonderful, there is so much to discover and enjoy, and I do hope the young get enough nourishment from their current education and semi-digested scientific and psychological treatment. Truth is simple, but it ain't easy. That's something we come to discover, don't we? Worth the effort, too.

Reggie is in Africa. I never like partings but I go on being *so* grateful for the joy we share. I hadn't heard either *War and Peace* or *Emma*, dammit. I've read Enid Bagnold's autobiography with some amusement – pleasure, although I don't think she's very – what? – aware of spiritual values, I guess.

I'm also reading Edith Sitwell's autobiography, and she is *so* spiky. But she had a wretched childhood, and her arrogance can be traced to a need to push I suppose. I don't think she's a *real* poet either, but a talented versifier.

Longing for your 'Women' book. Nice thought.

I must go and buy some food.

With love,

J.G.

7 *March*   *Elm Park Gardens*

My dear K.M.,

First of all, thank you for the book which, so far, I have only just *looked* at and read the first eight pages, but I am *so* looking forward to the rest, and I must tell you what pleasure it gave me to see my Aunt Nancy Astor on the cover! My mother was her youngest sister. There were eleven of them, and Aunt Nancy was the one to make the news, with my Aunt Irene following in a less vivid way as the wife of Charles Dana Gibson, the artist. Aunt Irene was one of the original Gibson girls, and my mama, aged fourteen upwards, was a Gibson child, and is to be seen with a big black bow behind her head and in Peter Thompson sailor suits.

178

The book is attractively done, and I'm fascinated by the subject. I do thank you for letting me have a copy. It will join my other lovely K.M. treasures.

Forgive a short note. I'm learning words and notes. My husband is due home tomorrow, and I do hope the airport is open and it isn't snowing.

With love,

J.G.

My dear K.M.,

I have now finished reading and enjoying your *Women*. It's a wonderfully complete job, and aren't we an impressive lot? I have loved looking at the wonderful women who made possible our opportunities today. They were *really* wonderful when you think of the opposition and the climate of opinion. I still feel gratitude for being the *gentler* sex, but I'm equally glad to be able to pursue my work in my own way and be accepted on equal terms with other 'artists'. I knew Lady Richmond, Gertrude Bell's sister, and I once *saw* Gertrude Bell. Mrs Wintringham was often at my Aunt Nancy's house and was a close friend for many years, a *dear* woman. My grandmother (my papa's mama) was Dame Jessie Phipps, who chaired a committee at the L.C.C. in some pioneer way. I *think* it was education. She was American, too, from New England *via* Dundee, where her papa came from. *Thank you* for the book. I *enjoyed* it very much.

My spring tour has begun.

I did two charity performances at Aldeburgh on Friday and Saturday last. Cambridge was on Wednesday. The new material seems to work well, which is a relief. Seven new items in all. Forgive brevity. I must start assembling my stuff for Cambridge and on for Easter to a friend in Herts.

May Easter be lovely for you – with love,

J.G.

Have you read *Akenfield* by Ronald Blythe, a record of Suffolk rural life? I find it delightful and very informative and enjoyable.

My dear J.G.,

It was sweet of you to write *twice* about my little book. I am so glad you enjoyed it. I was most interested to hear all about your relations (I knew Lady Astor was your aunt). My connection with the Bell family is rather a nice one – Sir Hugh Bell gave my husband sixpence for saying the Lord's Prayer correctly when he was four years old.

This is really to wish you a happy Easter, which I am sure you will have. I love Easter. I went to the St Matthew Passion at the Festival Hall, and it was more wonderful than ever, if anything. (I had a nightmare a short time afterwards and woke up saying to myself, 'It is *all* right, remember BACH.')

I wish it were warmer. I am going to my nephew's wedding on Easter Monday. Trevor Huddleston is marrying them, and it is the only day he could manage, but it's not a very convenient day for getting about. I *should* like the sun to shine then. I *wish* I could hear some of your new material, but I expect I shall get an opportunity some time. So glad it went well.

The fate of the Direct Grant Schools has been foremost in my mind lately. I wish there didn't seem to be a sort of hatred of excellence about nowadays. I don't think we want 'logical schemes' in education – we want variety and individualism and compromise. The Direct Grant Schools are a splendid compromise and have worked well and have served *all classes* of bright children. Why should they be forced to lower their standards *or* to become the privilege of the rich? I am sorry – I didn't mean to make a political speech. It is a thousand pities education should have become a political issue anyway.

Aren't reviewers odd sometimes? Audrey Laski in *The*

Times Educational Supplement ends a good review of my *Women* book by saying 'it is a pity such a civilized and well-balanced book should be slightly prim and puritanical – girls need some frivolity, etc.' I simply don't know what she means. It's not meant to be a manual for girls' behaviour, anyway. I don't *mind* this, it just strikes me as so odd. I would like to get the Suffolk book you mention. I don't know it.

I went to *Wozzeck* last week – Geraint Evans was wonderful in it. He and the music and the child at the end were almost unbearable. I had to remember Bach again – but the compassion is really what makes it great.

This letter is very disjointed, I fear, but it is the very end of the day so you must forgive. I knew if I left it till tomorrow I shouldn't have time to write it, and I did want to get an Easter greeting to you. Much love

K.M.

Forgive scrawl too – I am very rheumaticky just at present and everyone else seems to have colds – throats, etc.

3 July   *Elm Park Gardens*

My dear K.M.,

All is well with you I hope?

What a pretty spring-summer it's been. Now it's too cold for me, and I don't like it when the elms look black.

I write to tell you that yesterday I did a lunch-time talk in the pretty fifteen-century church of St Olave in Hart Street, E.C.3, where Pepys is buried – he used to pray there and lived locally. I thought it was to be a dialogue with the Vicar, Mr Claxton (as I've done before at St Mary-le-Bow with Joseph McCulloch), but it turned out to be me. I had suggested that I might speak about my experiences in America talking to students, and then I decided I'd like to talk about Tolerance. So I've been having a lovely time again, with your *good* book. What a joy it is! I read several quotations and began with your piece on the Open Mind.

Several people asked about the book. I do hope it is still available, because I recommended it most warmly, and enthusiasts seemed eager.

It is useful to look at the real meaning of Tolerance versus Permissiveness, and I think a *useful* exercise just now. So once again I am very grateful for your book. It's a treasure house, it really is.

It's been a busy time. I'm off to America in October for a short tour. The universities and colleges are very nervous, and whereas I expected to visit fourteen, as before, most of them have cancelled all concerts because of uncertainty and unrest. *Sad* – not for me exactly, but for the situation. So I do only six there and only three of those are colleges. I play there before I go.

Aldeburgh was lovely – sunny weather, flowers, buds and MUSIC. The newly restored Maltings is a joy. I spent the first week rehearsing for a programme of Noël Coward songs with Cleo Laine, Richard Rodney Bennett and Ben Luxon, a good young baritone. We were a success, and had to put on an extra show at midnight. We also appear again at the King's Lynn Festival at the end of the month. Between us we learned to sing thirty-six songs! Hard work. I quite enjoyed it as a change, but I'm afraid doing my own programme is more exercising and rewarding for me. This isn't *just* conceit. It is because singing Noël's songs isn't really very creative. There they are – period pieces of wit or charm – and there ain't much else to be got out of them. They are first-class in their own realm and stand up to time, so I'm not denigrating them. I suppose I've hogged it alone on the stage for so long that I feel a bit repressed having to fit into a frame and meld with other performers. Very disciplining and good for the ego, no doubt.

This is the season of visitors, and we have so many really good friends from Australia and America among us, and it is a bit tricky finding spaces to see them all in a *leisurely* way.

This fruity time helps the catering, doesn't it. Have you tried the tiny seedless grapes mixed with strawberries and added the juice of two oranges? You can use brown or white sugar 'to taste'. It is a delicious mixture.

No more time. B.B.C. due to tape a few words on the keeping of diaries. More Australians for dinners, and I must go out and get my grapes and strawbs and oranges.

With love,

J.G.

My dear J.G.,

I had been thinking of you lately and felt I would like to write again soon, and then your letter came yesterday and made a warmth about my heart. It was *so* welcome, as life is rather full of family problems just now, and also of sadness for various old friends now in trouble of one kind or another. Also there seem to be so many tragic happenings at the moment, outside one's own circle. Anyway, I loved hearing from you, and of course it pleased me greatly that you like my Tolerance book so much and found it useful for your address. Yes – I think it should still be obtainable, though I find booksellers strangely averse to selling one out-of-date books these days. Every now and again I get appreciative murmurs about the book and requests for inclusions in other anthologies.

By the way did you hear Enoch Powell's 'Personal Choice' on the radio? His love of Carlyle made me look up the passage of his (Carlyle's) on negroes, that I had quoted as an example of *in*tolerance in my book! I thought the letter in last week's *Listener* on Enoch Powell's choice very interesting. His interpretation of Beethoven's Ninth reminded me of E. M. Forster's exactly *opposite* view in *Howards End*. Humour and humility totally lacking in Enoch Powell?

I thought of you enjoying Aldeburgh and wished I was there. I read an enthusiastic review of your programme, but I understand what you felt about it. I got a record of yours for a birthday present and it gives us so much pleasure. As usual I prefer the sketches that are a subtle mixture of humour and seriousness. I think my favourite on this record is 'Lally Tullett'. It is so vivid – while you are speaking I am there, right in that world, and it is a shock when it stops. I have been that woman.

We had a good time in Salzburg again in May in spite of persistent rain. The Janáček quartet were there and played Beethoven (130) and Czech composers Dvořák and Smetana with what seemed to me peculiar magic. They play without music, which makes them a perfect unity.

We made another Austrian friend – a brave old Viennese Jewess (refugee in England in 1938) nearly eighty, but cooking and enjoying her guests in a remote Styrian village – full of life and humour and love of books and music.

Goodbye – I am sorry about your American tour being so reduced *and* for the cause, but hope you will enjoy it all the same. I suppose you will be seeing your brother and his family.

A very good journey to you and much love and many thanks, as ever,

K.M.

Excuse bad writing. I have broken my pen.

20 September   *Riverside House*

My dear J.G.,

Thank you for a *good* afternoon in Smith Square yesterday.* We were very grateful to you for moving everyone nearer, as the acoustics in St John's are not all that could be desired. I was struck once again, as I looked round on all of us listening there, with how very good it is for people (especially with the world as it is today) to be amused and touched and made happy by your lovely art. And I so appreciated what you said about *live* entertainment. It *is* a bit of an effort for us, in what is called our declining years, to walk, train, and bus there, and then back again to get to it, but it is always well worth it. It certainly was yesterday to

* A matinee performance in aid of The National Trust.

184

get to *you* and with an entrancing view of eighteenth-century houses topped by the twin white towers of the Abbey from the steps of the church thrown in. I don't believe I have been in Smith Square for about forty years, since we used to frequent the little struggling Labour Club which was in Tufton Street then and meet people like Harold Laski and Nevinson and Ramsay MacDonald, etc. I think your latest Oxford sketch – 'Eng Lit I', 'II' and 'III' is perfect, and, having just come back from six weeks in my beloved university (you get exactly the right intonation of this word) I especially enjoyed this. 'One is one and all alone' I thought so poignant and funny and I was thrilled to hear 'Nicodemus' because I remembered you telling me about him after you had met him. But I could write on and on about your programmes. It was such a good ending – 'Slow Down' and the 'Lullaby'. I had already begun to fidget over trains in my mind, and then came 'Slow Down', and I just stopped bothering.

I have taken a week to organise myself after being away, but have now got going with coaching and writing and friends and family again. My youngest granddaughter aged five came to tea the other day and asked for her grandfather. I said he had gone to London, and she said, 'Oh, I only wanted to exercise a little courtesy towards him.' By the way I don't think I ever said much about my husband to you, and as you have told me quite a lot about yours, I think I shall have to devote part of a letter to mine sometime. We shall be celebrating our forty-eighth wedding anniversary at the end of the month by going to Canterbury to see *Murder in the Cathedral*. I am ashamed to say I have only heard it on radio and seen the film. To put beside 'the exercising a little courtesy' story is another when my granddaughter was gazing thoughtfully at her father, and when asked what she was thinking about, replied to him, 'Oh I was only thinking what a dear silly old oaf you are'. Somehow these two remarks, both I think impossible in *my* youth to *my* grandfather and father, illustrate a change in relationship to older people which is so healthy and good. One may be sure that both courtesy and affection are absolutely spontaneous and sincere nowadays, and criticism outspoken and not bottled up. I do *like* the young, but I wish I liked how they looked. However, they look a bit better than they did a short time ago, don't you think? Much less dingy. The men's clothes are so pretty, but I still don't like them hairy.

I know you are going off to America again soon. I wonder how you will find things there. I can't talk about the things happening in Jordan. Poor, poor humanity.

With much love always and thanks for you. Don't bother to write, you will be busy before you get away in October.

K.M.

I was glad for the National Trust on Saturday – all power to their effort. I was for many years one of their voluntary lecturers in Kent, and we do need the Trust more than ever now.

What gorgeous weather – the nicest time in the year – the garden is rich with dahlias and much daisies and fruit and weeds.

13 December   *Riverside House*

My dear J.G.,

I wonder how you are, and hope all goes well with you? It is a troubled world. We had some American Quakers (from Vermont) to tea the other day. They were most interesting, but greatly concerned with the state of things generally in the States.

For me it has been rather a sad autumn in some directions – old friends dying – a much-loved brother-in-law, whom I had known all my life – others in trouble. Of course this sort of grief is inevitable at the end of life. But there is much to be thankful for. I have enjoyed a bit of teaching of my beloved seventeenth century this term, and the grandchildren are all doing well and *being* so nice.

My daughter is working hard for gipsies in this neighbourhood and should have an article on them coming out in the *Guardian* soon. The atmosphere and the social conscience of her family permeates to Sophie, now aged five; and Jane found a letter – profusely illustrated – from Sophie to two of the gipsies which ran as follows: 'Dear Christine and Levi. I hope you will soon get out of prison. If you do not my father and mother will help you. I think they will give you money to get you out, as they are both very kind and helpful people. From Sophie to Christine and Levi.' The illustrations were all round the margin like an illuminated manuscript of cats and tortoises looking at fireworks.

The plight of the gipsies is indeed a sad one – a tiny minority, helpless from their illiteracy, unable to cope with forms, licences, etc., disliked by farmers and respectable citizens and unable to fit into modern life at all – yet most of them brave, uncomplaining and honest, and only wanting to be left in peace. The answer is integration of the younger generation, but it is hard even to teach the children to read and write.

I mustn't take up more of your time. I enclose a Christmas poem I like, especially the end. The process of eternal recreation by the power of the Holy Spirit goes on endlessly. Of this I am sure, however dark the gathering clouds seem.

Goodbye and a blessed and happy Christmas to you.

My love,

K.M.

The Nativity. 1656

Peace! and to all the World! Sure One
And He, the Prince of Peace, hath none!
He travails to be born, and then
Is born to travail more again.

Great Type of passions! Come what will,
Thy grief exceeds all copies still.
Thou cam'st from Heaven to Earth, that we
Might go from Earth to Heaven with Thee:
And though Thou found'st no welcome here,
Thou didst provide us mansions there.
A stable was Thy Court, and when
Men turned to beasts, beasts would be men:

They were Thy courtiers; others none;
And their poor manger was Thy throne,
No swadling silks Thy limbs did fold,
Though Thou could'st turn Thy rags to gold.
No rockers waited on Thy birth
No cradles stirred nor songs of mirth.

But stay! What light is that doth stream
And drop here in a golden beam?
It is Thy star runs page, and brings
Thy tributary Eastern Kings.
Lord! grant some light to us; that we
May find with them the way to Thee!
Behold what mists eclipse the day!
How dark it is! Shed down one ray,
To guide us out of this dark night,
And say once more 'Let there be light'.

Henry Vaughan

15 December   *Elm Park Gardens*

My dear K.M.,

It was good to see your handwriting today, and I saved your letter for the last because it looked fat and promising, and so it proved to be. Thank you so much for writing. I'm so glad the teaching has been good to do. I *very* much like the sound of your gipsy-championing granddaughter. When I saw *Let's Make an Opera* was on for Christmas, I wondered if it was your daughter's production. What a shame that it isn't; but let's hope when it *is* it will be a winner.

Yes, it does seem that as one grows older one sees sadness among people one loves. But you know more and more and deeper and deeper I begin to *trust* my sense – 'intuition'? – that *in spite* of what *we* see, the spiritual man, the eternal man, is untouched by time and disease, and it is only 'the limitations of our view' that prevents us seeing this fully. I've come to realise that what one loves in a person may *seem* to be the way the nose sits, the eyes light up, the sounds, sights and touch seem to mean, etc., but when you analyse it, what you love is their humour, courage, warmth, kindness, etc., etc. *These* are the true being; that's why man's life is spiritual and eternal – or so it seems to me.

I've got a dear friend, seven years younger than me, a brilliant musician at the top of her particular world, who has become disabled in less than two years. Can't walk, can't play any more . . . It is such an exercise in patience to watch her move, slowly, slowly, and remembering the quicksilver of her mind and her walking and running, one can guess a *little* what this new frustration must be like. It is *so* difficult to know how best to help. She is on endless lists for a housing association with accommodation for the disabled, but no one knows *when* or *where*. Today her beloved Steinway grand – a beautiful one – went to a singer's house, where at least she can go and pat it from time to time, but this was a very hard parting.

Dear K.M., I have a feeling you can imagine what an agony all this is for a very sensitive, creative, not-of-this-world sort of creature, who was once so free and so mercurial. *Almost* a genius in some ways.

In spite of all this, I do *know* that all *is* well; that the Kingdom of Heaven *is* within; that God is all good.

My friend is a *sort* of believer. Her pa was a clergyman and a *dear* man. But she has a sneaking feeling God is a punisher, and she really does, I think, believe in evil as a power and not, as I do, as the *absence* (or *illusion* of the absence) of Love. Love *is* always present; so the evil is the mistaken view of what life is about and for. And it can never have the last word for Truth *is* Good and the original, the *only*.

America was good to me. Six concerts that went well and were so warmly received. The young flocked and responded. The final concert was in the little North Carolina town where my mother lived for twenty years and where many of her old friends made me *so* welcome. They have founded a Fine Arts Centre, where music, crafts, paintings, sculpture and plays are done, a lovely little three-hundred-seater theatre and a good piano. It was a perfect finale to the little tour. I was on two of David Frost's shows, and appeared on Dick Cavett's show too. Then two weeks in New York, which is a rough, tough hell of a place now, although it looks magical by night seen from a skyscraper.

It isn't a happy place just now. Much fear and doubt around. Not a place to live in unless you must.

I saw a lot of my brother and his family, and can report that Sally, sixteen, is growing up into a reasonable very nice young woman; over-energetic and full of self, but with the right instincts; and Lang, fourteen, is as nice as can be, a bit of a lazy scholar, but friendly and humorous and far too good-looking.

Among my farseeing friends there is a certain relief that the telephone (for instance) simply can't cope with the demands on it; nor can Con Edison, who provides the light. Emphasis on dependence on 'things' is being shaken. There *must* be other values. There is a real and active concern about pollution and conservation, and the young are full of it and working at it. So good things are happening.

I must cook supper. More later. (Excellent pork chops done under the grill and followed by grapes and satsumas.) One of the encouraging signs, I think, is that the big corporations in the United States are having great difficulty in getting young lawyers to join their companies. *They* do the interviewing now. What amounts of time and money does the concern give to problems like racialism, pollution, conservation? If this doesn't seem adequate to the young lawyers, they don't take the job. Unfortunately unemployment is becoming very widespread, and I wonder how long the young will be able to hold out on these lines? I think the young, the thinking young, *are* going to make a better world. They really do believe in values, and quite a lot believe in God as Love.

I am trying to take a kind of sabbatical from concerts in order to try and do some writing. I'd like to write a book, but may only have time to plan how I'd do it if I did it. I've got various radio talks to write, and I need more material for the concerts I'm to do in late September 1971 for a season of touring. In the meantime Reggie is taking me to Uganda and Kenya to look at birds, and we fly off on January 16 and will be away till March 1. He has work to do, and a friend is going to join us in the Cape, where I hope I may be able to do a little writing as well as swim in the Indian Ocean. I feel *so* spoiled. If only I could gather up all those I love and take them too . . . I hate leaving my ill friend, but she will be in most loving hands in Suffolk.

I hope 1971 will bring you deep joy and new views and some lovely discoveries – With love,

J.G.

P.S. I almost forgot to thank you for the lovely card and the Vaughan poem. Particularly, as you said, the last part. *Thank you*.

No more time. This brings love,

J.G.

1971

Riverside House

My dear J.G.,

I must write a note, *which does not need or wish for a reply*,
to thank you for your gay Christmas card, and for a most
interesting and beautifully long letter, and to send you my
very best wishes for a lovely bird-watching holiday in
Africa. Yes, you *are* spoiled, and I envy you dreadfully, but
it is a loving not a grudging envy and you deserve it!

I know you are off at the end of this week, and I am not
going to attempt to answer your letter this time, because it
raises so many endless questions such as the problem of evil,
the mystery of individuality, etc., with which experience is
constantly facing us, all our days. But I shall hope to talk
about some of the points you make some time or other.

I have thought a lot about your friend – it is so strange
that some people and those often the finest natures, have to
suffer so much. Death in itself is never so terrible because
everyone has to accept it. It would be dreadful indeed if only
some of us died, but it is so very difficult to accept the
suffering of those we love.

I have, since Christmas, lost another dear friend and
contemporary, but for the last two years she has suffered
much I fear, and it is a release for her though a great miss for
her friends.

I am sure the thing that must help *your* friend is the love of
those near and dear to her, and so we come round to the
power of love as the ultimate reality again.

Goodbye – God speed. May 1971 bring you time for what you most want and need to do.

Much love

K.M.

2 April   *Elm Park Gardens*

My dear K.M.,

A happy peaceful Easter to you in this rough and torn-apart world. I think it is possible to experience peace of mind even in these times when one acknowledges that Truth is unchanged and unchanging. Thank God. The Resurrection is so much the most moving of all feasts and is the whole point, isn't it?

I hope you are well and enjoying the signs of spring. Can't *feel* it yet in this cold east wind, but lots of buttons on branches and the birds, even in S.W.10, are improvising with great variety in the late dawn.

We had a wonderful birding safari in Uganda and Kenya, and saw 305 species (all identified!) in ten days. We were quite unaware of the trouble in Uganda and flew out of Entebbe at 10 a.m. on the day before the coup and the bombs. We saw no sign of tension or fear anywhere. The Ugandans are the most attractive Africans I've yet seen. Very black. The women have long necks and lovely wrists and ankles and walk proud. Some still wear the dress they must have been put into by Victorian missionaries: leg-of-mutton sleeves and wide skirts with a sort of over-drape, made of nylon and terylene and such man-made stuffs, but still cut in the old form; wear their hair high (in some sort of shape under the turbans) and have a faintly Nefertiti look. Lovely country: we went up the slopes (lower) of the Mountains of the Moon or Ruwenzori where there are tea plantations. Very green and lush and tropical. And we saw red-headed colobus monkeys, *rare* and fascinating with their white fringe beards and long thick tails ending in white tassels. After this, ten days in the Cape and various times up at the mine in the Northern Transvaal. No time to go into the situation, but I did get a new feeling that more people, in particular the young, are *concerned*, and there is a lot of anti-apartheid practice going on very quietly but effectively. No one has any hope of the National Government changing, *but* the young, who are the future law-makers, are not Nationalist. The Progressives are *slowly* making some progress I do believe.

What a waste it all is! Such a beautiful country and room for *all* to expand and develop in, and I don't only mean materially. Ironically the only happy faces I saw were black! They were naturally happy people and obviously can't go on being depressed, even if oppressed. And, of course, large numbers have known no other life, and are not the kind to protest nor have they the learning. *That's* the bad part. Even the Nationalists are going to have to do the right thing for the wrong reasons – economy – and already black nurses are nursing white patients, etc., etc.

I wish more people could go and see the place for themselves and appreciate the *problems*. For they are legion. *Then* with some evidence of real concern, something might be done *here* about race relations, too.

I'm in process of going through papers and letters because I'm hoping – vaguely – to try and do a book. Not a straight autobiography but, rather, a sort of memory book (I wish there was a word that isn't 'memories'). I have kept your letters and have been looking at them again. *So* good. Would you like to have them back so *you* can do your own book? *If* not they *should* be kept for your grandchildren. They are lovely. I've got them neatly stacked in a big buff envelope and will send them when you say what you'd like done. We are well and glad to be home. Away for a few days at Easter, but not *working* till September. I'm trying to write and finding it difficult. But lovely to read the old letters.

With love,

J.G.

My dear J.G.,

Again many thanks for your Easter letter. We came here for Easter and go home next Monday. It was a beautifully symbolic Easter this year, wasn't it! Grey gloom and rain all Good Friday and Saturday, and then a glory of spring sunshine all Easter Sunday with the flowers bursting visibly into blossom against a deep blue sky. There is a big pink magnolia just outside our window here and a plum tree smothered in blossom.

I am sending you a copy of the short memoir I compiled of my son. I finished it in the autumn, but it is only just ready. I should very much like to know if his personality emerges for you – who never knew him. I really did it for the younger generation, because I did not want him to be just a name to his nephews, nieces and godchildren.

About my letters – I feel flattered that you have bothered to keep them. At first I felt, no, I did not want them back, for I don't think I shall ever write the sort of book that will need them. But then, your suggestion that my grand-children might like to have them some day took hold, especially as I believe letter-writing is dying out. So perhaps I would like them after all, if it is not soo much bother to send them, any time that is convenient to you. I have all yours – would you perhaps want to refer to any of these for your book? I can't imagine any better letters, but I expect you have plenty of material to draw on.

I was *most* interested in your Uganda and Kenya descriptions and the number of birds you identified took away my breath.

What you say about the young and anti-apartheid feeling is cheering, and how interesting that the only happy faces you saw were black! I don't think the black and brown faces one sees over here are very happy. They mostly look rather lost and sad but the children are all right.

I really wanted to say a little more about your earlier letter. Since you wrote it and since I lost two people I loved about Christmas time another shadow has fallen on us. My youngest stepdaughter (now in middle age) has had a third return of cancer – this time I fear fatal. The first was twelve years ago, the second eighteen months. Now there is little if any hope, but she is at home and still able to get about a little. We are going to her at the end of this month. She is very brave and cheerful and determined to live till her son comes back from Australia this year, after five years away.

You told me in your December letter about your dear musician friend who is now disabled and I am wondering how she is now. It is so sad not to be able to help more. But I *do* agree that love is in command ultimately – that it is really the only Power that *counts* in the Universe. My stepdaughter is so reserved, and married to a rather bitter agnostic, but I have tried to tell her what I believe, and I know she has found it comforting, for she writes and phones me continually, and says that it helps her, though she can't talk about it in any detail. I am sure *your* faith does help your poor friend.

I have often thought along the same lines as you that what one loves in a personality is their reflection of the eternal values of humour, courage, sincerity, etc., etc., yet there is an individual twist to the way these are expressed which is inexpressibly dear and unique. Sometimes it seems indivisible from the physical appearance and sometimes almost *in spite of the body*. But it is queer how some people's bodies seem to *reveal* their *spirits*, and others to be just a rather badly-fitting garment, perhaps passed on by parents, etc., and not really belonging to their personalities at all.

I always want an earthly Paradise to include people as we have known them at their very best *and* animals and even places, and next, a more abstract spiritual heaven, and lastly a sort of Dantesque absorption in God or good.

But this is only dreaming. One must leave it all to love and simply trust.

Forgive red pencil, paper and scrawl. I am writing in bed – no other time at my disposal!

Always my love and thanks

K.M.

The underlining in this scrawl reminds me of the letters of Queen Victoria.

20 April   *Elm Park Gardens*

My dear K.M.,

Christopher is *very* clear to me and I love him already after only twenty-two pages. And what a face he has! Thank you *so* much for letting me see this book. I will write more fully when I have read it all. As I imagine you have only a limited number of copies, would you like to have it back later? I will send the letters in a few days. I'm off early today to tape an interview about birding and the wonderful times I've had doing it in Australia and Africa, etc., etc. Have to be photographed on Hampstead Heath with other contributors to the series. *Mustn't* forget to take my binoculars.

This is written in a rush at 7.30 a.m.

Thank you for letting me know your son. He is obviously one of the specials.

With love,

                                              J.G.

24 April   *Elm Park Gardens*

My dear K.M.,

I am still full of the little book and I feel I have been with a most exceptional and attractive creature, your son Christopher. I finished reading it last night at 12.30 a.m., and I was swept over by feelings for all you have had to endure about him . . . That the book brings him so clearly to life and is so full of gaiety and light in spite of all his experiences is a tribute to you both. The sense of continuity – of what Life really is – comes through for me. I look again at the enchanting lifted head and the beguiling smile and I can tell he was one of the rare ones.

I feel honoured that you have let me see the book and will hold it in trust for you, so if you want it, here it is.

I'm waiting to get one of those splendid padded envelopes in which to mail you your letters, and then you'll have them. My husband goes past a Rymans and will get me some. I think they have quite taken the sting out of packaging books for the mail.

This wet is making everything smell lovely, and I know the gardens and fields need it. Wish it could have done it in the night. We'd hoped for tennis. The writing goes on a bit uncertainly – I don't have the practice of *sustained* flow. I think in bits. Perhaps I can learn?

With very much love to my unseen friend, to whom I feel closer for reading the book about Christopher,

J.G.

2 *May*   *Riverside House*

My dear J.G.,

I have much to thank you for: telling me about your broadcasts – the radio bird one itself (alas, no opportunity for the T.V. one) which we enjoyed *greatly*, and then, also, for what you have said about Christopher. I wanted you to read the book partly because your attitude to life always reminded me of his. One of my nieces pleased me so much by saying, 'I don't know why, but reading Christopher's book cheered me up tremendously. I had been feeling so depressed, and it made me feel quite different.' This is the effect he had on people, and which I know you have too, and I longed for his personality to go on doing this a little through this book.

I was in Suffolk last week visiting a stepdaughter who has been ill, and I thought of you when we drove through Snape and past the Maltings. Reed buntings were busy there. By the way, our martins and swallows are very late this year, and I am quite anxious about them.

I had a rather nice birthday letter from my youngest grandchild the other day (aged just six). It was illuminated and had a golden heart with I LOVE YOU round it and said, 'I have grave doubts whether you will like my present, but I

198

sincerely hope you are spry and welthy and I send you my deep congratulations.'

We meant to have a birthday picnic, but the weather said 'No', so we had a Shakespeare reading of the *Dream* instead. One grandson was a marvellous Bottom, and the above grandchild, whom I had intended for a fairy, insisted on reading Titania, tackling the text (which she was seeing for the first time) with a real feeling and love for the words. It made me think, not for the first time, that we tend to spoonfeed our young too much over intellectual things and expect too much of them emotionally. I mean they are burdened with so much *choice* and also made to grow up emotionally too soon – yet intellectually they are often not allowed to stretch their minds.

Have you seen the O.U.P. paperback of Blake's *Songs of Innocence and Experience* – facsimiles of Blake's design – it is *enchanting*.

I've had such a nice day, beginning with cherry orchards and bluebells, and ending with Bach. Goodnight and *bless* you! K.M.

5 May   *Elm Park Gardens*

My dear K.M.,

Thank you for your letter. So glad the birds gave you some pleasure. Yes, Christopher comes through the book very clearly and with *charm*. I do love that picture of him.

I loved your granddaughter's message; and her choice of Titania. I agree about under-rating the understanding of children. On a much lower level I remember my brother Tommy aged four standing at the end of his bed *enthralled* by Ruth Draper doing the monologue about the train crash on the Western plains. This letter is to come with an envelope full of your *good* and lovely letters to me, for which again I thank you very much. I do enjoy our pen relationship so much.

Funny things we do in life: yesterday I went to Woolwich Arsenal at two-thirty to a retiring party for an elderly, shy bachelor who is a member of my church and who, three months ago, invited me to attend because 'my step-mother – well, she was my foster-mother really, has died, and I don't have . . .' He left the rest of the sentence in the air. So I was his only 'outside' friend, and with forty or fifty of his colleagues stood in a glass-roofed area of a vast shed-like building nibbling snacks and orangeade at 2.30 p.m. There were tiny thimblefuls of reddish sherry, and two little speeches were made, and Albert thanked and was given a fat envelope with twenty-one pounds in cash, bedroom slippers, gloves, a scarf and at least forty retiring well-wisher cards.

It was a very dear occasion. I was the 'surprise'. Only a few had been 'told', and the reaction was heart-warming and gave Albert a big boost. I was given pink roses, carnations and sweet peas with a card: 'To our visitor welcome and kind thoughts'. I had a word or two with all present – said 'Yes, Sydney is still the bad boy in my nursery-school sketch' – 'No, this occasion isn't at all like St Trinian's School – and yes, I do enjoy "Facing the Music",' etc., and went home at 3.30.

I think of Albert this morning for the first time with no dirty work ahead, and I wish him well. Lonely, I fear, and full of courage. He is one of those quiet, mild, saintly people who oil wheels. Everyone said, 'He's *so* kind and always cheerful'. And his boss said: 'The most conscientious man I ever met and a wonderful worker.' I wish he had a wife and children to enjoy in his retirement. He speaks boldly of seeing America.

The weather is so beautiful, and the suburbs are full of double cherries. I bet the bluebells are out now. We aren't going to Cumberland till July, and I am *so* envious of those there now among the birdcherry and larch tips so green-o, and cowslips, and all. (I'm doing 'Desert Island Discs' on Friday – taping – so I think it will be on the air soon afterwards, but don't yet know when. It's my second go, 1951 last time.)

This pen needs a good washout. Sorry.

Love,

J.G.

My dear K.M.,

A little bit of bonus time has been given me this afternoon. I thought I had to go and see someone in S.E.1, and at
the last moment they decided to go in another direction, and
truth to tell it's like being given a present to be given two
free hours. In it I've already swept and dusted the flat and
laid the supper (our daily is 'off' with 'flu) and now I have a
little while left so I can write to you and say I love the poem
and your letter and thank you for both. I love the idea of
telling the heart to 'screw thee nigh, up to the angelic cry,
Sing Glory, do'! It's very dear, and how nice must be (have
been?) the Hadfields.

As a very brief résumé of projects for 1972, I write to say
that after the summer when I wrote *at* my possible book, I
worked to prepare a concert programme and set off and did
it. I think I said this in my Christmas card? What I also said
is that the T.V. programmes start January 7th, but now I
hear its Friday January 21, and three other Fridays to follow
– should you care to know. We are well, happy, busy. I
think I should have said happy, well, busy. It's the true
order, isn't it.

I'm sad about your grandson. Don't let him be got down
by this sort of rejection. It is so stupid of Oxford; like
depending on the Welfare State or a computer to do their
jobs. The human (or spiritual?) element is what's needed,
too. Perception, in this case. I *hope* he gets in via music.

The 'world' is so hard to think about and the burden of
my five-minute address at a carol service at St Martin-in-
the-Fields tomorrow evening is that the getting on together
of neighbours, work-mates, families is the first step in
building true peace on the large scale and *the only way* to do
it. Love, in other words, *is* what makes the world go round.
There'd be no need for the agony if any of us truly practised
what we know to be the power of Love.

I too, loved Iris Origo's book and have been in correspondence with her about Ruth Draper whom she knew in
her 'Italian' period – when she had a romance with the

anti-fascist poet who learned to fly, had printed thousands and thousands of anti-Fascist leaflets and flew over Rome to let them loose. He was never seen again. Iris Origo is doing a piece on Ruth; I'd just been working on a chapter about her when she got in touch with me. I knew Ruth *all* my life, so I was able to fill in some gaps for Iris Origo, and we had some to-ing and fro-ing. She has asked to be allowed to quote from my piece. (I sent her the manuscript.)

Did you read her book about Byron, *The Last Attachment*? Very good.

I haven't read much lately, but one or two American books about theatre people came my way – were diverting but no more.

We are having our usual Christmas lunch for ten, two of us are now over ninety. Boxing Day, or rather Sunday, will be ten, too. Busy days. I hope our Mrs Agos (Cypriot) will be back to spruce us up a bit before it all happens. Reggie and I do it all at Christmas, but it helps to have a swept and polished flat. I'm amazed at how little dust there was when I flicked at it just now. It's been five days!

My American family are well. In April we take my brother and sister-in-law to Greece for two weeks. A big trip being very carefully planned now.

May you have a deeply loving Christmas, and may 1972 be a bit more enlightening than 1971.

With love,

J.G.

1972

My dear J.G.,

I have never answered your very welcome Christmas
letter, but I have had it in mind all this time and have been
thinking of you. It has been perfectly enraging and frustrating, but I simply have not been able to get B.B.C.2 in order
to hear and see you on these Friday broadcasts. The hills,
trees, etc., are all wrong in Shoreham for B.B.C.2, which is
one of the reasons we have never bothered to get a set. Then
we went to stay in the Wye valley in mid-January for ten
days, and I thought 'good, I'll be able to see J.G.', but only
to find they were in the same plight – no B.B.C.2 available.
Do you think they can be persuaded to repeat the programmes on B.B.C.1? I am sure they are popular enough.

Do you know and love Kilvert's *Diaries*? We were in the
Kilvert country, and I was really ravished by the beauty of
the Wye. No wonder he wrote as he did, and Wordsworth
loved it too – next best to his own country. I made a new
friend down there – a blind Quaker of over eighty, indomit-
able and vital, going for long walks by herself – very good on
birds. Her brother, William Hughes, had translated Rilke
and was a Blake enthusiast. Do you know Rilke well? I love
his poetry, though, alas, I cannot read it in the original. In
case you don't know his poem about a poet I'll enclose it, as
I like to send you special poems, and this one I feel you
might specially enjoy.

I agree so very deeply with what you say about love being
the answer to everything, and with love goes naturally
forgetfulness of self, or perhaps one should say enlargement

of self – 'a going out of ourselves and an identifying ourselves with others'. It is odd that as children one of the first texts we learnt to print on Sunday afternoons was GOD IS LOVE with a wriggly border round it – and it takes a whole lifetime to realise that this is really true in a perfectly practical and provable way.

Yes, I've read Iris Origo's Byron book. I also remember reading or hearing somewhere about Ruth Draper's poet and his flight with the anti-fascist leaflets and his loss. I went to hear Ruth Draper whenever I possibly could, and never forgot anything she did.

I've read an absorbing book lately, *The Sword Dance* by Priscilla Napier (née Hayter). It is about the Napier family – a really splendid lot. It is so sad to read about the Irish troubles then (1800) and to realise they and we are still full of hate and misunderstanding.

I am not having much luck about my own book on Victorian Wives in Fact and Fiction. I get loving and appreciative letters from publishers calling it charming and succinct and discerning, etc., etc., but for some reason they think it won't sell enough to be profitable for them. Heinemann's head reader thinks they are wrong and that it is very topical and would sell well, but Heinemann's business side would not listen to her. She says if I could get a well-known name to write a foreword it would do the trick. I don't much like this, but publishing is so much big business now that it is much harder for them to take risks, and I have put a good deal of work into this book and don't want to waste it. It will probably be the last I shall write, except the history of the school where I taught for so many years which I have now been asked to do.

I wondered if you knew of anyone who would be interested in the book which is related to the Women's Movement (though certainly not fanatically so). If you were not so busy I would send you the manuscript, because you have always been kind enough to like my books, but I really hesitate to do this because I feel you have every minute filled. I never understand how you find time to write to me.

My youngest granddaughter (now six) confided to me

that she would like to be a saint. I said, 'You'll find it very hard.' She said, 'Oh, I know, Granny, but once the idea has got hold of you it won't let you go, and anyway, if I try hard, I'll end up a little gooder than I am now.' Rather touching, don't you think?

How lovely to be going to Greece in April. But how lovely also to have been twice in my lifetime and to remember it for always. It is the most beautiful place I have ever seen.

Goodbye. I am so glad you exist.

My love

K.M.

4 *February*   *Elm Park Gardens*

My dear K.M.,

I'm *so* sorry the hills didn't let you see the T.V.s. They seem to be going well, and I had hoped you might see them. Never mind. Not all *that* important. This can't be a proper letter. I'm being inundated with letters after the programmes. They are *so* nice, and I do like to answer them, but it takes time.

Yes. I love Kilvert too. Fascinating.

Thank you for the Rilke. It is a very *interesting* poem. It assumes God knows I'm in pain, doesn't it? The God I know couldn't – for the God I believe in is all spirit, all good, and Him I can and do praise. Constantly, I hope. I know there is an 'accepting' kind of faith, but I'm afraid it isn't for me. Am I wrong in seeing that this is what Rilke means?

How tiresome about your Victorian Wives. Is it *very long*? Could I read it in two, two-and-a-half-hour train journeys to Manchester, where I go to tape 'Face the Music' again? I just don't have much other concentrated time just now. I'm trying to write material and not getting very far. I don't think an introduction by me would help, do you. I mean I'm not very Eng. Lit., am I? But if I can help I'd certainly love to.

Love – in haste,

J.G.

My dear K.M.,

The book is safely here and I've read Louise McDonald and poor Mrs Benson and the introduction to Viola. She enjoyed it all as much as I did. More today.

No time to write more. Must go to the shops.

Love,

Joyce G.

We wondered if there would perhaps be a footnote about the three Benson sons and Maggie, as we long to know *what* they wrote. I know about E. F. (a little) but nothing of the others, and I think readers would like to know this.

My dear K.M.,

It is *so* odd that quality isn't recognised and *welcomed*. I'm loving the book. It has had to be laid aside for a while because I've been involved in a pile-up of stuff and the Truro Cathedral address. (Over a thousand came, and it was a most moving occasion for me. Entirely non-denominational and the vast Victorian pile filled with the colour of clothes and the punctuation of black-robed nuns here and there. A whole hour of it listened to without coughs or shiftings about. All the work and praying that went into it allowed it to walk on its own two legs if you see what I mean, and I was hardly there. I was *very* grateful indeed. The Cathedral talk of printing it, and if so I'll send you a copy in case you'd be interested.)

How soon do you need a piece by me and how long do you think it should be?

I was about to write to you when your letter came. I am truly sorry about the disappointment but I do hope a proper and right home will reveal itself.

Love,

J.G.

My dear J.G.,

There is *no one* like you in the world for writing the nicest possible letters by return, and when you must obviously have no time to spare at all. I *really* did not mean to worry you just now but only to give you information, though, needless to say, your letter was a great comfort and joy.

I am *so* glad about Truro, glad for you and glad for all those people, and *of course* I'd love to have a copy of your address.

I have been heartened and strengthened lately by a small group of our Quaker meeting who come together in each others' houses once a fortnight (mostly youngish). There is such honesty and humility and tolerance and humour. We seek together and we often find, at least I feel I do and am so grateful to them.

I listened to David Storey on 'Desert Island Discs' last week, and he wrote eight novels before any were accepted, and then it was only after trying fifteen publishers. The fifteenth took the eighth, which became a bestseller.

I am enclosing an Easter card, rather early, but we are going to Oxford for Easter, and until then life is rather full, though it sounds silly to say that to you.

St Matthew's Passion on Sunday, with a grandson.

Much love, blessings and gratitude

K.M.

My dear K.M.

Yes, I heard Henry Cecil talk about his seventeen tries before he got a publisher. Courage. Is there any hope of it as a blue Penguin? Thank you for keeping me up to date with the book. I do hope it will work in the end. It must. It's good.

It has been a long pause in our letters. Sorry. First of all Greece. *Have* you been? Were you as knocked sideways by it as we were? It is so wonderfully un-disappointing, even

after all one has heard. We went at exactly the perfect time –
end of April early May when *all* the wild flowers were out in
profusion. Drifts of deep red poppies as well as our pillar-
box red kind. So many cistus, mallow, campanula, blue
pimpernel, all kinds of yellow daisies, orchids, etc., etc.
And the smell of thyme. And sun on pines. We rented a car,
and four of us – my brother Tommy and his darling wife
Mary – came with us. First two nights in Athens and the
museum, the Acropolis, etc., and a drive by the sea to
Sounion and the temple of Poseidon. Then four nights at
Nauplion, and from there we went to Epidaurus, Mycenae,
Corinth and Akra Corinth. From there up the coast to take a
ferry to Delphi. *Oh* Delphi! The great gorge and the
temples rising up the mountain, the air, the silence, the
scents, birds – the whole magic of Greece. We also went to
Rhodes for five days and *loved* it and to Crete for the same
time. Knossos and Phaestos are thrilling and the museum
superb, *but* Rhodes has more charm for us; nicer and more
beautiful people too! So it was all a big treat and we *all* loved
it. I wonder if I'll ever go back and whether it can ever be so
wonderful again. I'm glad I wanted to go there and really
didn't have many preconceived ideas about it.

After this the next outing was our annual time at Aldeburgh for the Festival. Much enjoyed in spite of wintry
weather. I'd spent some time making up a programme of
poetry for a recital. *Hard* to choose for other people to read.
Max Adrian was the other reader and George Malcolm
played the piano and harpsichord. I thought it was a *good*
programme. It went well – was sold out.

In late June we put the car on a train to Carlisle and drove
north to Scotland where we visited two of Reggie's half-
sisters. One lives in Ayrshire in a 1720 farmhouse set against
enormous beeches with a wide-open view across sloping
meadows to the sea two miles away and Ailsa Craig sitting
out of it like a bee-hive slightly to the right. The other sister
has moved from a Pembrokeshire farm, now run by the
eldest son, and bought a sort of dark rose stone house that
might just as well be at Weybridge or Ascot . . . It is in the
rhododendron belt of Kirkcudbrightshire, and I am not one

for rhodos. Plate-glass windows and gravel sweep, house built about 1860. Not that I mind that, but my mind can't take in the wish to run a *big* house in these days. Not big 'stately home' but big 'private'. Give me Laura's little old, rather shabby 1720 farm, and its curved stone stairway. Both sisters *love* what they've got, so it's good. After these two three-night visits we went to lovely Cumberland for six days' silence, curlew calls, cold winds but blue patches, wild roses and water fit to drink. And three nights in a Yorkshire dale with dear friends and then down old A1. and home two weeks ago. So a lot of 'away' this year, varied and pleasant, and I'm grateful for it.

All of a sudden we've been rather royal – with the Queen Mother, who is a dear, simple woman, rather lonely I think, gay of spirit and that smile isn't in any way false, or forced. The flat where we go for week-ends is made out of what was once the maids' floor in the house of the Queen Mother's late brother. His widow is one of our oldest friends. Indeed I have known her *all* my life; her nurserymaid left to come to my mother when I was born, and I spent much time in her nursery, and we lived with her family in the 1914–18 War. So when the Queen Mother came here, to her own old home, last week-end, we were included in the party, although we slept in our corner of this beautiful Queen Anne house. At least the front is beautiful Queen Anne. Our bit (which gets all the sun and light) is a much later addition – perhaps a hundred years old. It was a very quiet informal week-end, just eight of us. She brought no aides or ladies, just a maid and a truckload of trunks. There was a detective and a policeman, but I never saw them obtrusively, although doubtless they were on the *qui vive*. As a matter of fact when we all went over to a neighbour's new house (a Norwegian log cabin set in a Herts wood, raw and motel-like, very much out of its proper element) and were leaving, the little green car that suddenly appeared on our heels and dogged us all the way through the winding lanes was the faithful caretakers of Her Majesty. How it knew just when we were off I don't know. It was another very informal occasion, and no pre-arranged signals – as far as I know.

When we got home on Monday there was a call from Clarence House bidding us to lunch there on Thursday to meet Noël Coward. This was a sort of fairy-tale setting, for we had lunch under the great plane trees on the lawn, with sun flickering through the leaves on to a long table laid with green and white cloth and three big bowls of massed carnations. It was so pretty it made me whistle! There was a Garden Party later in the day, so the Queen Mother was dressed for it in a lilac and white organza coat over a silk dress of the same design; and a big hat in lilac organza too. She is tiny – and slimmer – and on her green lawns against the cream coloured house she looked enchanting. Noël is *very* frail, shuffles along, but is on the spot and still funny. The Snowdons with young were there and Princess Alexandra in apple green; she has all her mama's looks and charm and has a vulnerable quality that pulls at the heart.

Princess Margaret, too, has lost weight and was in really very good looks. She has the most exquisite skin and her eyes were untroubled and shining.

Keep all this to yourself, please. I thought it might interest you, although it is not important in any way.

We had delicious summery foods, and I went without a hat, and it was very easy and friendly and made 'a nice change' from doing my own cooking and meal planning – and the washing up! Not that I mind, do you? But then I only do one *real* meal a day. We have a very light breakfast, Reggie is always out for lunch except at week-ends, and I make do with cheese and fruit or soup. Life is full of variety.

Have I written since I did the 'holy' lecture in the series for Lent in Truro? It was in the Cathedral on March 16, and it was a thrilling experience of *sharing*. I seem to have been doing a lot of 'talking' this year. Just now I'm working on a fifteen-minute piece for an international gathering of young students of Christian Science to be held at Keele in early September. And I'm trying to write some new theatre material . . .

Many Australian and American visitors, *lots* of kitchen life. Enjoyable if time-consuming.

I thought I was to do a tour in the United States this

autumn, but it didn't work. Election, apathy, unrest on campus – those were the reasons given me. *Relief*. I didn't want to go one bit. Instead a tour here, a week at Brighton end of October and just possibly two weeks in London if a theatre is available. I don't mind either way. I don't *exactly* want to retire, but I'm not avid for work. This brings love, and thank you for your letter and news of your grandson, who sounds a good one – if problematical. I feel that extra effort to love those in whose path one finds oneself is the only step toward peace elsewhere. Do you?

Ulster is so daunting – what does one do?

Love,

J.G.

27 June   *Lane House, Oxford*

My dear J.G.,

How very nice it was to find your long lovely letter waiting for me here. I *do* thank you. Yes, Greece! I've been twice, in 1957 and 1961, and to me it is the most beautiful place I have ever been in. It has a sort of noble austerity about its contours and colours which I find infinitely satisfying. I've never been so drunk with beauty – almost ill with it – as on the long drive from Olympia to Delphi (*not* through Athens) arriving at sunset. I think of all places I'd like to visit again I would choose Mistra, a place of utter enchantment, and when we saw it, so remote and unvisited, and with no one in charge of all its marvels, and simple friendly people at the one humble inn – and, of the islands, Kos and Delos. My husband and I went alone by country bus full of Greek peasants to Delphi and stayed there some days. There were only two hotels there then – both old-fashioned but so nice, and the Greek people were so friendly towards the English. I remember one woman saying to me: 'Greece is first in my heart and then England', and in Rhodes, when I stopped to admire a climbing rose over a wall, a woman from the house came out and made us go in and have coffee with her, and we managed to have quite a satisfactory conversation though she knew only a word or two of English and I only a corresponding amount of Greek. Another man loaded us with lemons from his orchard – no money transaction thought of. Oh, I could go on for ever about Greece. I feel so sad about the tyrannical government they have now. The Greeks above all are a democratic people by rights.

It was strange your writing about your holidays there just then, as I had just finished re-reading aloud my diaries of our Greek holidays to my husband – the reliving of old holidays through diaries and photos is a favourite evening occupation of ours. Also, what had led me to get out *my* diaries was that my brother had lately passed on to me my mother's diary of 1901, when she and my father were in Athens, and I had been reading that for the first time with great interest. A visit to Greece then was something of an achievement, and Athens was small and primitive. I remember my mother being away then, for she scarcely ever left us for so long (they went to Egypt as well), and I missed her so much I used to shut myself in her wardrobe to smell her clothes – I was three.

Another glorious memory of the Acropolis was being there by moonlight, when the proportions of the building are even more purely stated than in daylight, and when, at a little distance, one can easily imagine the Parthenon in its entirety. Only a handful of people were there, and far down below, in the Roman theatre, they were rehearsing Aeschylus, and the voices of the actors and the Greek choruses came up to us clearly and so beautifully in the silence and the moonlight. Now I *must* stop about Greece, but I'm *so* glad you have been and found it as wonderful as I did. I too went in the flowering months. Oh, I must tell you one more thing, we met a rather wonderful old English lady in Greece – she was in her late seventies, had come of a poor working-class family, had left school at twelve and gone into factory work, became *enchanted* by the Ancient World (through her own thirst for knowledge and the British Museum); had taught herself Greek and Latin and read widely in the classics and saved up all she could for travel. She now ran a little business employing a few craftsmen, making gas appliances in the basement of her little early Victorian house near the canal in Islington. This was her eighth visit to Greece. I visited her several times during the next five years – she would never pay visits herself, but liked me to come to her. She had a houseful of stray cats and dogs she mothered – they all had names like Agamemnon, Socrates, etc. She was one of the most interesting and alive people I have ever met, with a *passion* for the Greeks. She died about five years after I had first met her, having continued her classical journeys to the end.

I was interested in your impressions of the royal family. I have always felt drawn towards the Queen Mother ever since I read an article about her and her brother as children, and they sounded so nice in this, and also since. And because I went over Clarence House once with the National Art Collection Society and there were many old favourites of mine among her books and, in that wonderful room of priceless treasures like the Fra Angelico, there was a thoroughly messy and untidy table full of junk and clutter and odd little objects obviously treasured because of associations.

Thank you so much for your kind encouragement about my book, which is now with an unknown firm – Allison & Busby – recommended to me as being interested in books about women. Because of the present state of publishing I haven't much hope, but I shall go grimly on.

I'm glad your programme of poetry at Aldeburgh went well. I wonder what you chose. Also I'm glad about your Truro lecture. Don't retire yet please. I am looking forward to hearing you next week on radio, and wish it could happen more often. It is always a *delight* and refreshment.

No – I don't mind the amount of domesticity I do now, which is the minimum. We both like living simply and are the better for it, and the older one gets the less one wants, anyway. I'm really lazy over cooking, but I hate bad cooking, waste and poor materials. I can't bear ugly-looking rooms, but don't mind shabbiness nor dust (as long as it doesn't *look* horrid). Your description of your two sisters-in-law's houses was very vivid. I *hate* rhododendrons (except growing as great white and pink *trees* in the Himalayas). I don't much like sandy soil vegetation, anyway. But variety is always amusing, and the contrast of people's lives and homes.

Oh dear – I've just heard the news, and that the dockers have voted against accepting the report, even when Jack Jones was for it. If *only* the militant extremists everywhere were not so able to influence events to the detriment of *everyone*, themselves included. Yes – one must love and not hate, hope and not despair and think about the whole range of history and how the apparent impasse never *is* the end.

Must stop now. Have you read *The Bonhoeffers – Portrait of a Family* by Sabine Bonhoeffer? I think you would like it.

Love, thanks and blessings.

K.M.

10 *October*   *Riverside House*

My dear J.G.,

We have been friends now for so many years that I feel I must write and tell you of my *great* loss since I last wrote to you. My darling husband died suddenly in Oxford at the end of August. He was a good deal older than myself, but always so young in spirit and physically so strong and active for his years, that I never felt the difference and indeed relied on his strength to the last. I have never said much about him to you in my letters, perhaps because he was *so* near, so much a part of me. Do you understand this? We were looking forward to our golden wedding, which would have been just a month after he died. We have had a perfect companionship for these fifty years, and I am so thankful for that and that he did not have to face any time of helplessness or loss of personality. He would so have hated that.

I think, as I never have told you anything about him, I will enclose a copy of the appreciation that was read at his memorial service. There were two bits in *The Times*, too, after his death, but you would not of course connect them with me, or indeed have any cause to read them.

I should like you to know the sort of man he was. You can send it back any time.

Of course my daughter and most kind son-in-law and the family are my greatest comfort, but she is not well just now either, and the children are *so* good and clever, and *so* unable to pass exams (because of the time complex, which now is affecting the girl too) that this is an anxiety of all of us. They are both trying for Oxford this November in Music and English.

I wonder if some time I may have the copy of my book back (*no* hurry). I have lost heart about it and the last publishers (whom I know nothing about but who were recommended to me as being interested in books about women) have had it for eight weeks and haven't replied to my request for it back – so yours is the only safe copy extant, and I may sometime feel like pushing it again.

I feel at present so utterly diminished and just fight on from day to day – luckily there is a lot to be done, and I have some coaching and other work to be done. And of course part of me is full of triumph over such a life and such a love, though this also makes the pain worse in a way.

Goodbye, dear J.G. One of the joys and interests we shared was your letters and your sketches and songs. He was so interested in our friendship.

K.M.

11 October   *At Euston*

Oh, my dear friend, my heart goes running to you. Thank you for telling me, and I do thank you so much for letting me read that *lovely* list of tributes to your dear husband. All he was shines through the words, and no wonder you had a wonderful marriage. That kind of goodness, the timber that does not bend in times of pain, is what Life is for discovering, isn't it.

Last week, in Bath, I passed by the Friends Meeting

215

House and read this: 'Quakers believe when you speak to the good in man you get answers.' (I do this from memory, but this is the general fact of the statement.) Clearly your husband did *exactly* that. (I'm sure you've seen that before, but it is new to me.)

When the bruising shock is over you will resume the confident centre of all you know to be true and what's more I believe you will find the *continuity* of Life is a fact. We know so little about 'what happens', but somehow I am convinced that because we don't remember being born, we shall not remember dying, and all we know is that *we are*. Do we see each other again? Why not, since the qualities of which we are actually compounded are spiritual, and that is why they are eternal. We only recognise by our spiritual perception even now. Because, although one may think it is the way a person looks, walks, laughs – shape of head, touch of hand, etc., that are the man, surely the fact is that it is the warmth of understanding, humour, kindness of generous heart, wisdom, selflessness, etc., etc., that are *really* what one loves and knows and acknowledges to be the actual and eternal. I'm convinced this is so, and when you are over the present bad time I believe you will find it to be true.

I am married to a good man, too, and every day I am grateful for all he is, and I know that this *is* enduring. We are nearly at our forty-third anniversary in December, and I am continually grateful for all the loving understanding my marriage has been to me, so I can imagine something of your feelings, dearest K.M., and I send you very much love and thoughts and the certainty of all *is* well. Of course you know that prayer that says: 'Death is an horizon and an horizon is but the limitation of our view.' I bet that's it. I believe it was said by Bishop Brent, whoever he was. Anyway I love it, and bless him for it.

Just now I am full of thoughts about what Life is. My darling paralysed friend is now totally immobile except for her neck, and we are told it won't be very much longer. What I find a sort of miracle is that a rather diffident and complex character has dissolved into a wholly warm, appreciative, generous and grateful woman, with all her humour and high intelligence developing all the time.

This physical dwindling is so hard for her; she was like quicksilver, moved through the world, a room, a crowd with a deftness that matched her beautiful playing of the piano. To be totally helpless must be the final lesson in humility, and, of my word, she is learning it so well.

One's sadness for her is no good; one's acknowledgement that the spiritual is the real, untouched by matter, is my kind of praying.

She doesn't want my Christian Science teaching, because she thinks it is rude to God not to believe in matter. But the concept behind the wonders of flowers, music, words, mountains, light, etc., *are* the reality. The rest goes to dust. Even light seen by our limited view fades . . .

Next week I do a concert in aid of Save the Children in the Maltings at Snape and we'll be at Aldeburgh (where she lives with *marvellous* friends and a helper to care for her) and can spend some time with her.

Dearest K.M., forgive me for going on about my friend when I meant only to speak of your husband. Thank you for writing to me.

I'm *en route* for Rochdale via Manchester in a rocky train. I will return the book later – I'm home for two days from Thursday. All going *very* well on this tour. A new item, four characters involved in a story. It's quite long and I was a bit afraid of it, but it seems to work. More another time.

With my love and sympathy and thoughts,

J.G.

17 *October*   *Riverside House*

My dear J.G.,

THANK YOU for such a lovely letter of sympathy and kindness and warmth. I do so agree with everything you say. I do know and love the lines about death being only a horizon, and I have always felt that what one loves is the spiritual personality of which the physical presence is in this life the medium. But what a mystery personality is – it is, as

217

you say, 'the warmth of understanding, humour, kindness', etc., that one really loves and knows, and yet this has a different quality in all one's friends which is indefinable. It isn't just these abstract qualities which one loves, but the subtle combination and difference which makes us all *different* though sharing in the same fountain of spiritual life. That is why one longs and hopes for a glorious renewal and fulfilment of all personal relationships after death, though in what way we cannot now grasp but must trust in Love. Meanwhile it is hard to bear the desolation that sometimes overwhelms, though *at times* the continuity you speak of is dimly felt.

At the moment I am away for the weekend, and shall be going away fairly frequently till after Christmas is over. Then I must rearrange my life. My chief need is to find some *useful* work, not just odd bits, and this I fear may be difficult.

I have thought so much about your friend – indeed I have thought about her since you first told me of her earlier in this year. It is sad that spiritual help for her is so lacking. Personally I have always got more help from books than from people. I think it is rare and very lucky to find a true spiritual guide in real life (as Rose Macaulay did for example). Perhaps it is one's own fault. I have met *many* people who are far far better and further on in the spiritual pilgrimage than I am, but somehow they are not quite on the same wavelength, whereas in books one has a much wider range. I know just what you mean about being too near a person to be listened to. But I am sure all the same that you are of very great help to your friend, and I shall pray that you will be able to talk to her in the way you mean when you see her this week. I don't think I am afraid of death – in fact I tend to think of it rather too much as Vaughan does in all his poetry – as a friend and a release. What I fear is a helpless and burdensome old age. I wonder if your friend's fear of death will suddenly go. I have known this happen. I do hope so. I think of her as gloriously released one day into light and joy and a fulfilment of all that has been so tragically interrupted here.

I have just lost another friend, who for a year has been suffering a dreadfully sad mental breakdown, in which she has been engulfed in black misery. Now a physical illness, which the doctors mercifully did nothing to check, has released *her*. I am going to her memorial service next week, which will be a thanksgiving service. How dreadful it would be if death only happened to some of us, and not to all, and yet many people behave and even talk as if it were a fate only meted out to 'poor' so and so. Why 'poor' – any more than it is 'poor' to be born? The sadness is always for those who are left. 'They are all gone into a world of light', and yet the world of light does penetrate into this world, too, and your friend's spiritual growth through all the darkness and suffering of this illness is a penetration of the Eternal Light.

This all sounds much braver and more confident than I really feel at present, but I know with the best part of me that it is true, and that I have got to cling to it.

I am so glad your tour went well and that your new item was a success.

Much love and thanks

K.M.

P.S. I am getting a T.V., so perhaps may be able to see and hear you more in the future.

18 October   *Elm Park Gardens*

My dear K.M.,

Home for two blessed nights and lots of time to glance again at your *good* book and find an envelope to return it to you.

I suddenly wonder if it would perhaps work as a series of articles in, say, the *Guardian*? Or one of the Sunday magazines – except I doubt if anyone reads those. Or on radio? For the latter I dare say some adjustment might be needed, but the material is all so interesting, and so timely with Women's Lib in the news.

I hope my letter from the train and the *beautiful* address

and tributes about your husband reached you all right. I mailed it in Manchester on Wednesday at about 1 p.m.

I'm thinking of you and winging thoughts of affection and friendship in your direction. We who have happy marriages are so wonderfully blessed. Nothing can ever rob us of the understanding and marvellous *silent* companionship that this relationship produces. I never cease to be grateful for my marriage.

With my love,

J.G.

21 October   *Riverside House*

My dear J.G.,

Thank you *very* much for sending back the book. I think I shall go on trying to get it taken *as a book* for a bit longer. I am thinking of you and your friend so much this week.

I feel more and more now that my husband is still with me in a way, and that our love is always there. I am so very glad about your marriage, I can't help feeling it is the crown of life here. We too used to rejoice in 'the silent companionship' you mention, and now I feel sometimes that is mine still. But, of course, times of desolate longing for the actual physical presence come too. Luckily I have much to do and *many* friends, and my daughter and the children are often here.

Goodbye again. Thank you for being such a very great dear to write as you do.

Love

K.M.

1973

My dear J.G.,

Thank you so much for a gay and lovely Christmas card, and for your message inside it. I had a quiet and friendly Christmas away from home with a dear and lonely friend – we had two really good church services, full of life and hope.

Now I find life very full, and though the great blank is there, especially in the evenings and when I come back to the house, I do not feel so hopelessly lost. But the adjustment is difficult. I saw the Impressionists at the Hayward Gallery today, and the whole time I kept on referring to my husband in my mind and saying, 'I must tell him that, he would like that – we saw that together at –' It seems incredible, and a nightmare from which I *must* wake up, that he is no longer here with me.

I am really writing to tell you that my book has been quite enthusiastically accepted by some publishers called Allison & Busby who are interested in books about women – they have had it ages, and seem very nice but rather slow. But I like their attitude; for instance, they want it just called *The Victorian Wife*, because they think it more satisfactory for a book to have a title that actually tells you what it is about. I *do* agree and have always disliked the fancy titles Heinemann forced upon me. Then I brought up the possibility of your writing a foreword, and they said on the whole *not*: 'It looks as though we haven't faith in the book on its own merits.' This too pleases me, and I am sure will you. But I shall always remember your kindness in agreeing to do this, and also I was and am so grateful for your encouragement over the book. Curiously enough this firm has taken another of Heinemann's rejects – a hitherto unpublished Turgenev, which their reader wanted Heinemann to take, but their sales manager turned it down. These publishers want a longer introduction and more historical data and a good many illustrations, so I shall be busy over that and over finishing my school history. I am also going to Cyprus with a friend for two weeks in March. We nearly decided not to go, because of the slaughter of little birds that goes on there, but decided to try and help the Cyprus Ornithological Society, and also to write to our members to try and get this sale made illegal. Apparently they are sold to English restaurants as a special delicacy called *ambeloboulia*. There was an article in *The Times*, followed by a letter from Professor W. Bourne, Department of Zoology, Aberdeen University; and I wrote to him. He says, 'It is said the Secretary of State for Home Affairs could introduce an order under section 707 the Protection of Birds Act (1954) barring the sale of such birds immediately, if he would only take the trouble.'

I wondered if you felt like doing anything about this – such as writing to your members, speaking to anyone influential, etc.? Apparently thousands of song-birds are being packed and sent to Britain from Cyprus for this purpose. It has certainly put me against going there, but my friend is very keen and depending on me, and, if Britain encourages the trade over here, we are being just as bad as the Cypriots – alas! – alas!

My granddaughter, whom I was coaching, has got safely into my old college at Oxford with a glowing report on her work, which is a source of gratification, but my darling grandson has failed. He had a good interview at Merton, and they said they were impressed by his playing and personality, but he just *can't* write enough in the time. I do wish we did not put such a premium on *quick* thinking and writing from eleven-plus onwards. There ought to be an alternative. Daniel, like others that I have taught in the past, thinks deeply and with originality and could do a thesis well, but simply can't cope with the paralysing effect of a time limit.

I do run on – I meant only to tell you about the book. Of course I am pleased, but again cannot now care so much about it, but I know my husband would want me to go on with it – in fact it was he who did it up and sent it off to these particular publishers.

Are you going abroad in the spring?

Isn't it a tremendous relief that Vietnam is over – if it *is* over? In a sense it can't be, but at least something terrible has stopped.

I am reading a book on Pascal and Cowper's Letters. I want to buy the new Common Bible.

Do you know an author called John Fowles who has written a book called *The French Lieutenant's Woman*? Highly recommended to one.

How is your poor friend? I often think of her – the musician one I mean.

Please forgive a muddled wandering letter. I have been in town all day and am tired, but I did not want to wait longer before writing and the week-end is full.

With much love and gratitude as always

K.M.

Friends are marvellous.

3 February   *Messina, Northern Transvaal*

My *dear* K.M.,

Your letter reached me yesterday in Johannesburg, where we were for five days – ugh – and I'm afraid you won't get this for some time, because mails from up here take for *ever*. I was so pleased to hear about the book, and of course I'm delighted that it isn't to have a foreword for *all* the reasons! Sensible publishers. And nice to know they are so enthusiastic. Quite right, too. So I rejoice for you. And about the other books.

No time to write fully. After two years' absence I do notice a good deal of difference here: growing awareness of the *need* to change. And I meet so many who are already doing a lot – quietly and in secret, to further understanding. What we don't know in Great Britain is what a lot of liberal hard work *is* going on here and is, like water on a stone, wearing down the solid wall of prejudice and fear. It isn't ever going to happen quickly, I think. But we *must* keep the lines open, encourage those who are working at it here. The Afrikaaners themselves have many in their ranks who are liberal. When one sees the complexity of it all and the incredible backwardness – 'our' fault – it seems insoluble, but of course nothing is – with God's guidance.

I'm trying to get on with writing the possible book I began in 1971. I'll have ten days here and nothing else to do. I should get something done. Reggie has to go away in the middle, and otherwise we are here to see the old friends who work for the mine. He has to do a lot of visiting the various depts.

It's late. I must pack our overnight bag.

So forgive the rush – we are off to the ranch deep in the bush where at least two inches of rain has fallen, so the birds, who hold back till it comes, will be building. It's a paradise for birds.

This brings love and wishes, and thoughts about your lonely times. I am sure that one grows more aware of the unchanging continuity with time. But it is the presence that is hard to be without, I'm sure.

With love,

J.G.

5 April   *Riverside House*

My dear J.G.,

Thank you *very* much for your cheering and most interesting letter about South Africa. I have also been encouraged by recent articles in *The Times* and accounts of the Christian conference (inter-racial) at Durban and the Intersports meeting, and the enquiry about wages, which at any rate shows concern – all bearing out what you say about lots of changes in the right direction.

I am so glad you had a real ten days' holiday in the Cape. I had two weeks in Cyprus in March with a friend and found it more interesting, though less beautiful, than I had expected. It has been a devastatingly dry winter there, so the flowers were not good, and it was sad to see the poor thin crops and already great tracts of dust in many districts. I wonder if you saw the correspondence in *The Times* (mine amongst them) about the alarming growth in the destruction of song-birds in Cyprus for commercial export as pickled delicacies? I got my facts from the recorder for the Cyprus Ornithological Society – a very nice man living in Nicosia. I think there *is* a good chance of getting something done about this – at any rate as regards the United Kingdom.

I have now got a young couple and a baby sharing my house, which, on the whole, I enjoy. They are here for six months as they were homeless. After that I want to find a single suitable lodger.

Life is very full, which is a good thing. I find it still hard to adjust, but I do feel (at times anyway) that I am still sharing things with Harold. He and Chris are so much part of me for always. I may enclose a poem I tried to write at Christmas, which tried to express the sort of double existence which the death of those with whom we have shared this life in love seems to force upon us.

I am spending Easter with my dear Oxford friend who, since I was there at Christmas, has developed severe arthritis, which is crippling her, and for which apparently nothing can be done. I shall look out for you on the radio Good Friday morning. I've got T.V. on hire for a year, but don't use it much. I really *prefer* listening to looking. However I do enjoy 'Face the Music' always.

I'm re-reading Rilke's wonderful Letters.

Good luck to your book. I do hope you'll get some time for it. Can you go by sea to Australia and write then? Harold Nicolson and V. Sackville-West always did a sea voyage when they wanted to get on with a book.

Goodbye and bless you. My love,

K.M.

I will add the poem. I am no poet, but sometimes it is a relief to try to put things into words, and words which are not exactly prose. I don't think you *do* feel the duality of time and eternity (?), but the longing for the physical presence forces it upon one, I find.

Christmas 1972

My littleness cannot admit death's magnitude.
Neither the void, nor immortality
Consorts with dear familiarities.
The 'pure and endless light' tortures these eyes,
Used only to the coloured chequered shade.
Humanity crouches within the chrysalis,
Craves and contrives for Eden, not for Heaven.
Death will not have it so.

Those who have lost
Must learn the strange and difficult ways
Of incompatible, simultaneous worlds,
Dispossessed of earth, alien from Paradise.

Yet angels sang to shepherds (and why care
Whether in fact, or in the minds of men?).
A stable lodged Divinity, so it is said –
And in the very saying two worlds meet.

Be patient then, take courage, Wanderer.

7 April   *Elm Park Gardens*

My dear K.M.,

The poem is lovely and says *so* much in a clear and concise way. Thank you for writing it out for me. I *like* it. It is a *real* poem. I particularly stir to:

'Humanity crouches within the chrysalis,
  Craves and contrives for Eden, not for Heaven.
  Death will not have it so.'

I find that I'm beginning to realise a huge fact – that we are not born, and that is why we cannot die . . . We simply are. I don't believe we suddenly explode into being. I think we are part of God's be-ing, and because this is wholly spiritual it has *always* been. This is partly intuitive (in me) and partly, as I see it, logical if one accepts that spirit *is* substance, and I do.

Yes, I *did* see the correspondence about birds in Cyprus, and I salute you, and hope something *will* be done.

I like the idea of the Lewis Carroll exhibition and hope I'll see it sometime, but can't think how. Busy days, and we go out to Australia again on July 2 for a long concert tour. I wish we could go by sea, but there isn't time. And, second thought, I don't think I'd like ship-life for four weeks.

No I don't think I feel the duality of time and eternity . . . I am beginning to feel eternity more as I get older, and I *know* it is always Now as well as Then and When – and is real. Time isn't.

Isn't it difficult to sort out the difference between acknowledging that because man *is* spiritual he includes *all* that is good and the egocentric point of view that oneself is real. (And I don't mean only the human being so much as the misconception of what the true ego is.) As I see it, it is god-and-man and when I see it clearly (in glimpses) so I experience the sense of universal harmony – True *being*. I don't know much about Jeremy Taylor, but I do love this: 'What is the chief end of Man? To know God and enjoy Him forever.' I believe we must experience more joy – not 'happiness' but that deep reverberation of all's well – confidence in Life.

Love and a happy Easter time at Oxford.

J.G.

Good Friday   *Northcourt House, Abingdon*

My dear J.G.,

I have been listening to you with great interest and enjoyment as usual. Thank you. I am not sure I agree with you about the 'Three Brothers' song. There *is* something sad about a life which has not developed any independent personality, but exists only for the sake of and in others. If she had become a full person herself the brothers would not have written only once a year. But of course she was much better off than a selfish or self-centred person. I was very interested in all your autobiographical bits, some of which were quite new to me.

I have another letter to thank you for. I am so cheered you like the poem, because I am always very uncertain of myself on the rare occasions when I try anything but light verse. I am sending you another one, which I think may appeal to you, but it needs explaining. I have a friend (young) who is one of the happiest people I know, independent of her circumstances, which are not very favourable. She said to me one day '—— came to me the other day and asked me if I was happy. I knew if I said I was, she would tell me all the reasons why I shouldn't be, and I felt I couldn't quite bear it, so I said I wasn't, and that was all right'! So I wrote this verse (I won't call it a poem).

> She said, 'But are you happy?' And I knew
> She wished, for my own good, to set me right –
> 'Lead kindly Light to the encircling gloom.'
> That the deluded rose must fade and die
> I should admit, that birds and beasts and men
> Live incommunicable and apart,
> That all my books gave only dusty answers.
> So I replied – 'I am *not* happy.'
> She smiled approval, and went on her way.
> The Star that danced when I was born
> Winked at me from the dark but dazzling night.

I like your idea that we are not born and therefore cannot die (you always manage to stretch me theologically), and that we are part of God's being, and I think I can fit into this the importance of individual personality, which I think must be of eternal significance, because it is so marked a feature of your life here and because Christ stressed the value of the individual. Yes 'to know God and enjoy Him forever' is very satisfying as a chief end, because God means so *much* – that is where my conception of God has grown.

I am here for Easter with a very dear friend (not quite so old a friendship as yours with Virginia Graham, but going back fifty-five years now, so a good stretch). She is badly crippled with arthritis, but still carrying on her school and very cheerful.

Jane's Lewis Carroll exhibition a great success – very good notices. I went to see it last week.

Don't trouble to answer this, because I *know* how busy you are, but I always like to answer yours, and always have much to thank you for.

Did I tell you I now have a young couple and baby sharing my house – so warming – and they bake lovely home-made stone-ground bread (as I used to do long ago), and the house smells nice, and I find a loaf on my table? She is American, and they are feckless and happy, and the baby always has a welcoming smile for me.

I can't find a really nice Easter card, but I do like *open* windows and flowers.

Much love

K.M.

26 April

Forgive a postcard, but unless I write one now I fear I won't get down to a letter for a while. Owing to a broadcast (oh, you heard it – thank you for saying kind things) I've had a huge mail . . . Thank you for the pretty open window that Dufy did. Pleasing.

Just back from 'Facing the Music', twice, in Manchester. Lovely sun up there, too, and I had a lunch in Cheshire with an old friend between tapings, so it was very pleasant.

I read a very good piece about the Lewis Carroll exhibition and wished I could have seen it. I love your poem. Very pleasingly done. You are good at it. Made me laugh. About individual personality – isn't it truly individual reflections of one mind?

So glad about the smell of new bread and the company of a smiling baby. Nice.

Wish I had time to go into more but I know you understand so no more excuses.

Love

J.G.

My dear J.G.,

I don't know where you are, or when this will reach you, but it seems a long while since we communicated, and I suddenly thought I would like to write. I have wanted to say how much I enjoy 'Face the Music'. Since I acquired a T.V. and can now get B.B.C. 2 this has been my favourite regular programme, and it has also been thoroughly appreciated by my grandchildren when they have happened to spend a Monday evening with me. We generally get about half right between us per programme. Do you remember an old shot of Myra Hess playing at one of the National Gallery wartime concerts which came up on one 'Face the Music' programme? You talked about it, and I was so pleased, as I had been at that particular concert, too. For the first time then it struck me that I must have often seen you at the Lunch Bar there, before I knew anything about you. I have a dim memory of one particularly nice and tall dispenser of lunch. My husband and I and my children came so often to those concerts. It is curious how one looks back to those war years with nostalgia, though at the time this would not have appeared possible.

This has been a sad year for me. I think I did tell you that following my husband's death I have lost both a very dear niece and stepdaughter – both quite young. But friends have been very good, and life is still full of interest, though I cannot help a feeling of inner loneliness and emptiness without my husband, who was my anchorage, and with whom I shared so fully all life's joys and sorrows.

My book, I *hope*, comes out at Christmas, though printers have been causing delays. I am now at work on a small educational book on Caxton and early printing for Long-mans and this has meant a good deal of interesting research, as I really knew very little about it.

Sharing my home with my young couple and baby has been an unqualified success, and I shall miss them greatly when they move on to their new job at Bristol at the end of September. I am now looking for someone to succeed them. It is quite possible to commute from here to London, and I am sure there must be people who would be glad to come if they knew, but I don't want to advertise. I have told all my friends to look out for me. I have two rooms to spare and have made a separate kitchen. I expect the right people will turn up eventually – in fact I am feeling rather Micawberish about life in general just now. My daughter is fearfully busy and is likely to be for some time to come over various jobs. The two elder grandchildren both start college in October.

I shall be sorry when 'Face the Music' stops – as well as being thoroughly amusing and stimulating, it provides a link with you.

I was very grieved to see in *The Times* that Joseph Cooper had lost his wife. He has all my sympathy.

I am, at the moment, re-reading William James' *Varieties of Religious Experiences* – a great book. It is interesting that Alister Hardy is trying to do the same thing for religious experience today. Have you read William James? If so, do you remember his classification into the once born and twice born? You, I think are, undoubtedly one of the happy 'once born'. I seem to myself to belong, at different times. to both, but I have never had an outstanding religious experience. I wish I had. Mine is a slow plodding pilgrim-age.

Did you enjoy *Death in Venice*? I think you must have heard it. I would like to do so if I possibly can when it comes to Covent Garden.

Goodbye and bless you. *See you tonight* (alas, the last time for a long while I fear).

With love

Katharine Moore

My dear K.M.,

Lovely to hear from you. I've thought of you so often and had planned to write while we are away for three weeks at Aldeburgh, Marske-in-Swaledale, Ballantrae, Ayrshire and Howick, Alnwick, Northumberland.

Rather a lot to tell you – a sinister phrase. But things are O.K., after a roughish time. It's a saga. We were supposed to leave for Australia on July 2, and for some time I'd rather dreaded the length and size of the concert tour, sixty-eight concerts in two and a half months, with all the press and T.V. stuff to do in each different place. As you know, I am a student of Christian Science, and it has always healed me of *every* problem large and small. This time it was a bit slow – Oh, I forgot to say I'd had a problem with an eye. To cut it short. My husband who isn't a Christian Science or a (conventional) believer was very concerned because the eye became inflamed, etc., etc., so he asked me if I'd go and see his doctor, who is a dear friend of ours. He sent me to an eye specialist, and between them they said: 'Whoah! Stop! Cancel Australia!' So with ten days to go before we were due to arrive (but nearly three weeks before I was due to appear in Perth) we had to cancel . . . I felt so sad at letting them down, and at missing Australia, for I love it, and we have so many very close friends there, we'd been looking forward to seeing. So, for the first time in my life I took pills and hated it. The feeling of being a zombie, the side-effects, etc. My husband was absolutely superb. He took over completely. Because he was supposed to be away he was free to do so – he shopped, cooked, cared for me, and was funny, kind, gentle and strong and wonderful. He lost six pounds in a week (I lost ten and was very pleased). All the horrible part is over, and I'm *very* well; back to normal. 'They' say that they can do no more for me. I'm free of drugs and drops, and I am full of faith and at peace. It is remarkable what one can do with one eye. I'm even allowed to drive if I want to. I don't, yet. I still wear dark glasses in the street, partly because it stops people saying, 'what have you done to your eye?' But in the house I don't bother. The eye is now fully open again, and though still a little pink looks much more reasonable.

So that is the story of this summer. We are now off for a little change. We've been absolutely quiet, and I've *loved* it. So has Reggie. Friends come in for tea. I've been out to lunch with one of two special friends. But I've been gloriously *un*demanded. I'm writing again. Short, light pieces. I hope to go back to my 'Book'. Whether I go on doing concerts is entirely up to me. And I don't *mind* either way. *If* I do – O.K. If I don't – O.K. It's a lovely free feeling. Anyway, nothing at all till 1974 and then I'm to do another season of 'Face the Music' – if I look all right. I'm sure I will. And I could easily wear specs – or even a patch. Well, no out-lining. Let us just trust and see.

So, dear K.M. that's what I've been up to. But before that happened I had a lovely time at Windsor Castle when the Queen asked me to come privately and entertain her friends after dinner. It was in Ascot week, and I didn't much fancy all those horsy people, but they were so generous and quick and friendly, and it was great fun. I will send you a copy of a dictated account of the evening I did for my brother and a few friends abroad. Please sent it back to me.

Must now rush – This is unread.

Love and I'll do better at answering your letter next time.

                                                                    J.G.

9 *September*   *Northcourt House, Abingdon*

My dear J.G.,

I am so *very* sorry about your eye trouble. I cannot quite make out from your letter whether there is permanent injury? I do *hope* not. I think during all the fifteen (?) years of our pen friendship this is the first time you have spoken of any physical trouble. I am so glad you have had the experience of extra love and care from your husband. That is also something I have been privileged to have had in the past. I can't get used to being without him now but feel I am bearing this loneliness *for* him and *instead* of him, and am glad about that.

As I have said, this has been a sad year, and last week another thing happened. I was staying here with my dear arthritic friend, and we were looking forward to going for a little holiday together in Dorset. Instead, she fell on the stairs on Wednesday afternoon and broke her hip-bone. It was over three hours before I could get a doctor – then she was taken at once to Oxford. She is in much pain, and the arthritis exaggerates the trouble. Drugs for this upset a sensitive digestion and she is also anaemic. I hate to see her suffer, but she is as brave as a lion. I spend my time going in and out of the Radcliffe (where my husband died this time last year – it is strange and sad that I should be visiting there constantly again) and trying to cope with things here. My friend runs a school, and term is almost upon us. However, a niece comes to take over from me at the end of the week, and I shall go home, but probably come here again later.

I *loved* your account of the Windsor Palace banquet. Thank you *so* much for letting me see it. I do love perfection. I too would have enjoyed the flowers most, I think – in going over 'great country houses' the wonderful arrangements of flowers give me intense pleasure. But it is *everything* being perfect of its kind (including, of course, the Entertainer!) that makes an experience of that sort so deeply satisfying. Thank you very much for letting me in on it. I am so glad the Queen was so nice.

Do you like the enclosed poem? I don't know the author but it was in a recent copy of *The Friend* (a Quaker periodical). I liked it so I thought you might.

I hope you are able to go on writing and that you really are getting *quite* well again. I am very sorry you had to give up your Australian tour, as I know you love going there, but it sounds a most exhausting programme. I wish I felt a bit more reassured about your eye trouble. I gather it was a really horrible attack.

With so much sympathy and good wishes for the future, and love from,

K.M.

My dear K.M.,

Thank you so much for your letter and the return of the Windsor piece. So glad it was of interest to you. Yes, I am a very 'well' person and have always been quickly healed of things that cropped up, serious or not. This eye thing is very slow and the doctors say it is *no* good, and they can do nothing. I continue to hope and pray . . .

Thank you for the 'Faith' poem. I like it. For me, though, I think the future tense in it isn't quite enough . . . 'You *will* be there,' I believe 'You *are* there' is more powerful.

I wonder if you will like the very brief lines I will enclose. I find it a good 'prayer' and think about when I'm working in the house or walking.

Yes, I am writing again. I've done some brief 'light articles' for the *Christian Science Monitor*, and now I'm trying to get on with the 'book' I began two or more years ago. I think I try too hard to write *well*. I'm sure that my only hope is to speak in my natural voice; but it isn't the way I'd like to be *able* to write. When I try to write 'literature' it comes out stilted and lifeless and phoney.

I've done about twenty thousand words – I think I've told you this, earlier on? – about my parents, grandmother, nanny and Ruth Draper. Portraits. Now I'm writing, not in any chronological way, about going on the stage, staying away in big houses (as we did when I was young), and about what I think. Tall order. I have no overall shape for 'the book' – so far – but am getting down the matter. Then I'll edit, I hope, and shape it.

We had a happy eight days in Ayrshire staying in my younger sister-in-law's low old whitewashed muddle of a friendly, shabby house set on a high hill against trees, and with a huge open view over falling meadows rolling down to the sea, three miles away. She has morning help three days in the week but does all the laundry – sheets, towels, clothes – and cooking and housework the rest of the time. This isn't unusual, but my brother-in-law Bernard Fergusson (do you know his books? *Trumpet in the Hall* is *well* worth reading) is a compulsive inviter, and they rarely sit down alone to a meal. He is also a compulsive smoker, and everywhere is covered with ash . . . This is something about which all your lovely book on Tolerance is needed by me! I resent the imposition of clouds of smoke that cause my hair and clean clothes to smell as horrid as his do. He is a very vulnerable man, but totally insensitive about his smoking, and the effect it has on others. He is pretty self-indulgent, and my dear Laura is very like Reggie – totally *without* self. She has become a good and imaginative cook, and thanks God for a deep-freeze. Up there this is a necessity if one is to be faced with last-minute calls for three extra mouths to be filled at an hour's notice. She does it with grace and flourish.

Now we are in Northumberland in Reggie's mother's home, where he spent so many happy holidays as a boy. He responds to the scents and scenes, and is wreathed in smiles as he explores old familiar places. I find it a bit over-treed. Howick Hall is a colossal stone pile of eighteenth-century elegance, empty now, and dry rotten from top to bottom. Young Charlie Howick lives in a wing of the great house, entirely rebuilt into a small elegant place incorporating mantelpieces and floors from the big house. His mother, Molly, with whom we are staying, lives in a charming double bow-fronted stone dower house half a mile away, set in lawns and a walled garden where she works every minute she can spare. I find the area a bit claustrophobic compared to Cumberland. It is partly the North-East Coast weather that seems so enclosing. Sea mists and low clouds. No views. The Greys (Howick is the Grey family house – the Great Lord Grey was Reggie's great-great-(maybe great?) grandpapa and has a statue on a column in the centre of Newcastle), are great tree people. Charlie, Reggie's uncle, made a most beautiful 'wild' garden of rhododendrons and hydrangea and lilies and varied shrubs, called Silver Wood because he began it the year of his silver wedding. It is open (free) to the public, and they wander down the grassy paths at all seasons. It is *lovely* but I find it too enclosed for my needs. Give me vistas to wider views.

I've just done my part in a two-handed article – Pro and Con Nature as a holiday – Virginia (Graham) Thesiger is Con Nature and Pro the hand of man. I'm for Nature *sans* too many men at all. We've enjoyed ourselves. Her piece is far more elegant than mine, and I feel now I should re-write, but I can't.

We go south on the eighteenth.

Thank you for writing and for the poem. I do hope your brave hip-broken friend is mending well and as painlessly as the Radcliffe can allow. I hope you are well and I'm glad you are working – you *are*, aren't you? – on a book?

Love,

J.G.

13 October   *Riverside House*

My dear J.G.,

Thank you so much for such a good letter from North-umberland. I am so *very* sorry about your eye and hope and pray that the doctors are wrong and that it will improve. I am sure your own attitude must help.

I have been laid up with heart trouble and anaemia since I last wrote, but am on the upward grade now and able to crawl round and look after myself again, which is a great comfort. I miss my two older grandchildren dropping in so much. They have both departed to college – one to London and one to Oxford. Bless them! I do hope they will be as happy as I was and make as good lifelong friends.

I am very glad you are writing. I am sure you are right, and that you should write as it comes. Your letters are so good that I am certain your book will be alive and swift and natural in style, for that is the way you naturally express yourself, and that *is* 'writing well', and I don't see how anything could be better – for that sort of book especially. I am longing to read it, so hurry up with it – do!

I loved your description of Ayrshire and of Howick Hall.

Talking of writing – why have roots now always got to be *grass* roots? And what a lot of them seem to be about. And why has this age always got to have a day tacked on to it? And why is almost every simple statement prefaced with 'in fact' – often erroneously and nearly always unnecessarily – sometimes three times in one sentence? And why is the simple 'yes' discarded in favour of 'definitely'? While I was laid up I listened to radio more than usual, and all the above occurred with maddening frequency. And it isn't only in speech – grass roots in fact tangle up many an article in this day and age – definitely.

My very dear lodgers and their baby departed this morning for their new home in Bristol, and I feel very lonely without them. I have a new lodger – a bachelor in his forties, arriving soon. I don't know him, but he has had a sad life and is in need of some security and peace for a time, anyway. He works in London, so will be away all day.

I am trying to work out what one ought to be able to learn from old age – because I do feel, since my husband's death (*not* really before) that I have entered into that 'last mansion' (see Keats's letters). I think it is primarily acceptance in a positive sense of limitations and a certain degree of loneliness. Small pleasures must become large (and they can if one gives oneself to them). I *do* think radio music and some T.V. programmes are a wonderful boon when one cannot get about much. But I *wish* some of the best T.V. items weren't so late, and so many of my friends suffer in this way too. We just *can't* keep awake. Now if they were in the middle of the night – how one would welcome them!

The news is so sad – my Jewish son-in-law is very disturbed.

No more just now. My love as always and I think much about your eye and pray for its restoration.

K.M.

1 December   *Elm Park Gardens*

My dear K.M.,

I see your letter is dated October 13 . . . time does fly, no doubt of it. I'm so sorry you have been ill. In October you were on the upward grade. I do so hope this is maintained.

You wrote with an irritation that I share about the English language being abused. 'This day and age', 'in point of fact', etc., etc., and there are also the awful vowel sounds – in-VOLved (as in low). I do dislike that. And SOLT for salt.

I hope your new lodger has proved pleasant.

I think you have seen 'Face the Music' sometimes; perhaps you will like to know the last series is to be repeated on B.B.C. 1 at 4.30 on Sundays from January 6, or so I'm told (we do a new series for B.B.C. 2 later in the year). It's a great compliment to have a quiz repeated, and to have it done on another channel is a *great* honour! I'm off to Manchester on Monday – rail strike permitting? – to tape a special 'Face the Music' for Christmas. I'm told my eye is really not too bad to look at, and the cameraman is going to avoid zooming in too close on that side. I am *very* well and leading a full life, but staying at home.

Yes, I am writing away at the 'book'. Slow it is, but I am enjoying it.

On Thursday I am to be made an Honorary Fellow of Manchester Polytechnic. Isn't that nice? Sir Charles Groves is, too, and there are five or so others (northern) people being honoured. Reggie is coming up for that. And on Friday I open a Community Centre in Bradford, so you see I'm back in the swim. But no concerts. And that is a great relief – particularly in cold weather – oh, those draughty stages and long journeys.

I have so much to be grateful for.

I meant to write you a long letter, but the time has gone and I must get to the shops for the week-end foods. This 'arvo' as Australians say of the afternoon, we see Laurence Olivier at the Vic in *Saturday Sunday Monday*. We hear it is charming.

Reggie enthuses over David Cecil's book on Hatfield, and I'm about to read it. *Emlyn* was distasteful to me, not because he is bi-sexual, and says so, but because I think a little reticence is becoming, and there ain't much around. As I've said to you before, I am NOT shockable, but I am offendable. I found it self-indulgent.

May you have a peaceful Christmas with some of those dear to you.

Do you turn on any of those all-night programmes when you can't sleep? A friend tells me that they are very helpful in sending one back to sleep! Just words without ideas, and not well said.

Love to you and thoughts and hopes,

J.G.

We have our forty-fourth soon. What a blessing it has been all these years!

1974

My dear J.G. (I think I like this better than Joyce – it is more distinctive to me of you and our long pen friendship),

I was so very glad to hear from you. I had been thinking of you a lot lately, and I was on the point of writing, but waiting every day for my 'Victorian Wives' book to come and was hoping to send you a copy. It was promised, first for Christmas, then for March and then for mid-April! Now I am writing this hastily hoping it will catch you before you start for the United States. It brings my Easter greetings. More and more, Easter seems to mean so much, and this year the flowers and trees seem almost more beautiful than ever. Yesterday I was sitting with an old crippled friend of eighty-eight in Hampstead Churchyard in the lovely sun. She has suffered loss of home and personal belongings (she has a tiny room in a Council Old People's home). She had two gifted children – one whose poems were published by the Hogarth Press when she was eighteen, has been for years in a mental home – the other a gifted composer is in an alcoholic home, and though cured, is worn out and old before his time. Yet she was radiant at the spring, at all Easter means and with our companionship. The human spirit is amazing. Did you read or *hear* the article by Hans Keller on his experience with the Nazis? It has been haunting me ever since. The height and the depth to which man can rise or fall. But it seems to give the Cross more significance than ever.

Anyway this began with my Easter good wishes to you. I

am so *very* glad you are well. I am looking forward so much to meeting you again on 'Face the Music'. I wonder how much difference your eye trouble makes to your actual sight? A great Oxford friend of mine has to do with one eye and she says it only makes judging distances difficult. I *do* hope you don't suffer much from it in any way.

I am getting along pretty well with my re-adjustment to life. If I keep busy and see a good many people I manage, but I never realised before how much enforced loneliness differs from chosen solitude, nor how the beatitude of a loved and loving presence always in the background acted as a kind of anchor to one's whole being. But I feel that presence still in many ways, and all the richness of my past life is still with me.

My daughter's Lewis Carroll Exhibition is now at Greenwich. It has been at Longleat and Sheffield Art Gallery and has given so much pleasure. She says how much she wished you could have seen it. But it closes at the end of April. It has been a joy, as it was an original conception of showing how the actual happenings of L.C.'s life were woven into his books. Jane arranged a Victorian nursery, schoolroom and kitchen with many of his actual books and toys and with the figures from the books – e.g. the Red Queen's shadow was the figure of Alice Liddell's real governess – the Frog Footman stood outside L.C.'s own little doll's house – the figures of the old Happy Family cards (which were designed by L. Carroll himself) the Sweep, Miss Bun, Mr Bung the Brewer, etc., were peering down the basement of the Victorian kitchen where sat the cook and the Duchess and the Cheshire Cat.

The children were fascinated – one little coloured boy came up to me and said, 'Please Miss, does this open on Saturdays – I'd like to spend the whole day here.'

Jane has broadcast several times about it. She now wants to do a Caxton exhibition if she can find a sponsor. I am so glad your book is going ahead so well and am longing to read it.

I am rather fretting after some work and am being kept hanging about waiting to know if I have got a commission to do a book on the 'Seventeenth-Century Lady' or not. It would be fun.

I have had a lodger since last November when my original family moved to Bristol. This one is a bachelor of about fifty, very sweet and considerate and with a sad past, so that I think I am of use to him. He goes to London every day, is musical and loves Nature, but doesn't read, except the papers. He is really hoping to buy a cottage here, but is in no hurry.

My youngest grandchild aged just nine generally spends one night a week with me. She loves reading to me and last week read for three hours on end! With a very short break for supper. She *had* to finish the book which was Nicholas Gray's delightful *The Stone Cage*. The next morning she said, 'Shall I begin it again to you Granny?'

I must stop – I hope you will have a satisfying time in America.

Please excuse this scrawl, written against time. There is so much I would like to say to you about books and birds and music and even politics but that must wait.

Much love

K.M.

16 April   *Elm Park Gardens*

My dear K.M.,

Lovely to get your letter. Thank you. I look forward to your Victorian wives – I loved what I read in typescript. All wishes for it.

Yes, I heard Hans Keller do the talk on radio, very moving. So was the Dutch Jewish woman, now Mrs Douglas, who spoke at 6.15 on Sunday on B.B.C. 1. She seems to have done a book called *Live* – I *think* (see this week's *Radio Times*).

I now have a superb 'cosmetic contact' for my poor eye, and it entirely disguises the problem that it isn't working. A clever German refugee man specialises in cosmetic eye work and it is quite *marvellous*. I do not give up hope of healing.

So sorry I missed the Lewis Carroll exhibition, it sounds *so* good.

Loved hearing about your granddaughter reading to you. Nice child.

I think I have now finished the *shape* of my book, but there's lots more work to be done. In the letters to my mother I've found lots of funny things, including a dressing-room behind the platform of a village hall, with a print of a classical Nativity hung over the dressing-table. I did a wartime concert there and noted a piece of paper stuck under the picture that said, 'First prize for skipping to music'.

We are due home May 10th.

Love and I'm glad you are 'managing'.

J.G.

I grow more sure that all *is* well – spiritually I mean.

30 May   *Riverside House*

My dear J.G.,

I hope you had a good time in the United States. It is so nice to see you again on 'Face the Music', which, together with 'Dad's Army', is my favourite T.V. programme. I couldn't see anything wrong with the eye.

At last I am able to send you a copy of my book – if you don't want to read it again, and I don't expect you will, perhaps you will find someone to give it to – but anyway I wanted to send you a copy. I can't feel quite the same about it as about my other books, partly because it's been so long on hand, partly because my husband isn't here to be pleased about it.

I have been asked to do a huge book on Women's role and influence on religion. The subject enthralls and appalls me. I think I am too old and nothing like learned enough. I should have to get a lot of help. Yet I hate turning things down. Personally I would like to write a children's historical novel in my own leisure time, but at present there is the great disadvantage that I can't think of a plot.

My dear musical grandson has successfully dealt with his Intermediate (in the London Music Degree). As he has an infinite capacity for failing in exams, we are all greatly relieved. His tutor has said such very nice things about his work and his personality and his influence for good on the other students.

How are your American nephew and niece?

I paid three rather exhausting but very interesting visits to Wales in May – they were to three completely different worlds (1) farming, (2) literary and artistic, (3) Quaker philanthropic. On getting home however I had to take in more iron to recover!

My lodger, who came only for three months, is still with me, and we get on very well. He needs help and reassurance after a rough deal in life, and he gives me in return physical help. We share music and politics (Liberal) but he never reads. Occasionally I make him listen to poetry, which he can take in very small quantities.

So many people are so very depressed about the world today. I don't think they read enough history. Fanny Kemble in the nineteenth century describes Manchester in horrific terms, for instance. There *has* been progress – and look at China and one's hopes for Portugal.

I must stop. With my love and blessing on you as ever.

K.M.

5 *June*   *Elm Park Gardens*

My dear K.M.,

We got in late yesterday after a glorious week in our favourite Cumberland valley to find *the* book. I'm so pleased to have it and I look forward to re-reading it. Thank you VERY much for sending it to me. I do appreciate it. Doesn't it look nice, too? I'm *very* fond of Pre-Raphaelite painting.

My own 'great work' is pending – that is, I've done about

245

60,000 words and now Rupert Hart-Davis has read it, and we've been through it together, and he's given me such *great* help in suggesting cuts, where amplification should be added, going through every comma and spelling mistake, etc., etc. – We had two three-hour sessions of high speed concentration after he had read it quietly before I arrived. He is a most skilled editor and did mammoth work on his aunt Lady Diana Cooper's books. He also edited Wilde's letters and wrote a very good biography of Hugh Walpole. So now I am longing to get down to work again, but until we've been to Aldeburgh for the festival, and to see my dear paralysed friend, I can't really get at it. But we are *not* going to take our trip to Australia this year after all, so I can get down to work and complete the book at *leisure* and not at a rush. I had thought of calling it *When I Wasn't Looking*, but Rupert doesn't like it. Must try again.

Cumberland was glorious – we were lent a house, cosy-warm, easy to run, and how we enjoyed the peace and the clear air and the water that tastes like water! We birded and walked and lazed and slept and slept and slept. *Very* good it was.

No time to write more. Yes, of course, if your publishers write to me, I'll do what I can about the book. It's easy when you like something to do something about it! I can always find out who to get in touch with through Joanna Scott-Moncrieff – ex-editor of 'Woman's Hour' and now a free-lancer. I must catch up a bit with an accumulation. Love and *all wishes* for your book. It's good.

Love,

J.G.

14 June

I loved your pretty postcard. What an enviable-looking house you live in! And there really *is* a 'shore'. Thank you for showing me. We are off to Suffolk tomorrow and are lending the flat while away. This means tidying it up . . . Very good for one. Have begun to revise the manuscript before I go on to the next bit of writing, but I must wait till the festival is over.

Isn't it lovely to be warm? Long may it last!

I haven't yet cast one vest. I rarely do, but I'm about to remove my nether garments in view of the sun, but will take them to East Anglia, you never know there. Love and again all wishes for the book and you.

J.G.

15 September   *Riverside House*

My dear J.G.,

I have been meaning to write for some time to thank you for writing so kindly to my publishers. It pleased them very much. They have written to 'Woman's Hour' but had no answer yet. I expect they are booked up anyway for some time, but if nothing comes of it I am none the less grateful.

I also thought I would like you to know that the book club has ordered ten thousand copies* – these won't be ready before next spring, but I am very glad for my publishers' sake (and for myself too of course!).

I do hope your own book is progressing well. I am looking forward so much to reading it. I am now just in the middle of Enid Starkie's life. I knew of her at Oxford, of course, though I never met her. What a queer, tortured, gifted creature she was.

I am busy with life on a small scale, trying to finish my short life of William Caxton, and I've begun a purely imaginative work which I find terribly difficult and exciting and I tear up more than I write.

A good deal of time is taken up with my lodger. He will have been with me a year next month. I knew before I took him that he had been in prison, but he only managed to tell me all about it in June. I much admire the courage with which he lived out his sentence and is trying to build up a new life. He came to me quite by chance, and I only knew of

* This order unfortunately did not materialise.

his past by an accident just before he moved in. (He did not know that I knew.)

Apart from my lodger, of course, my family keep me busy and interested, and I have just come back from being with my arthritic invalid friend near Oxford. She still continues to run her school in spite of pain and constant *extraordinary* domestic details. She is consistently robbed and exploited by a wicked but fascinating Irish cook.

My grandson is so happy with his music now, specialising in Opera and French music for the next two years. I am looking forward to 'Face the Music' beginning again.

Much love always and so much gratitude for your good wishes and help about my book.

Katharine

18 September   *Watching How, Lowewater, Cumberland*

My dear K.M.,

Good to hear from you. Thank you for your letter and interesting items. I'm sure you have been a huge help in more ways than one to your lodger, how good for him to have fetched up in your house where he has found security. How splendid about the book club order. Hooray!

I am still writing my book – and rewriting it constantly. I'm anxious to get it right, but I'm not sure I'm not cutting it down *too* much. Rupert Hart-Davis has the manuscript now – about 70,000 odd words of it, and I await his advice about whether I'm going in the right direction. He had read the first half earlier, but this is the redone version with cuts and expansions and five more chapters. I do wish I wrote well. I have enough sense to know I don't. Therefore I mustn't press too hard, but try to stick to a conversational tone.

At least that is what I *think* I'm doing!

I've still got at *least* three more chapters to do. I plan to take it up to when I first 'went solo' – that is, 1954; but I did solo shows long before that in music clubs, and I was solo all during the war when I went to fourteen countries, playing in hospital wards and to isolated units. My paralysed friend

248

has died. Last Saturday at Aldeburgh we had a Thanks-giving memorial service for her, almost entirely music. I read from Wisdom and from Philippians. The Bishop of Ipswich, who'd only known her for a year, exactly caught her quality and was just the right man to do a three-minute address about her, much of it quotation – Revelations and *Pilgrim's Progress*. The English Opera Company were at The Maltings doing two operas, so the chorus – thirty strong, sang at the service and we all made a *most* joyful noise unto the Lord. Over two hundred friends came.

We have been lent this house in Cumberland where we always stayed when Ella Milburn was alive. She ran the hotel where I originally met her when I was on a concert tour in 1957, and we made friends. She died two years ago and left the house to a nephew who is stationed in Germany, and he lends it to us from time to time. I *love* it up there.

The local Show happens (in a steep field against a dra-matic backdrop of mountains and lakes) tomorrow, and we are watching a watery sunset this evening with some misgiv-ings – it will be gummers and macs, no doubt.

Home on Tuesday next.

I wish I had a title for my book, but so far I haven't got one I like. It is an autobiography, but not strictly chrono-logical and not detailed. I'm leaving out *lots* – I didn't much like the early 1930s when my parents parted and I was a mess. Or so I now feel – non-productive, self-centred, un-canalised. Dabbling, I was, and I didn't realise it. I wish Patricia Napier hadn't used *A Late Beginner*, because it is exactly what I was. *L for Learner* would be more accurate, but it's a bit too twee.

Bath-time and then fresh farm eggs for supper. Reggie and I are both pre-supper bathers, and this is usually popular with hosts because no one else wants to bathe at that time, and it gives the boiler time to hot up again. At Home I get into a dressing-gown but here the retired vicar is apt to drop in, so I wear a house-coat.

Love to you – keep in touch.

J.G.

My dear K.M.,

It seems a long time since I wrote, and now it is almost Christmas and I want to send you my love and thoughts, hopes and wishes. I know feast days are hard for you, and I hope so much that the great love you experienced in your marriage sustains you with real nourishment. Reggie and I had our forty-fifth anniversary on 12 December and we rejoiced over sausages for supper (his choice of a special meal!) and otherwise did not celebrate with presents or any trappings. We never have. Last year he chose boiled eggs (two) for his treat supper. Simple pleasures *are* best.

Apart from continuing to work on my book, mostly in spasms because of a lot of other activities this autumn, there isn't a great deal of news to tell you. But it's been a good time. The book starts to settle. You who have written so many will be amazed at my slow progress. I have now written sixteen chapters and am reviewing the whole, revising as I go. Reggie is a big help in watching out for repetitions and inaccuracies. He also edits in a friendly way, and, though I argue a good deal, he is usually right. Did I tell you I am calling it after the first solo show I did – with three dancers, so not quite solo – *Joyce Grenfell Requests the Pleasure*? I *think* I'll end volume one with the end of the war, because after that came all the big tours of Australia, United States, Canada and New Zealand and the development of T.V. in my life.

The most demanding occupation in the last two months has been my job as chairman of the Arts Category in the selection of Fellows to go overseas on Churchill Memorial Trust grants. I've aided Sir Trenchard Cox for two years in this category, and now he's made me take the chair for 1975, and he is aiding me. 'Teachers of the Arts' is the precise category and I have read (several times) 550 submissions. I selected about seventy from this pile and Trenchard and I whittled it down to twenty for interviews in January when we finally give nine fellowships. It is fascinating work, but one feels very responsible, and I long to *send all* the applicants on their dreamed-of travels. I must hasten to explain I don't judge their qualifications. My job is to assess calibre, and whether the applicant would benefit himself (herself) and the community if given the grant. A sort of intuitive business. Sponsors write about the qualifications. As the Trust was set up to provide for those without degrees who would otherwise not get the opportunity to pursue their particular interest overseas, I look for the often quite humble applications, for it seems to me that those with high qualifications and degrees could in all probability get overseas *somehow* without a Churchill grant. Ages range from sixteen to sixty-seven and men and women are treated equally by *this* chairman. It has been so interesting but *very* time-consuming, for I take it very seriously, and, as I said, read the papers over and over.

If you are near your 'telly' at Christmas I'm on both the 25th and 26th in the evenings on B.B.C. 2 – 'Face the Music' on Christmas Day night, and in a programme with Joseph Cooper on December 26 night. I didn't want to do monologues again, but have been persuaded to 'support' Joe in his first big programme. And we are attempting a rather risky thing – improvising a song together. We've done it to amuse ourselves, and it has worked well; but to order? I've made the producer promise to delete it if it doesn't come off. We tape it on Friday next, 20th.

Tomorrow I do another dialogue in the double-pulpits at St Mary-le-Bow with Joseph McCulloch. A book of dialogues done there is just out. I'm in it: *Under Bow Bells*. Some are rather good. If you see it in your library you might be interested in some of them.

We are happy, well, busy. Reggie takes me with him to South Africa at the end of January for five weeks. I hope to work while I'm there.

This comes to bring you much love at Christmas and may 1975 bring us all wisdom and more understanding.

Love,

J.G.

My dear J.G.,

Thank you for your wren card and the booklet and your wonderful letter. It was wonderful because it put into words what I feel most deeply – the nourishing and sustaining power of the love that I have been given. I was re-reading just that sentence of yours, when the phone rang with the utterly unexpected news that my closest and dearest friend had died suddenly. We had shared our joys, sorrows and interests since we were at Oxford together fifty-six years ago. For all that period we had never missed writing once a week, and had never been more than a month or two without meeting (except when I was in India). After my husband's death it was to her I went, and I spent the last two Christmases with her. This year I was going to her on December 31st and was talking to her on the phone the night before she died. She had been crippled with arthritis for two years, but was so brave and cheerful and carrying on her school, and although I have lost so many dearly-loved friends and relatives, I somehow always thought *she* would be there forever. Except for my husband I think she was closer to me than any other person – a sort of sister and mother figure in many ways. So I came back to your letter, and, though I cannot realise what life will be without her – I know too that in one sense it won't be without her. On Christmas Day I was alone in the afternoon listening to the King's College Carols, which I had listened to with Harold for years, and with her for the last two years, and I felt so strongly and happily that they were with me still. Of course this feeling isn't constant, and one has to fight waves of grief and longing, and yet one *is* sustained and nourished. I am so lucky in having many friends still, and my beloved daughter and son-in-law and grandchildren (but they must never be battened on emotionally by one, because they are the kind that needy people *do* constantly batten on, and I am *not* needy).

I loved your description of your wedding anniversary treat – so like us, only it would probably have been toasted cheese with us and my pancakes which Harold loved – and coffee (made by *him* never by me). Our wedding-day was September 30th, though, and it was always a lovely day, and we used to have long country walks, a sort of goodbye to summer picnic. Sometimes we managed to include the date in a holiday. I remember one *lovely* anniversary, in Scotland, and one in Siena. Oh! how *lucky* one has been.

I am sure your book is going on fine. I am longing to read it. I have begun two more, but I wonder very much if either of them will ever get finished. I couldn't look and listen to you on Christmas night, because I was entertaining my family and my lodger, and we were making music ourselves. But I did *very* much enjoy the Joseph Cooper programme last night, especially the hidden melodies, the Satie piece and the Rossini, and above all the Debussy song, and of course, your sketches. Yes – it was a wonderful oasis. *THANK YOU BOTH*.

You will be tired of reading all this, but it has helped me to write it.

I do wish you so many wishes for 1975 and especially for the book.

With much love and gratitude as always.

K.M.

31 December   *Elm Park Gardens*

My dear K.M.,

Thank you for telling me the story of your lodger and its ramifications and complexities. How fortunate he is to have found you and been able to talk freely to such an understanding heart. Poor man – he has been through a good deal . . .

I can, I think, imagine the sense of desolation over the death of your dear girlhood friend. I have one of those – Virginia Graham of *Punch* and, at one time film critic of the *Spectator*. She and I have known each since we were about seven (fifty-five years), I think, and write regularly whenever we are parted. The relationship of two women all through childhood, girlhood, marriage, and in her case widowhood, is very special. I feel blessed and enriched by such a wonderful, easy and stimulating friendship. Of course, we don't tell each other *everything* – I don't think one should ever do that, but to know that one *could* and the friendship would remain firm is a great blessing. So I send you thoughts and sympathy and affection over this blow, dear K.M. It's hard not to be able to say, 'Do you remember?'

How interesting about your lodger that he is not bitter, and that his Roman Catholic faith sustains him – I think it is a very *personal* kind of faith, and it does seem to comfort people. But I don't respond to priests and sacraments – I love the feeling of God and His children as *one* – cause and effect. The spiritual relationship is the one that I find works for me, and this is arrived at by prayer and silence and study. But it is good to know your young man feels as if he *belongs*. I think that is the useful part of the Roman Catholic faith; particularly for the lonely.

Did you chance to see the T.V. interview with Hugh Bishop, once head of Mirfield, who has leapt over the wall – after thirty-seven years soul-searching and agony.

I honour him for facing up to his doubts, etc., but to make a T.V. programme and *justify* his needs (homosexual but not specifically mentioned) and to tell us how wonderful it is to belong wholly to someone who will *always* be there . . . What a risky claim! And somehow the cheapness of the whole exercise was distasteful to me. He had every right to quit the church, but surely sensitivity should stop him gloating over his new relationship. It was the *self*-will and *self*-love I found so unattractive. I think those three weaknesses are *the* stumbling block to spiritual understanding – self-will, self-justification and self-love.

His T.V. programme has wounded so many who loved and trusted him as a good, holy man, and while I think it is right to be *honest* if one can no longer continue in the faith, I feel the self-indulgence and show-off attitude was *sad* and hurtful. There are ways of withdrawing quietly . . .

We are taking an Australian actress friend to see a musical

called *Billy* – her choice. *Hope* it is enjoyable . . ??

1975 is just a man-made name for another segment of time and I refuse to be hypnotised by it. 'New Every Morning' is the way I try to look at it. Times are rough for *so* many. And likely to get rougher.

But the verities endure – timeless eternal and full of their own spiritual power – Life – Truth and Love – God is *all* that is good and nothing else.

Much love,

J.G.

1975

11 January   *Riverside House*

My dear J.G.,

Your last two letters have helped me and it was so *very* good of you to write again. I must just get this one in to thank you before you leave for Africa.

Without my husband and my closest friend I sometimes feel like a ghost, but your sentence about the love one has been privileged to have sustaining and nourishing one still is *true* and I have always been *so* privileged.

I didn't comment on all the demanding and responsible work you have been absorbed in for the Churchill Memorial Trust Grants. This wasn't because I wasn't interested. It rejoices me to think that someone so conscientious and *sensible* as yourself should be involved in this kind of work which means so much to people. I know so well what you feel like, though, in having to reject people: I always wanted to give *everyone* prizes at school!

I agree with what you say about priests and sacraments and the R.C. faith generally. I can't do with it either, but I will say this for them – they *do* care about their people. John, my lodger, has two obviously saintly priests whom I have met visiting him here. They are very different types – one old, traditional, gentle – the other young, socialistic, the worker priest type. I didn't see the interview with Hugh Bishop – nor did I ever know he had left Mirfield. After your letter I read again an address of his on 'Suffering' which is in a book of Mirfield essays – I liked it, though there was nothing very new or vital about it. It seemed a sadness that he appears to be less of a person than he could be – certainly rash and not right to belong *wholly* to anyone.

You say about Hugh Bishop that the self is the 'stumbling-block to spiritual understanding'. Don't you think the whole battle of life – what life is about I mean – is to get rid of the wrong sort of self and pierce through to the reality of the self you find when you lose it? I read an exciting book about Keats, *The Nightingale and the Hawk*,* which showed how he did this through losing himself in beauty and could then face death. I've just been listening to *Death and the Maiden* which always reminds me of Keats.

I'm trying to get time to write, but it is hard. I've got a lot of letters to catch up with – many in connection with this dear friend so I won't make this longer. But THANK YOU again, and I hope you will have a lovely time in Africa.

Much love,

K.M.

13 August   *Riverside House*

My dear J.G.,

It is some time since we exchanged letters, but I often think of you, and I wonder how your book is shaping? Mine is the greatest comfort. I am just finishing a chapter on Julian of Norwich and Margery Kempe. Margery is a sort of religious Wife of Bath, and I find her fantastically improbable, but yet very human at the same time. Julian is wonderful. Isn't it striking and somehow most reassuring that all mystics, from whatever age their voices come down to us, seem to agree that the nature of ultimate reality is inexpressible and ineffable love. Julian and William Law and Blake and Wordsworth (sometimes) and Plotinus all seem to speak with one voice.

I might possibly include Aldous Huxley whose life by Sybille Bedford I have just finished, and which impressed me very much. He was one of the influences of my youth, but I think really he belongs to that class of creative human beings whose personality was greater than his work – among

* By Katharine Wilson.

which I include Charles Lamb, Johnson, Charles James Fox.

How I ramble on – it is the result of living alone. I always used to criticise the elderly and solitary for being garrulous. Now I no longer do so. My lodger is away, and so is my family, so I am more than usual on my own. I really meant first to tell you a nice story. A few days ago a friend of mine brought a cousin of hers to see me whom I hadn't met before, who said that her son when thirteen had chosen to go to one of your shows for a treat. A little while later he was taking part in a Youth Group 'Any Questions', and he was asked, 'If you hadn't your own mother whom would you choose for a mother?' His answer was immediately 'Joyce Grenfell'.

I wonder if you are in London or having a nice holiday somewhere? I had mine in May, two weeks in an old Spanish house belonging to a friend in Shoreham. It was in the north in lovely country where nightingales were singing all day and night.

I am having another week with a friend at the end of the month. I don't like the heat and worry about the farmers, the birds, the lack of vegetables, etc., but have come to the conclusion that it's no use letting the weather interfere too much with one's life, so I am doing a stint for the National Trust at Wolfe's House at Westerham today and some reading at the British Museum tomorrow and some visiting of friends again in London on Sunday. But all the same I *hope* it will be cooler. Another book, besides Huxley, that has absorbed me lately is Georgina Battiscombe's life of Shaftesbury. What a triumph his life was, and how much he did for humanity! I never knew about all his work for lunacy – housing – India – education besides his well-known factory and chimneysweeps fights. It took seventeen years to get the Ten Hours Bill passed. To read this book is an antidote to despair about the present state of things. Both Shaftesbury and Huxley had wonderful marriages – a fact which pleased me greatly. Much of what Huxley says about music and about transience and the loss of friends came home to me so much.

He says *exactly* what I feel about Bach – 'an expression of the essential all-rightness of the universe . . . including death and suffering with everything else in the divine impartiality which is the One which is Love.'

Bach gives me more reassurance than any other musician, which is exactly the opposite to what Bernard Levin said in *The Times* not long ago. I wonder if you read that article and what you thought of it?

I miss 'Face the Music', but it is a bad season just now for T.V. Geraint Evans is a joy – also the nature films, 'Private Lives', also the archaeology. Did you by any chance see the Yugoslav film after the Shostokovich on Sunday? Very well done and much better than the book (*The Master and Margarite*), I thought. Satan's acting and sad despairing face haunts me still.

Much love,

K.M.

24 August   Riverside House

My dear J.G.,

Many heartfelt congratulations about the book, but *of course* I knew they would love it, and of course I equally know it will be a bestseller of the right sort.* I can hardly wait to read it.

I do so love writing mine, which certainly won't be a bestseller, if it is a seller at all – but it is an enormous interest and consolation to me, and I greedily look forward to any time I can spend on it.

I read the extract from the Mitford book in *The Times* yesterday. I feel so like you, only of course I didn't know the Mitfords personally, but I couldn't help admiring and being amused by Nancy Mitford's earlier books, though I didn't *like* them, and I was astonished and pleased that she attained the heights of true and patient scholarship that she did in her French histories, and I enjoyed them very wholeheartedly. I think forgetting herself in writing them

* *Joyce Grenfell Requests the Pleasure* had been accepted for publication.

259

must have deepened her as a person – or perhaps it was the other way round. I knew she had suffered in her last years, but not whether she had written the books before this.

You aren't quite fair to Bernard Levin when you say music for him begins and ends with Wagner, because he does adore Mozart, though I can't think how he or my grandson can do both! If and when I am occasionally bowled over by Wagner, which doesn't happen often, I always resent it. He always goes on too long for me (I went to sleep at *Tristan* during my honeymoon at Munich). He bullies me into being swept away by him almost like being raped (though I don't really know what that is like either!). Bach is so entirely the opposite, and I suppose that's what Bernard Levin doesn't like. My grandson once said Wagner always wants total control – not to be limited in any way, and Bach is content to accept divine control.

I have had a worrying week with my adopted grandson's little boy (aged three) very ill with meningitis. They live in Wales, and he is an only adored child, and his mother is diabetic and can't have other children. But I think things are going to be all right now.

I won't write more as we've just exchanged letters. I am glad you are reading Volume Two of Aldous Huxley. I do so like him and Maria, and his second wife sounds nice too. I'd like to read her book sometime.

My love and again so many congratulations.

K.M.

No need to answer this scrawl – it is only a congratulatory note.

1976

My dear J.G.,

Your delightful Christmas card is still cheering me and has pleased so many of my friends and your admirers. It and a lovely Byzantine Madonna in red-brown and gold I have kept out still, rather a contrast, but *both* so happy. I generally keep some favourites about from Christmas until they go into books for markers. Today I have also got out an old valentine my daughter did for me when she was a girl. It is a red and gold heart with on one side a dried bouquet of rosemary, buds and corn, and on the other, this rhyme:

> 'Spring, summer, autumn, winter see
> What various blooms are picked for thee,
> The darling kitten coat of spring,
> The heart of summer, honey sweet.
> A ripened blade of corn to bring
> The harvest's minted wealth complete,
> And then these antique leaves to say
> That love grows evergreen as they.'

I think she was in her teens when she made it, but I've always liked it so much, and I send it to you as a late Valentine greeting.

Oh dear, this horrid blotchy cheap ballpen – and the fat cat is on my lap and we are both too lazy for me to go and fetch another.

I do miss seeing you on 'Face the Music' at the moment and indeed hate not having the whole programme, which is a very favourite one with me. I am *much* looking forward to your book and glad it is going on satisfactorily.

Mine is my chief resource when depressed and lonely. I have reached the end of the eighteenth century. The next two chapters are going to be the most difficult because there will be too much material. I want to put in one section on American women and Christianity and shall certainly want to include Mrs Eddy. Can you kindly tell me of a good short life of her and account of her work? . . .

23 February *Elm Park Gardens*

My dear K.M.,

We got home from South Africa (four and a half weeks, *quite* a lot of sun and a great deal of fruit to eat and lovely country to see) to find your good letter of February 14 awaiting me. *Thank* you. I love the valentine. I *love* 'the darling kitten coat of spring'. Vivid. Thank you.

'Face the Music' is to have a ten-week season in September. I'm to be in five. About a book on Mary Baker Eddy's life and work: have written today to Henrietta Buckmaster, who did a book about important American women who made their mark, or rather she did chapter on Mrs Eddy for the book. It was for schools I think – so is brief, accurate and authentic. Henrietta edits the Home Forum page of the *Christian Science Monitor* and is a very remarkable woman. I've asked her, if possible, to send a copy of the little book (short) direct to you and let me know what it sets her back. It gives me *great pleasure* to do this, and it will save you having to read a whole life, some of which (H. Fisher's for instance) were hostile, inaccurate and missed the point of Mary Baker Eddy's discovery.

I only hope it is still available . . . All my records have been deleted . . . only the million-sellers (pop) seem to last.

So glad about your daughter's success with the exhibition. It deserves to succeed.

This is a short note, because I must get on with answering a lot of business letters – will I open, perform, speak, be present at ????? Answer: *mostly* NO. Hurray. I *have* retired.

The book is due in proof from *next* week. We did galleys

before we went away, and Reggie is working on the index in South Africa. I laid plans to promote it there next October when we pass through *en route* for Australia to do the same and stay over Christmas. It is our travelling year and includes the great treat of a Swan's Tour of Greece and Turkey on April 15th–29th.

I have begun to do some work for volume two. Not as straightforward as Vol. 1 but in some ways more interesting. I had the Pilkington Committee; B.B.C. Advisory Council; Churchill Fellowships and 'Face the Music' among other activities to write about.

Forgive incoherence. The telephone keeps ringing. I must prepare supper. Home is *very* nice but getting into a quieter rhythm seems to take time after an absence.

Love, J.G.

5 March   *Riverside House*

My dear J.G.,

No one but yourself would reply so promptly and be so generously helpful, especially after only just having got back from Africa with all you have to do. It made me feel so happy. I shall look forward to receiving the book on Mrs Baker Eddy, and I am sure it will be just what I need. If it is unobtainable, they may have it in the American Section of the London University Library.

I am finding this end part of my book very difficult and often wonder whether any of it has much point, but I plod on. I am very glad yours is making such good progress.

I went to a thrilling lecture on bird and animal life in Africa by Dr and Mrs Harrison. Perhaps you have heard of them? They live in Sevenoaks, but birds are their hobby, and she has won outstanding awards for photographs from the Geographical Society. They had been on a trip photographing birds, wild animals and flowers up from the Cape to the borders of Angola, and their pictures were unforgettable. I thought of you as I watched them.

I shall look forward to 'Face the Music' again. I have undertaken to give some talks in conjunction with our music lecturer (W.E.A.) in the autumn on Shakespeare ('Falstaff') to illustrate Verdi, Nicolai, Elgar, etc. I can't think what made me, as I am quite terrified, and it doesn't help that our music man (Christopher le Fleming) is a very good, fluent and amusing talker. His charm just overcame my reluctance.

I *may* have met my future lodger. On coming back from a great niece's wedding in Gloucester last week-end, my train was much too long and I couldn't get out at my station, but was carried on to the next stop, three stations away. Waiting dismally on a freezing cold little country platform for half an hour to get the train back, I started a conversation with a nice woman with a bunch of catkins and dried bracken. At forty or so, she has decided to be a primary school teacher and was doing practice work at this place – wants to come and live in the country – has a little girl of eleven who loves reading and writing stories. I liked her and in ten minutes between stations we exchanged addresses. 'Oh Granny, you *are* so impulsive' said my grandson doubtfully, but I'm not generally let down, and anyway nothing will probably come of it and need not till the autumn.

I'm reading the Bible as if it didn't matter and finding it *extraordinarily* refreshing and apt, especially the Psalms and the Epistles. When I was a child I thought if I read it right through once a year it might earn me a bit of merit to get me to Heaven because I was *very* doubtful of getting there. But I usually got bogged down by Deuteronomy. Since then I've always read it in a worried sort of way. Now I'm just enjoying it and finding it – as the Quakers say – speaking so vividly to my condition night after night. For instance, the other night I was haunted by fears and came across this splendid message. 'For God has not given us the spirit of fear but of power, and of love and of a sound mind.' (Timothy)

Much love and *many* thanks

K.M.

Everyone who saw your Christmas card recognized it at once except one person who thought it was ME!

Have you read Colin Middleton Murry's account of his childhood? Terrible and so sad in parts, but well written and moving. Middleton Murry has always worried me – a sort of saint without a *grain* of common sense and therefore has done a lot of harm. *Common sense* – oh how I *love* it, in Dr Johnson, Falstaff – Jane Austen and my husband (among others, of course!).

Just as I was shutting up this letter, the book actually arrived from America. It is *just* what I want and I shall be also very interested in the other chapters.

THANK YOU ONCE MORE.

K.M.

8 *July*   *Elm Park Gardens*

My dear K.M.,

Your letter dated *June 20* – got here *today*, and I write at once, this evening, to enquire how you are and to bring you my love and thoughts.* I'm so sorry you are having to go through this business. Bless you for writing – and for a lovely description of the gipsy girl and her kin who crept in through the window.

Did someone forget to post your letter, I wonder? You must have thought me *so* unfeeling. I'm NOT. I hope so much that you are experiencing the feelings I had so supportingly when I went through a horrid time with an eye and found it hard to pray, BUT at the same time I had the most marvellous knowledge that my spiritual identity, which is the only infinite one, was whole and untouched by the goings on. This has been a reality ever since and confirmed all my beliefs as *actuality*. Lovely. Do you know – have I said this to you before, I wonder? – I'm coming to the conclusion that my yardstick for what is real – (i.e. eternal) is measured by whether it is touchable – hearable – tactable – seeable, etc. If it *is* then it *ain't* 'real' in the sense I mean.

I did one of those St Mary-le-Bow dialogues with Joseph McCulloch just before Easter, and we discussed a quotation

* At this time I had to go into a hospital for a cancer operation.

265

he'd found that we both liked. This is: 'We have to accustom men's minds to the notion that it does not matter what the politicians do, does not matter even if our bishops seem to betray us, we belong to a spiritual kingdom complete in itself, owing nothing to wordly alliances.'

Can you guess who said this? It's twentieth-century and, I think, it's unexpected. It's Ronald Knox. We decided that this didn't mean we had to ignore the world, the opposite. We had to bring to bear on all problems the knowledge that we are essentially spiritual creations, of a spiritual kingdom, and what we did here must prove our awareness of absolute values.

My book is beginning to move, as it were, *long* before it's published. It seems there's a good deal of interest and orders are most encouraging. Macmillan are re-ordering before they begin to sell. Do *hope* they know what they are doing . . . I speak here and there nearer the time (September 16), and in late October I go with Reggie to South Africa and on to Australia, promoting as I go. Isn't it a glorious *excuse*! We longed to go out to Australia again and now I can pay for some of the trip as expenses. I'm to have a Foyle's luncheon and various other occasions. It's so *strange*.

I have just wriggled out of doing an ad for W. H. Smith and Son with a reference to my book . . . I saw what Marjorie Proops's ad was like in yesterday's paper and recoiled with horror . . . I was supposed to do the interview today and be photographed here, and I knew I *couldn't* do it. Oh the relief! Macmillan agreed with me when they saw the layout used for Marjorie Proops . . . and are apologetic for having urged me to do it. I was a fool to have accepted it in the first place. I've never advertised anything, and if I ever did it would have to be something I *truly* believed in.

Dear K.M., I meant to write earlier to tell you we'd had the holiday of a lifetime going on a two-week Swan's tour of Greece and Asia Minor at the height of the wild flower time – April 15–29th. Perfect timing. Flew to Athens, boarded the *Orpheus*, unpacked and settled in for two happy weeks. Four wonderful lecturers including Lord Wolfenden and Peter Fraser. Also Barry Cunliffe and Rev. Guy Pentreath.

And a botanist, young Christopher Brickell of Wisley. Oh, the *wonders* we saw! Ephesus – Patmos – Xanthos – Olympia – Delos. Mycaenae, Epidaurus (*not* in that order). On Rhodes tiny wild white cyclamen with pink noses in profusion on the mountain Prophet Elias. Also wild peony, cream with yellow centre and a red eye. Nineteen kinds of wild orchids and orphyrs, etc. It was energetic. Up at six, on the bus by eight and off to see the sites! Agreeable people on board. A *lovely* holiday. We were only at Aldeburgh for six days this year, but heard Ben Britten's new work for Janet Baker – lovely. Before that – in May – we had a week up in Cumberland – bluebell time but *no* pied flycatchers while we were there. Drought?

This great heat suits us – we both like to feel our spines uncurling in the warmth. But I hear on the radio tonight the spell is over. If only it will rain *hard* and then let the sun come again.

Dear K.M., be better. And *when you feel like it* please write and tell me how you are doing.

Reggie is away in South Africa for ten days. I don't like it when he isn't here, but a telex to his office says he had a good flight (yesterday) and finds it warm (mid-winter) but lonely in horrible Johannesburg.

My niece Sally is now twenty-two and working over here helping the remarkably courageous Erin Pizzey who runs the centre for battered wives in Chiswick. Sal is looking after and trying to get through to the adolescent sons of the poor wives. Most of them are already in trouble – drink, drugs, violence, pilfering, etc., fourteen-to-seventeen-year-olds.

I said to her: 'What is the end-product of your work?' She looked at me, pityingly: 'If it is possible to get *one* of them to realise that a real relationship *is* possible without sex or violence I think it's worth doing.' I was grateful for this. She is quite a girl. Dauntless. I couldn't *bear* it. Squeamish. But not Sally. I wish she was doing something a bit less alarming, and indeed sordid, but she is one of those people who are drawn to helping people who seem to be deprived. I also worry a little that in some ways it is a sort of opting out. I wonder what you think? Anyway I think she is *good* at what she's doing, so perhaps that's a good reason for doing it.

This brings you my love. Write soon.

Joyce   J.G.

My dear J.G.,

Many thanks for your letter – so full of encouragement, interest, discussable ideas, in fact as inspiring as your letters always are. Of course, I could never think you unfeeling – I thought either that you were away or that my dear daughter had forgotten to post my letter, or that in the general stress it had been wrongly addressed.

I am now blissfully at home again. The operation was successful, in that they were able to remove the *whole* growth, and there were no after complications. It was cancer, but at my age, and because it was compact and removable, there is a very good chance that I shall have no more trouble. I was three weeks at Orpington Hospital, during which time I had eighteen different nurses, and out of that number only *one* could be called unsympathetic or anything but kind. All the others, though varying in skill, were dedicated – though young student nurses, most of whom seemed to have wanted to nurse since they were babies – and extraordinarily nice girls. The patients were regular cockney types, all except my gipsy and one beautiful and sweet Irish girl. I got great interest, amusement and kindness from them. I wish you had been there to incorporate some of their remarks into a sketch. My next-door neighbour, a great platinum blonde, was extremely temperamental, either in tears *or* the nurses couldn't keep her in bed. She woke me one morning by swearing loudly: 'Gawd – my locker's covered with bloody ants'. She was swiping them all over the place, but suddenly stopped, and, looking at me seriously, said: 'But – you may know this – they are bloody hard-working clever little creatures.' She was full of surprises – a Barnardo child but now happily married; and she and her husband helped run a youth club. She wanted to 'set' my hair for me in tight pink rollers all over my head, but I escaped this by washing it myself while she was asleep. She was only one of many characters – nearly all brave and kind.

I rejoice in the certain success of your book, and in all the good it will do, for I am sure it cannot help but do good. I see I shall have to order my copy in advance. Hoorah! So glad you refused W. H. Smith!

What a lovely life you have – but I, too, have had sudden riches. I have been twice to Greece with my dear husband – both times in the fifties when there were few roads and few tourists. We travelled up to Delphi in a village bus – all friendly Greek peasants and on our first visit there were only two hotels. I think Delphi and *Mistra* were the most exciting places, but the island I long to revisit was Kos. I am now re-living all our lovely holidays. I kept full and illustrated diaries, and I used to read these aloud to my husband on winter evenings. We enjoyed doing this so much, and I haven't had the courage to read them alone till just now (four years after his death). Suddenly, I am able to do so, and to feel thankfulness instead of sadness.

Your niece Sally sounds a splendid person. No – I don't think it is opting out – in fact, quite the contrary. I expect with the idealism and *natural* intolerance of the young she feels 'her own kind' don't care enough – that *they* are opting out, in fact. My grandson is at present helping with his music in a Rudolf Steiner farm school for autistic and mongol children. He *loves* the children and has enough humour to appreciate and admire the staff, while amused at their serious intensity and fads.

My daughter is too tired. She has had the strain of my illness and Sophie (aged eleven) has glandular fever, and she has an unending supply of friends of all ages who sap her energy, agonises over her social work among gypsies and has her own design exhibition work (which is going fine, but is very demanding) so she is my chief worry, for I love her so much.

I must stop for your sake as well as mine. I have had a

marvellous and enormous number of letters and cards to cheer me, and I hate not saying 'thank you' to people – but your letter was too tempting not to answer quickly.

My love and gratitude as ever

K.M.

My dear J.G.,

I have been meaning to answer your last kind letter of July for some time, and now your face looking out at me from *The Times* this morning and the news of your book coming out next week thrills me into sending you a note of warm and *heartfelt* congratulations. I feel honoured to have been in at this book from the start so to speak. I know it will be an enormous and justifiable success, and I am longing to read it. I feel rather miserable about mine at the moment – my operation, etc., has disrupted it, and I can't seem properly to get back to it and long to finish it now, but have also got some awful lectures on *Henry IV* and *Merry Wives* to accompany some W.E.A. music lectures on Verdi, etc., to prepare for this autumn. I let myself in for these long ago, thinking they were too far off to happen.

I am distracted this morning at having lost an important business letter (involving other people) and have wasted nearly two hours looking for it. I never *was* orderly enough and get worse in old age. That is another reason why I am writing to you to remind myself that material things don't really matter, though when they affect others it is perhaps harder to make *them* believe this!

Seriously though, to revert to our former discussion about the soul and the body. I think basically we agree – I certainly agree that soul is spiritual identity. It is difficult now to remember the dark night of the soul that I experienced in the first week of my operation, but if it comes again in a similar circumstance when the body seems to take over and become the only reality I *think/hope* I shall be stronger to resist it and to wait patiently on the Lord.

I liked Sir Mortimer Wheeler, the other day on T.V. saying that *all* experience, even the worst, can be creative. This *does* fit in with my own conviction (the worst for me being bereavement of course, *not* physical pain). I am *so* much better after two weeks away – the last part on my beloved Sussex Downs.

In a village I saw this nice inscription on the wall of a house:

'In grateful affection for the life of our Doctor
Frederick Wallace Linton Bugle who died 1964
To heal sometime, to relieve often, to comfort always.'

I thought you would like this.

My daughter's Caxton and Printing Exhibition opened in Brussels last week, and is apparently a great success. The British Council received a special telegram of congratulations from Belgium, and this hasn't ever happened before. It goes on to Bruges – comes next March to Hatfield House. Perhaps you might like to see it there – it really is the history of printing, and is a very imaginative conception. I suggested as a title 'Mightier than the Sword', which I believe Hatfield are adopting. Jane is exhausted but happy about it. Meanwhile the grandchildren have been producing *The Beggars' Opera* and *so* enjoying it.

My thoughts and prayers are with the women of Ireland. I heard Mrs Betty Williams and Mrs Pat (?) (the Protestant leader) on the radio and was much moved. The trouble is today that a small minority of terrorists anywhere can wreak such havoc. I believe the *majority* of people are more tolerant and peace-loving and compassionate than they used to be, but modern technology (the car and the bomb) have put such power into the hands of the few.

Don't feel you've got to answer this. You will have masses of extra correspondence, interviews, etc., over your book – but so *many* good wishes and congratulations to you and gratitude for it and for everything; and love from

K.M.

My dear K.M.,

Lovely to get your letter. Thank you for your wishes for the book.

I write at Manchester Station before the train starts at 8.12 a.m. on my return from taping a 'Face the Music' last night. When I was up here a week ago I did a whole day's 'promotion' arranged by Macmillan – two radio and a press interview and an hour's talk to a 'Meet the Author' gathering organised by the local Booksellers' Association. In a local radio interview I met a rather uncertain man of Nordic appearance – Viking beard and blond hair to his shoulders, age uncertain too, who (*a*) hadn't done his homework and (*b*) was therefore aggressively out to win. I no longer react to such things and was blessedly undisturbed when he asked me what he prefaced with 'perhaps this is an awkward question': 'What makes you think you are important enough to write about yourself?' I said: 'I don't feel in the least *important*, but I've had an enjoyable life, and I'm very grateful for it, so I wanted to put it all down so I could read it.' And do you know, K.M., that is the actual truth. I said to my husband *ages* ago: 'Of *course* I hope someone *will* want to publish it, but the important thing is to get it all down, because I want to record it and enjoy looking back at it.' The inquisitor was a mite perplexed by this and gradually he stopped trying to goad, and we got on *all right*. Not a very adequate man, probably disappointed about not *really* being on top of his job. Anyway we parted amicably.

I do hope your book starts moving again, and I'm sure it will. It must be very frustrating not being able to get at it until you've cleared the decks of the lectures. I'm speaking ('talking' is a more accurate word) up and down the land until we leave for South Africa on October 20, and I'm hoping to get on to Volume two while I'm there – and maybe do a little in Australia, where we are to be for Christmas. It's a mixed visit, originally simply a social one, but now I'm to 'promote' as I go.

Today Macmillan give a small private luncheon for me

and Reggie; tomorrow is publication day, and I'm on Pete Murray's Radio 2 programme from 9.15, then I tape a few minutes for 'Kaleidoscope' tonight, and for the 'Today' programme on Friday, and at 12.30 I sign at Truslove and Harrison in Sloane Street. Whew! Friday is Oxford and Blackwell's with a lunch thrown in. A talk.

I hope the business letter turned up?

I love the inscription about Dr Bugle. Thank you.

And here, in return, is a quotation I can't verify in *The Oxford Book of Quotations*, but which I'm sure *is* somewhere. Emerson is supposed to have said: 'What you are speaks so loudly I can't hear what you say.' I find it *very* good. And it is another way of saying one must *demonstrate* what one believes, not just state it.

I hope I'll get to see Caxton when we get home in February. I'm so glad it's done so well in Brussels.

We're just off, and I know this line. It bucks like a bronco, so *fare thee well* – and love and hopes, from,

J.G.

For your information I'm also visiting Leeds, Birmingham, Glasgow, Norwich and Bristol, talking as I go!

4 December   *Riverside House*

My dear J.G.,

This is to bring you my very best wishes for Christmas and 1977 and my love. Thank you so much for your letter of October 18th. I hope you've had and are having a well-earned rest. I am lending your book to most appreciative friends. I am so glad Joseph McCulloch chose it as his 'book of the year'. More and more do I think people are grateful for hope and generosity and charity which your book is suffused with. I am not without hope that quite a new sort of force is beginning to get going – perhaps we can do without so much politics in future. I think of the Women's Peace Movement, for instance. People think it a failure *unless* it goes on to political pressure and power, but it works through individuals. Nothing can destroy the way it has bridged hitherto unbridgeable divisions, nor the influence it may have on the children of all its members. I went off to march with them to Trafalgar Square last Saturday, but, alas! alas! I fell on a curb before I got there, and bruised my shin so badly that I had ignominiously to go home! It is still painful, and I can only crawl about with a stick – all the more infuriating as my family is going through a bad patch of illness just now. My daughter has had to give up a good commission and is struggling to fulfil commitments. My younger granddaughter is still having unexplained temperatures – probably still glandular fever after six months – and has had very little school this term. This doesn't matter in one way, as she is a clever child, but is frustrating and a great bind. I have her here when she is well enough to come.

I am sure you will be very sad about Britten, but what a gloriously fulfilled life.

I have enjoyed giving my Shakespeare and music lectures, and they seem surprisingly to have been so much appreciated that I have thoughts of doing some private ones (on either the relevance of Shakespeare today or seventeenth-century literature, and/or Milton, or the Romantics from Cowper to Keats) for a group of about ten and having a collection each time for Amnesty International or some other cause. I feel so useless otherwise without a car, and with rather diminished energy this year (eighty in one and a half years). But I can still make people like what I like. I don't mind blowing my own trumpet to you because yours is such a much bigger trumpet – if you understand.

Yes – I had a lovely two days in Bruges and the Exhibition was a great success.

Oh dear – there is so much to say, and my paper is giving out. *How* I agree with you about class warfare – one of the worst things rampant today. Yes – I loved the portraits of your parents. I think your niece is splendid. I *couldn't* have done that job at her age or ever. I did work for poor boys and mums in Lambeth in 1921, but they were so different – depressed not violent. I found the Reith Lectures very interesting now they have got specialised – I did not like the first generalised old-fashioned mechanistic one. I am so enjoying 'Face the Music' again, but it is getting more difficult. Last week I only scored three, am still stuck on my last chapter – ordination of women, nature of God, etc., etc. I am out of my depth, but I do think we ought to stop thinking of God as a Male or a King. Love and all good wishes. Please live a long time and write a lot more books.

K.M.

1977

My dear K.M.,

I enclose one of 300 cards I've been forced to use, because there was such a huge pile of letters when I got back earlier in the month. And now I have got a space to write to you as I wish to. Your letter of December 4 came safely and was much appreciated. You had fallen and hurt your leg. Is it well again? I do hope it is.

Yes, Ben Britten's death is a continuing sadness, but what wonders he has left for us to go on enjoying!

It is good that you enjoyed giving your lectures. Are you still doing them, I wonder? And have you finished the book?

Yes, it's high time we stopped thinking of God as He or She or It. For me God is the power of all Good, all Love, all Life and all Truth. The Divine Principle of all that is real in the spiritual sense.

I'm sorry this is so brief, and so ill-written. It brings you my love and interest and wishes for the rest of 1977.

Macmillan are bringing out six Nursery School Teacher sketches I've performed and recorded down the years as a Christmas book with decorations by John Ward, *George – Don't do that*. I am starting to work on the second book of memoirs – slowly. Please let me know how you are.

With love,

J.G.

I'm reading my first book on 'Woman's Hour' – starting April 10. I tape it in March.

My dear J.G.,

It was good to get your note to say you were safely back in England. I do take it kindly of you that with such a pile of mail to contend with you spared the time to write to me. I meant to have written earlier in answer, but have been very busy lately, and I find energy depleted by such nuisances as my broken leg-bone (not quite right yet), 'flu, operation's delayed effects and, I suppose, age, as I shall be in my eightieth year next month. But I have very much enjoyed lecturing (especially to a most intelligent group of VIth formers), leading a study group in connection with our Quaker meeting, my music appreciation classes (we have been doing French music this term) and a certain amount of grandmothering and entertaining.

It is good news that you have begun on your second volume. My book, now finished, is being considered by my publishers. I am afraid it falls between two stools, being neither popular enough to please widely and not scholarly enough for the University Press. My publishers say it all depends on whether they can sell it in the United States. I am waiting for the verdict rather unhopefully, but shall try elsewhere if they fail me.

I have begun a children's book, but have got out of the way of purely imaginative writing and find it difficult. It needs more concentrated slabs of time than easily come my way now. However I shall plod on.

It will be lovely to hear you reading your book on 'Woman's Hour'. I must train myself to keep *awake* for it. I am furious at so often dropping off just now when I *really* want to hear Gabriel Woolf reading Thomas Mann!

Next week I am going to Oxford for four days, then I shall have the St Matthew Passion Sunday at the Festival Hall with my grandson and then I am having a week's holiday with a friend at Ross-on-Wye and the Kilvert country, so there is plenty to look forward to.

I am hoping to read Hans Kung's book, *On Being a Christian*, soon. The 'Anno Domini' interviews have been so good and stimulating this winter.

There are two kingfishers about our stream and charms of goldfinches and flocks of siskins.

Much love

K.M.

10 April   *Written in Hertfordshire*

My dear K.M.,

I see it's over a month since you wrote me that good letter and sent me the family card – *much* enjoyed. Thank you. Very pleasing.

I hope by now that your leg is mending more quickly and the flu is well over, etc., etc. It is being a very long winter . . . Iced roofs here today: pretty, but not cosy to the nose. *Freezing* hard. In fact I've been lazy and stayed put ever since we got here on Thursday night. Very nice, too. I wonder if the Hatfield exhibition will be open in May, as we have a plan to try and go there around the 16–18th? It is idiotic to be so busy as we *all* are, isn't it. Retirement? Ha, ha.

I have taped excerpts (curt and brief) of *Joyce Grenfell Requests the Pleasure* for 'Woman's Hour' and every day at 2.30 from Tuesday next, 12th, you can hear it for three weeks! I am also at the moment taping the complete text for the Royal National Institute for the Blind taped library. Arduous but worth doing.

My niece Sally is still working at Chiswick, but I'm glad to say her social life has developed somewhat. She dances with a group at a studio – 'modern dance' *à la* Martha Graham – three nights a week. Goes out a *lot* more, which we are glad about. No idea who her friends are; that is her business, but she *is* happier, prettier, plumper and more fulfilled.

I do hope your last book is making progress with a publisher. A children's book is a *good* idea, and I've always wished I could write one. All wishes for that too.

I saw many of the 'Anno Domini' programmes and thought them *useful* and nourishing – particularly a little red-headed Irish Jesuit (I think) in Japan talking about meditation, and making it clear that there are two kinds – the mental gymnastics, and the spiritual, consciousness of oneness with God. I *loved* him for being so direct and so *spiritually* aware. So often the 'holy' talks on air or T.V. seem to be devoid of *any* spiritual nourishment – or awareness. I sometimes wonder if the department at the B.B.C. really believes in God as all Good, as Life, Truth and Love? I mean to try and write about this, perhaps in my volume two.

Have I told you of my proposed title of the second book, from a Psalm I very much like: 'The lines are fallen unto me *In Pleasant Places*.' As there is to be a good deal of travelling in volume two this is apt – endless tours to the United States, Canada, Australia, New Zealand and frequent visits to South Africa.

I'm writing this in bed, electric blanket on, and I've just seen the time. As I am the cook I must hurriedly finish this very scrawly note that brings you affectionate Easter greetings and continued interest in your doings. Forgive its untidiness, and I only hope you can decipher it. My hand gets worse and worse. Yours remains a delight to see.

I hope the visits to Oxford and Ross-on-Wye were refreshing and enjoyable.

With love and thanks and wishes.

J.G.

It looks as if the first book will be done in America this autumn. A paperback, Futura company, comes out here.

18 April   *Riverside House*

My dear J.G.,
I feel like answering your letter at once but in instalments. Sometimes it is good to respond on the rebound, and also tomorrow (arriving for breakfast) I have my adopted grandson, wife and little son from Wales for a visit, and then almost immediately an old very dear blind friend from

Oxford, so it looks as though this may be my last quiet evening for some time. But I shan't post it till next week, because that might be a bit daunting for you just when you thought you'd polished me off for a decent period. I never get over your *goodness* as a pen friend.

I am glad you were keeping snug and warm when you wrote. It *was* cold over Easter, but I always love the festival. The St Matthew at the Festival Hall with my grandson was as good as ever – better in fact than last year, when I was feeling ill, and I had a lovely week in Herefordshire between that and Easter and a *warming* four days at Oxford. The wild daffodils in Herefordshire were at their best, and I *did* enjoy the churches and abbey we saw, and the beautiful heart-rending Kilvert country. We had one night at Malmesbury, where I had stayed with my husband about forty years ago, and I had a room looking directly out on to a glorious Early English window of the Abbey – floodlit with stars above. I was so excited I had to keep getting out of bed to look at it, and the Norman clerestory in the moonlight.

I *do* like listening to you reading your book and am thrilled at the thought of the second volume. I like its title. You are lucky to be able to dictate your title. It is very annoying to have one imposed upon you as Heinemann imposed *Cordial Relations* on my 'Aunts' book. Also Jane wanted to call her Exhibition 'Mightier than the Sword' but 'they' chose instead the rather affected title of 'Goodlie Printing'. I enclose a poster giving particulars and am *so* pleased that you will be able to go in May. I wish you could have seen it at Bruges.

Yes – I liked the little Jesuit from Japan *particularly* – especially the way he included the Buddhist practitioners of meditation in his friendly exposition. I am so very glad that you mean to write about 'God as Life, Truth and Love' in your book. I feel it would be much appreciated and perhaps do a great deal of good if you gave up some space in this second volume to what your letters to me have so often expressed and which has certainly helped me.

I have almost finished Hans Kung's monumental work *On Being a Christian*. It is a good clear overall account with which I mostly agree, and parts – especially upon St Paul – I found enlightening. Though a Catholic, he seems quite happily to dispense with the Virgin Birth, Mariology, the Apostolic Succession (in its accepted form) the Pope and even the priesthood.

Being a German, he can't put things concisely, but, on the whole, he is easy to read. He is good on bringing home to one the astounding originality and power of Jesus. I am glad to have read it, though I should much like to ask him about certain lines of thought.

Tuesday 19th. My first batch of visitors have come and gone, and all went very well – though I got a bit exhausted the first day when both parents went solidly to sleep from tea till supper and Nicholas (aged five) was very far from asleep. But one gets one's second wind, and being woken with 'Granny may I look at your scar?' seemed very right and proper. Actually I am his *great* granny to both our pride (or should it be prides?).

Now I am waiting for my blind friend to arrive. That visit will be very peaceful.

I have not yet heard about my book. I am planning to give a course of private lectures in my house once a week in June and July on seventeeth-century literature – charging 50 pence per person per lecture in aid of Amnesty International. The idea seems popular among our music group (which doesn't meet in the summer). I am terrified inwardly but outwardly bold and calm. But I may have told you this before.

Must stop and get going on house.

Love and thanks always,

K.M.

18 May   *In Hertfordshire for three days*

My dear K.M.,

Retirement? If that's what has happened to me, I know it is not a season of idleness. It is all this talking that takes so much time to prepare. Last week I did two, very different, and both exercised me for *hours* beforehand. The first was an informal lunchtime talk to the Six Point Group, founded by Lady Rhondda in 1921 to further the cause of women's rights. No bra-burning or Ms. type of aggression, but a quiet steady pursuit of the law and the moral rights due to us. About thirty of us sat around in a pretty upstairs drawing-room at the University Women's Club in Audley Square, and after a very good 'cold plate' I did a very little talk which had not got a title, but was about 'privilege' and discoveries of what that really means; about my experiences talking to students about ethics and values; about my job as performer, etc., etc. It was lighter than this may lead you to expect. They were very friendly, and it went off all right. But the second occasion was the most demanding I've ever had, and when I counted up the time that had gone to prepare it the sum was *fourteen hours* for a fifteen-minute address. The Dean of Westminster, Edward Carpenter, rang to ask me if I would attend an *ecumenical* service of thanksgiving for the Queen's Silver Jubilee, for Old Age Pensioners of the diocese, for *Westminster Abbey* – and 'encourage us', he said, 'by giving the address'. So last Friday Reggie and I went to the Abbey on a cold sunny (briefly, but for as long as we were there) afternoon, sat in the Quire (as I'm pleased to see it is spelt), and when the moment came a verger collected me from my Quire stall and I had to walk a long way up those shallow steps we have seen so often on T.V. in ceremonies at the Abbey, turn left and climb up to a tall pulpit. I was advised not to wear a hat because of the necklace-microphone. I put it on, heard the last of the anthem filling that superb building, looked up at the cleaned, almost white, fan-vaulting, put up a small prayer for God to be in my mouth, and I spoke. I began by saying that the talk had no title, but if it had it would be: 'You can only discover that which is already present.' It was about discovering that which is good – and therefore, real, true. That every time is a first time, 'New Every Morning' and it is never too late for discovering delight and WONDER. There were stories and illustrations, and I ended by saying

282

why I was wholeheartedly able to rejoice in the Jubilee, because we have as Head of State someone who is what she appears to be – dedicated, straightforward, un-selfed. Not a 'public image', but a private person publicly revealed. Six hundred believers sat with faces turned up, and were very responsive. Tea in the cloisters with R.W.V.S. ladies to serve us. A nice occasion, particularly when so many of totally different faiths all said: 'You said *just* what I believe!' So there *is* only One Cause! I was glad I'd worked so hard over the little piece, because it was possible to trust in the work (and the prayer) and let it happen. And it did.

Thank you for your very good letter, undated, but you put 'April?' oh, later on I see you put 'April 19th'. I have every intention of going to Hatfield – not sure *when* – and I will go on speaking about the exhibition.

More later. We're going to look at a bluebell wood while it isn't actually raining. *What* a spring! Brrrr!

19th May. The woods here are *full* of bluebells, bluer than ever, thicker than usual. Breathtaking sight. And all the new leaves on the beech, oak and chestnut are still damp as they uncrumple. Glorious time of renewal and symbol of eternity, for which thank God.

Now we're off to London by 9 a.m., and a day of home chores and the making of chicken salad to give John and Patricia Casson (Sybil's son), and I stay home to wash it all up while Reggie takes them to see Donald Sinden in *Lear*. I can't *bear* to see the play again ever. It is so agonising, and all the hate in it of Goneril, Regan and Gloucester's eyes . . . No. I don't feel I ever need to endure that again. Freedom. And *Heartbreak House* on television.

Thank goodness we are going to refuse entry to Amin – or so it *seems*.

This is a disjointed letter, but it brings affection and interest and hopes for your book. I've done a chapter of my volume two while I've been here. The first one goes *on* and on in an astonishing way – I 'signed' at Liberty's last week – *180* in one and a half hours. It makes no sense, but there is so much *friendliness* attached to the whole thing. I feel entirely un-responsible for the book – someone else *must* have done it.

Love,

J.G.

My dear J.G.,

Your last and unanswered letter was in May. Time goes so swiftly, his winged chariot runs faster and faster, although the days are not so full when old age draws almost imperceptibly on and on. But I have been busy for the last six weeks giving a course of lectures locally on seventeenth-century literature, which I suddenly felt moved to try out in answer to a request. I have been loyally supported, and was able to send quite a nice fat cheque to Amnesty International, as I had a collection on each week. I think people enjoyed it, and although it is now a bit of a strain, I loved having to *live* with the great writers of that period every day so to speak.

Your last letter described so vividly your wonderful experience in Westminster Abbey. How I should like to have been there! I enjoyed the Jubilee. We made much of it in our village with three different street parties and a fête and prizes for the best decorated house, inn, etc. My granddaughter made me a lovely golden Lion and silver Unicorn and bronze crown to go over my porch. The Unicorn now decorates my bathroom. At the fête we had thundershowers – the first one, which sent us all to the sheltering trees, was greeted immediately by an announcement through the megaphone: 'The rain is free, we charge extra for the thunder' – which I thought so very English.

Alas, the British Council have *now* no spare funds for the arts, and it is difficult to get sponsors for creative work in any direction. But I am glad to say my book on Women and Christianity has been accepted, though it won't be out before the spring.

I have written all this without talking about what is

uppermost in my thoughts just now. An appalling tragedy has happened to the dear daughter of a family I know who lived at Shoreham till fairly recently and then moved to Otford – the next village. She was going to spend a month in France and went off last week and never arrived, but her body was found in a wood near Paris. She was eighteen and comes from a very happy and devoted family with two other daughters. They were all children together with my grandchildren in Shoreham. It is just thirty years last week since my son was drowned, and I know how it changed life and how the morning I heard of it will always be with me, and this is worse. I cling to that bit from Romans – 'For I am persuaded that neither death nor life, nor angels, nor principalities, nor powers, nor things present nor things to come, nor height nor depth, nor any other creature, shall be able to separate us from the love of God.' This family *do* have faith and they have love, but the suffering in this world is hard to bear.

Our Katie has been to and fro to Paris by herself several times, and next week Daniel is going to Belfast to stay with a college friend but I tell my daughter that this life is given to us on terms of absolute *physical* insecurity, and we have to accept that. I am sure that one day we shall see the pattern, though now we see through a glass so darkly. I find St Paul more and more satisfying.

Must stop. Blessing on you and love

K.M.

4 *August*   *Cumbria*

My dear K.M.,

Heavens! I see your good letter is dated July 16th . . . So sorry. And now we are at the end of a brief visit to our favourite 'pleasant place', Loweswater, five miles from Cockermouth. It has been a very crowded summer, and we've been to South Wales – Pembrokeshire – and to Norfolk, Northumberland, and now lovely Cumbria. (I dislike all the new boundary names such as Humberside and Avon, but Cumbria is all right. Do you agree? *The Times* has had some correspondence about Yorkshiremen resisting Humberside and other ridiculous names for *Yorkshire*.)

I still resolutely refuse to use the postal code unless forced to by letters that don't give the proper *place* name and make do with those foolish mixtures of XYZ and 123. Ugh!

So glad about your lectures. I wish I might have heard them. Lucky locals.

I'm sorry to say we have never managed to get to Hatfield for the Printing Exhibition, and now I doubt if we shall because we go to America on September 6–October 21, and in between then and now a lot of things are happening, including the making of a double L.P. gramophone record of many of the songs and monologues I have never before put on tape. This means hard work. I practise daily and the voice is *there*, but it needs lubricating and using. Poor Reggie has to endure me singing in the car, because I don't feel I can sing *out* in a hotel room. Nor could I in friends' houses unless they were out. So I'm sorry to have missed the exhibition.

How good about your book! I'm looking forward to that in the spring. (My *George – Don't do that*, six of the Nursery School sketches and one extra called 'Writer of Children's Books' – is out on September 1. The cover has a very plain portrait of this writer! My ma would have hated it – but it is instantly recognisable. Otherwise the book is well presented although I've found two misprints.) Talking of misprints – do you share my joy in them when they are funny? Do you know the one about the funeral of one of the Sally Anny Booths – 'When the hearse drew up at Victoria and the coffin was carried to the train a large crow sang "Abide with Me" '. And I've just been shown one in a lush romantic 'historical' novel about Byron, no less, that reads: 'He looked at her with passion, and put his arm around her wasit.'

Of course, I read of the appalling tragedy that happened to your family of friends from Shoreham. *Ghastly*. How does one cope? I suppose, believing as I do that the spiritual

286

is *never* invaded, I do get consolation in this continuing truth. But all the attendant horror that has been endured is very hard to think about. Such terrible earthly blows are very very hard to cope with. My brother's young son was drowned in a sudden squally storm in Lake Erie about eighteen years ago, and *distantly* I shared in the feeling of horror and loss – when it is your *own* child . . . *Heaven* help you! And does no doubt.

I, too, love that bit in Romans, and I *know* it is true. When I had 'my problem' the glorious realisation that nothing fundamental had changed – that line 'I', the spiritual identity, was invulnerable and whole – gave me the most marvellous support. The continuity of all good is the *fact*. There is no such thing as 'Safe as Houses', but there is the certainty of spiritual continuity that is our actual being *now*.

Thank you for writing as you did. Bless you. This little job/and holiday trip has been so pleasant. We left London on July 26 for three days in Norfolk in an absolutely quiet corner three miles from Cromer, from which I went into King's Lynn to speak at the Literary Lunch of the music festival. Wild flowers wreathing the ditches in a profusion never before seen. Every kind of white, cream and lime umbelliferae, cranesbill, scabious, poppy, rose bay willowherb, chicory, knapweed and varieties of labiates and yellow coltsfoot type of thing. I'm told it is the result of economic cuts in council spending on scything. Hooray! Though I also hear that unless scything happens much of the time only the tough weeds survive and choke the rest. So we must hope for occasional economies resulting in a garden-like countryside. Really lovely – and *everywhere*. On the 29th we headed north and paused to 'pick our own strawberries' as we approached Alnwick. Four pounds to take to Reggie's cousin Molly Howick, who had two daughters and six grandchildren in the house. On the 30th I opened the Lifeboat Fête in the tiny harbour village of Craster on the north-east coast. (Kippers come from Craster.) I was stood on the roof of the shed in which the local inflatable rescue dinghy run by the R.N.L.I. is housed, and because we were overpunctual, and the lady running the occasion felt we must wait for the hour of two to strike before I 'opened' I decided we'd better sing, and so sing we all did. A large crowd of summery visitors in bright-coloured clothes, lots of childrem, all joined me, songs like 'Blaydon Races' (local), 'Little Sir Echo', 'Rosie O'Dea', 'The More we are Together' and 'Daisy, Daisy'. Then it was time to speak. After which I tottered down a perilous ladder in highish heels and over rough paths down to the harbour, went down another ladder on to the big Lifeboat borrowed from Seahouses next door, and went for a little trip out on to the glassy North Sea. An Air-Sea Rescue helicopter arrived to demonstrate the lowering of an airman on a rope to the stern of our boat – flew away – and returned to take him off again, and did the whole thing twice while we clutched our heads and were *nearly* blown away by the 'chopper's' wings that raised a whirling wind. It was a very dear, if arduous occasion. I made £16.50 in signing autographs at ten pence a throw for the Lifeboat Fund! Over an hour at a trestle-table. 'And what is your name?' 'Tracy – Stewart – Carolyne – Terry – Debby.' Names of our period!

And then on August 1 we crossed England *via* the wall and *en route* I began to judge the five finalists in the Best-Kept-Small-Village in Cumbria. You have to look at the state of the grass verges, telephone-boxes, litter bins; read the church and village notices – are they up to date? Are the church flowers fresh? Are there amenities such as benches at bus-stops or on the green? Play facilities for children? Is the village hall, school, pub well kept? Etc., etc. A little imagination helps a village, and we found a bird-box on a tree in a churchyard, a double-seater 'rustic' bench cut out of the root of a tree, among other items. Where there was a beck we had to see if it was free of old cans and bottles and plastic. Two out of five had becks, and both were *well* kept. It was a demanding job, and took two long days of inspecting in which we saw a lot of *lovely* Cumbria in lovely hot sunshine. Alas, today all is lost in mist and gales. We head for home tomorrow.

I'm making a little progress with volume two, but it must

now wait for 1978 when I plan to refuse *all* other engagements.

With love and thanks for writing. I love your letters.

J.G.

My dear J.G.,

I have left your last long letter unanswered so long, and if I don't write now Christmas will be upon us. I was very sorry you couldn't get to the Caxton Exhibition, but do understand how your time gets filled up. You sound as though you've had a good and fulfilling summer. I have only been away for short trips with friends and relations this year, on one of which lately to Norfolk, on looking too interestedly at some ruins, I tripped over a concealed step and banged, but not I am thankful to say, fractured, my knee. However, it was pretty disabling for a month and isn't really its normal self yet. It was the other leg from the bone I broke last year, and my granddaughter remarked, 'Thank goodness you haven't got a third leg, Granny.'

I am so enjoying having you read aloud to me every morning. What a good beginning to the day! It has set my own memories going, especially to the evening I first saw Kangchenjunga at Darjeeling. We had arrived the day before, and for twenty-four hours no sign of a mountain. Then my husband was laid low with Himalayan tummy, and I went for a walk alone. Suddenly the mist lifted, but only from the heights, the foothills were still obscured, and I saw far above what my senses took in as possible, this glorious range. No wonder people worship it – like you, I shall never forget the sight.

This morning you read about your German treasure of a housekeeper. I don't know whether I have ever mentioned my Christal. She came to me from Germany twenty-five years ago on her eighteenth birthday to help look after my little d.p. boy of two whom we had taken in, in memory of my son. I was then teaching and needed extra help. We were put in touch with her through an exchange schoolmistress.

She had an English grandfather and had longed to come to England for a year to learn the language. After the year she went home, but then asked to come back to us – eventually married a local builder – lived at the top of our house in Sevenoaks, and when we moved to Shoreham found a cottage here. They had one daughter who is now married.

This year we celebrated our jubilee together – it was just before the Queen's. I took Christal up to London, and we had the good fortune to see quite by chance a bit of rehearsal going on in the Park – the Queen's trumpeters, carriages and all.

Then we took a taxi to my club for lunch. We had hardly got seated when the driver turned round in his seat. 'What do you think of devaluation?' he shot at me. But before I could collect my thoughts he began to tell me his: 'I don't blame them – this country's done for . . .' And it was *all* due to the Blacks.

After a little I felt I must say something, which I did.

'You don't know what you are talking about, madam.'

I said: 'Well, fifty years ago I was working in the East End, and I can tell you things weren't all that rosy there then, though there wasn't a coloured problem, and so I might as well say, *you* don't know what you're talking about.'

And so it went on – Christal by my side in a panic all the while, as our driver was much more interested in the argument than the traffic.

In the middle of it I said, 'Are you a Christian?'

I know this sounds offensive, perhaps, but it was not meant or taken as such, and he said '*What?*'

I said, 'I just want to know.'

He said, after a pause for thought, 'Well, if being a Christian means putting other people before my family and my country I'm not one – but don't get me wrong, I wouldn't hurt a fly.'

I said, 'You might have to.'

But from then on he seemed a bit on the defensive, and when we got out and I was paying him I couldn't help saying, 'Look here, I'm an old woman, but I just want to say one more thing: Do try to think of black and brown people as *human beings* like yourself, and not as "them".'

And he leant towards me with a very sweet smile, and said, 'God bless you, madam.'

I've run on as if I were talking to you, but I thought you might like this story, though it began by telling you how lucky I've been, as well as you, and still am, with the dearest and kindest person to help me all these years. In fact I've *always* been lucky, because before that I had a wonderful Yorkshire farmer's daughter (who was descended from Sir Isaac Newton). She is still living near Oxford, now in her nineties, and I hear from her regularly.

Enough of my reminiscence – but I can't find your last letter – I usually keep them all together, and I can't remember it in detail, only that things seemed to be going well with you and you'd had a lovely time up in the north.

I'm pressing on with my children's story, though finding purely imaginative work difficult and much harder to fit into short periods. One wants to get warmed up to it, and then the phone goes or someone calls – not that I'm not grateful for human contact. When a marriage like ours is finished in this life, I find loneliness has to be fought with deliberate campaigns, or it is overwhelming – it is the close effortless *sharing* of life which is so irreplaceable, and a sense of pointlessness is always lurking in the background. This is in strict confidence – it is the advantage of having a pen friend whom one has never met and never means to meet – it is rather like a confessor. The funny thing is this loss doesn't get better, even after five years. I can say this to you because of your happy marriage, as I think you will understand. It is *not* a moan. I know I am privileged beyond measure to have had such a marriage.

Much love

K.M.

P.S. I am going to some good lectures on mysticism, such a sincere, intelligent keen *young* lecturer. It is heartening to find he teaches Religious Knowledge in a huge comprehensive.

P.P.S. The book is supposed to be coming out next spring. I don't much care for it. Great discussion as to title. I favour *She for God, Some Aspects of Women and Christianity*. Do you think that a good title? I would be grateful for comment or any other suggestion. But, oh, *don't* think you have to write. I always look on your letters as miracles, and I can't even remember whether you are in England or not. I'm very troubled about South Africa, and would also like to hear your thoughts about this. It seems so suicidal. I am also troubled about the growth of the National Front. Forgive the scrawl and general mess!

I hobbled round the Somerset House Exhibition of Thames pictures and *did* enjoy them.

28 October   *Exeter*

My dear K.M.,

Lovely to get your letter, and I loved hearing about your view of Kangchenjunga, about Christal, the taxi-driver (a particularly pleasing tale) and I'm honoured when you feel free to tell me of your loneliness. But as you say – after such a wonderful relationship one is simply not *used* to being on one's own; it doesn't diminish the joy or the appreciation of the actual good times. It *can't*. They are *real*, therefore true, therefore eternal. I'm glad you are going on with the children's book. What is it about? What age group?

I like *She for God* very much. (Do you know the anecdote about the man who died and came back to earth and was asked what God was like. He said, 'Well, to start with she's black.') It is the father-mother-God feeling I *best* like, and we need reminding of the 'She' inclusion. So I like your title – concise – eye-catching and *honest*.

I, too, feel so sad about South Africa and alarmed by the National Front. We as a nation have a feeling for order *and* freedom, don't you think, and if we aren't *led* to it, or don't find it for ourselves, we mistakenly take poor substitutes such as Fascism that *look* like order on the surface, and are really nothing but repression, fear-motivated. Horrifying.

I'm tortured by the realisation that South Africa is the only bulwark against communism in the continent of Africa, and that is the real issue. No one dares spell it out, but that is what it is about. Vorster is ham-fisted, a Boer, and he sees no alternative to his methods. What are the alternatives? Christianity, first and foremost, but what else – how else? It is the most complex situation. No easy answers. And how much *time*?

I'm in Exeter for the paperback of my book, and the publication of *George – Don't do that*. Plymouth for T.V. interview yesterday and a dinner (Booksellers Association) here last night.

30 October   *London*

Now I'm home again after a pleasant visit to the West Countree and a mammoth signing session in Blakey's Bookshop. I was hard at it for one hour and twenty minutes, and then they had to close the queue because I had to catch a train back . . . The whole strange phenomenon of bookselling – or marketing, as I'm called on to do it – is evidently successful. I realise that being an entertainer is a decided help. The face is familiar, and people respond to laughter. Even so I nearly fell down when Futura, who are doing the paperback of my *Joyce Grenfell Requests the Pleasure* told me on Friday that, since October 7 when it came out, it has sold over 100,000 copies, mostly in supermarkets. Isn't it crazy?

Yesterday we went to see the American actress Julie Harris do a one-woman performance as Emily Dickinson, and it was *so* good. Emily must have been a crackpot, wearing white as a sort of image-concept, never leaving the house, but she was also a poet, a real one. The 'play' is beautifully wrought and directed, and the lighting evocative and helpful to the changing moods. It is impossible to describe the way the whole thing works, but work it did for me. I was wholly engaged and convinced and touched. I felt Emily Dickinson must have been tiresome to live with, but being a dutiful New England Protestant and spinster, she was disciplined, if eccentric, and her inner life must have been boiling a great deal. I somehow equate her with Emily Brontë. I believe you would have enjoyed the performance. It was taut and springy at the same time – thought through to the very edge. And Julie Harris who is slight and still has a young figure (probably is about fifty-five) moves freely like a girl. And I suspect Emily Dickinson was always a 'girl', part of her slight craziness.

The American trip was lovely. I'd been a bit 'off' America in the last visits – New York is so *difficult*, distances are so vast, the melting-pot feeling is heavy, and one sees so few contented faces there. But I did try to see with a new eye and feel with my heart, and, of course, it worked. (I still don't like New York, but staying with a generous friend in a beautiful fifteenth floor flat in quiet with a terrace, trees and birds, was a help.) And then we had happy visits to my brother and his wife. The talking tour for the English-Speaking Union went *very* well. I have accidentally found a new art-form – after-dinner speaking (talking, in my case) at a reading-desk with illustrations from my repertoire to illustrate. I don't step aside and perform – I do it (quotations from the monologues) from a standing position, so I'm really telling *about* the characters and then turning into them. It called on a good deal from the audience in the way of imagination, and it *worked*. About forty-five minutes long – or sometimes a little more. We went to Washington, Philadelphia, Charlottesville – Nashville and Memphis, both in Tennessee, Louisville, Kentucky and Houston, Texas, and lastly to Ashville, North Carolina, only forty miles from Tryon, where my Ma lived and died, and where we have many friends. Reggie enjoyed it all, as I did. So *many* kind people and really generous with their time, and though not many were really on our wavelength, it was fun to see American in this way. Louisville was the high-spot because we knew our hosts and like them very much, and had an extra day with them in which they took us to see a restored Shaker village a hundred miles south of Louisville in country very like Yorkshire. Kentucky has charm and robustness, and we felt there was a good deal to recommend

Louisville. Its theatre is lively – a rep that sells seventy-five per cent of its seats *before* production, and *innovates* plays from unknown American writers. Has an orchestra. Lively-minded people came to the English-Speaking Union evening, not just the country-club set as we found it in the deeper South.

Finally a week more on Long Island at Southampton with my brother, cosy, quiet and restoring and then three days of promoting the U.S. hardback of the book in New York City – T.V., radio and interviews. I don't know how it is progressing over there. It seemed a bit vague compared to the way Macmillan work over here. I'm constantly discovering how much slower and less efficient are most U.S. businesses . . .! A lot of apparent action, but too much red tape and interdepartmental carry on.

The desire to please is attractive (as in Ireland) but somehow it isn't enough. But I enjoyed America more this time – in general. And it is *very* beautiful. You may have Houston – flat and green and lush and hot – and RICH – a sprawling town going on for ever. We had a morning's birding down on the Gulf where there are marshes in among industrial sprawl, and we saw roseate spoonbills among other lovely things. But it was the orderly beauty and craftsmanship of Pleasant Hill Shaker settlement that called to me. In the main house, pale Cotswold stone-built in severe Georgian manner, there are two spiral staircases of intense beauty rising up like song, in finely constructed wood, to the third floor. A strange cult – celibate, narrow, bigoted and fierce – but it certainly produced superb craftsmanship, simplicity of design and fully functional. The dumb waiter was invented by the Shakers.

Now I'm up to my eyebrows in reading submissions for Travelling Fellowships under the Churchill Memorial Trust auspices. This year it is craftsmen and women. So far over five hundred applications. I read them all with *care* three times. First time round I make three piles: C, no good; B, possible; A, likely. Then I go through A and B again, and just in case I've missed something in C, I do that lot too. Now I've reduced the first batch of about four hundred into 'possible' and put them under their own categories – silver, glass, leather, weaving, embroidery, metal, wood and potters. Far too many potters and ceramics. It isn't always easy to decide if some submissions really are right for the category of craftsmen. I'm sending my first selections to a fellow council-member for his views, and later we try to make a short list of twenty-four to be interviewed for ten places. Whew! The arts category is always the biggest one. Last time I chaired it we had over five hundred for Teaching on the Air.

I've gone on far too long. All this 'Churchilling' is keeping me busy for the next three weeks, and then there are still 'book' dates to be accomplished, but in 1978 apart from selection board for the fellowships and *Yorkshire Post* Literary lunch in Leeds for best-sellers (ha-ha), I am resolutely going to cut out all else and get on with volume two. I *hope*. And I wish you *very* well with your book and the children's story and all else you are doing.

It was such fun seeing Reggie's success in America. He was the beau of the ball, and enjoyed it so modestly.

With love and wishes and thoughts.

J.G.

1 December   *Riverside House*

My dear J.G.,

I hope you won't mind a rather early Christmas card, but, as I wanted both to answer your last most welcome long letter and to make a special request, and also, as I feel you must get so very many cards and I should therefore like mine to arrive before the multitude, I am sending it now.

You are quite right – no amount of loneliness diminishes joy which one has known, and it is extraordinary how joy and grief can exist together. It is not that I mind being alone, and I am still blessed by so many precious and interesting relationships – it is the continuous *sharing* one misses – though perhaps one does still share in a deeper sense. Another thing to be grateful for is that sometimes experience of sorrow makes it possible to be of a little more use to others. I had the mother of that girl who was murdered in Paris not long ago round to see me the other day, and I think she felt that my loss of my son (though in much less awful circumstances) drew us near. I was deeply impressed and touched by her courage and faith.

You are having a wonderful time about your book, and I *do* congratulate you. I am hoping to get some copies of the Nursery School one to give as Christmas presents. You ask about my children's story. I am getting rather thrilled with writing it – next week I am going to look up some early Parliamentary reports on 'Climbing Boys'. It is about a little chimneysweep. As to the age it is meant for, I don't quite know, but an intelligent great niece aged fifteen, who has been staying with me, said it was the sort of book she could have enjoyed when she was seven, enjoyed much more at twelve, could read with pleasure at her present age, and go on reading all her life – and this pleased me. About *She for God* – and now I am coming to my request, but let me say at once that I am only making it feeling that after twenty years of our pen friendship I feel sure that you will feel perfectly free to refuse it, and I shall completely understand. If you remember when I was trying to get Victorian Wives published I asked if you would write a short introduction, and you tentatively agreed, but we were both glad when my present publishers said they thought the book didn't need this. This time however they think that this is the kind of book that wants a *short* (very short possibly) foreword from someone trustworthy just to say it is *a sane and sensible book* – the subject being rather controversial. They thought that your word would carry a lot of weight, as you are known to be someone who takes religion seriously, but are not a theologian.

If you could write even a paragraph or two I think that would be all that was necessary, though, of course, there would be no limitations either way, but I know how busy you are, and this is my main hesitation in asking you, but you need not read the whole book – you'd get its measure from a few chapters! If you *should* agree, my publishers would send you a copy at once as the date-line would be the end of January. Now let me say again I only *can* ask this emphasising that I wouldn't do it if I didn't feel sure that *you* won't mind me asking, and that you will know that *I* shan't mind you refusing.

I hope your work for the Churchill Trust Travelling Fellowships is over now. It sounds most exacting, though interesting. (Oh dear – I feel pretty awful even suggesting any addition to the requests you must get, but it wouldn't take as long as writing one of your lovely letters.)

I am so glad you and your husband enjoyed America so much and glad to hear more about your niece Sally and her work. Did I mention that my granddaughter Kate has begun a job with my publishers and is loving it, they tell me she is a treasure. Meanwhile my grandson is doing all sorts of exciting things musically.

I too have associated Emily Dickinson with Emily Brontë, and I think both have something also in common with Stevie Smith, though she, of course, can be exquisitely funny. They are all three very good poets and sad people – or perhaps sad isn't the right word.

Although I like women very much, I am rather glad, having written three books about them running, to be now writing one where all the main characters are men and boys.

With my love and gratitude as always

K.M.

28 December   *Riverside House*

My dear J.G.,

I am so *very* pleased and grateful and apologetic – all in one. My apologies are because I know how busy you are, and because you'll have to read this tiresome book of mine. I don't call it tiresome in false humility, but because it is not what I would like it to be, and I am so very conscious of all I have left out. In my Foreword (which, by the way, I think must now be called Preface instead of Foreword, which must be kept for anything *you* write, as being the more appropriate term) . . . Oh dear, this sentence has become out of hand, so I'll start again. In my Preface I think I say what I meant the book to do. If you haven't time to read all of it may I suggest the Introduction – the chapter on Julian of Norwich and Margery Kemp – one of the eighteenth-century chapters and one of the Victorian ones, and I suppose the last, which I found the most difficult, and is perhaps the most inadequate. (Also the short American one.) The only thing I hope is that the book tries to do something which I don't *think* has been done before. THANK YOU AGAIN.

I hope you had a lovely Christmas. Thank you for a gay card. I enjoyed mine because I felt so much weller than last year and able to cope. I had a nice young friend (twenty-two) staying with me. She is delicate – and has fads – eats practically nothing but cheese. I am completely out of cheese by now, so I am glad the shops are open again! We had a good family party, partly here and partly at my daughter's. We played a game of choosing for each other the *most* unwelcome but *possible* presents, mine was an abridged Jane Austen. I won't make this a long letter – to take up more of your time and make me feel even more guilty.

With much gratitude and love,

K.M.

29 December   Elm Park Gardens

My dear K.M.,

I've *enjoyed She for God*. I read some of it more carefully than the rest, but I found it *all* of *enormous* interest, and I've tried to say so in the enclosed little piece. The modern women are a bit too close to assess very clearly, but I'm grateful for the paragraphs about Mrs Eddy who for my money was heads and shoulders over the rest, because she has made practical the teachings of Jesus. (It's not easy, but it is, for me, a *true* science, and I'm so grateful for it all it has taught me.) I love Julian of Norwich and you've brought her to life. It is a very fascinating tapestry – I see it as an unfolding strip of portraits linked by one important thread – the Love of God as a practical way of living. I've lived with the book for two days, and when it is in book form I shall read it (more carefully) again.

I don't type, and I can only hope you are able to read my hand. If it is suitable, will you forward it to the publishers. If not, send it back with suggestions, and I'll try and improve it. I'm so interested in those who were humanly good, and those who were spiritually illuminated – 'transparencies for truth'. All good is of God, but some is less powerful than the good that opens one's eyes and mind and heart. Then it is *recognition*, isn't it?

Thank you for your letter. It came today. Do you know if the publishers want me to send back the manuscript? It can be done – I've got some fat envelopes. It's a photostat copy.

I'll get this in the post to you first thing in the morning.

Happy New Year. Congratulations on the book. And all wishes for it.

Love,

J.G.

30 December   *Riverside House*

My dear J.G.,

If only everyone in the country were like you what a nation we should be – talk about delivering the goods!

I am extraordinarily grateful and beholden to you, and enormously relieved that you like the book. It has made me so happy.

I couldn't wish for anything better than what you have written about it, because you have seen what I was trying to do. There is one sentence in your letter which sums up so clearly and beautifully what it is all about that I would very much like to incorporate it, slightly adapted, in your Foreword. You say in your letter: 'It is a very fascinating tapestry – I see it as an unfolding strip of portraits linked by one important thread – the Love of God as a practical way of living.' I should like to put this in the Foreword after the sentence, 'I found it both interesting and moving.' So it would continue thus: 'I see it as an unfolding tapestry linked by one important thread – the Love of God as a practical way of living' – It would then read straight on: 'The courage and vision revealed in these brief histories', etc., etc.

I don't want to trouble you to write to me again about this, but if I don't hear to the contrary I shall take it that I may insert that sentence from your letter.

Last night I had an unexpected pleasure – that of hearing you in the programme about Myra Hess, which I switched on because I have such grateful and happy memories of the National Gallery concerts. Then I heard you giving that lovely description of Walford Davies and you and others dancing to her playing Bach. I owe so much to Walford Davies, too, in the way of musical education and joy. Personally I never felt Myra Hess's professional personality to be austere – the warmth seemed to come through, so, though I never had the privilege of knowing her, I always connect her with a sort of glow.

Oh, how lucky I am – now I can't go to concerts much – to have the radio and the Third programmes.

I do hope you will have a rich and rewarding year ahead and be able to get on with volume two.

Quite by accident (or is it?) I have come across someone who is writing a thesis on 'climbing boys', and we are lunching together next week and I am going to pick her brains. Of course she is a proper historian, and I expect to be awed and apologetic, but it will be very interesting.

Goodbye and too many thanks to even express.

K.M.

P.S. I am pretty certain the publishers won't want the manuscript back – if they do they can jolly well send for it or at least send the postage! I have run out of notepaper and especially envelopes, and as the shops seem perpetually closed nowadays I am falling back on some Athenaeum ones which I found in my husband's bureau. Did he purloin them I wonder? Anyway it gives me pleasure to use them, because the Athenaeum is so snooty about women, never allowing them past their portals.

1978

My dear K.M.,

I'm *so* relieved that you like what I wrote, and I'm delighted that you should add the sentence from my letter. Good idea. Thank you. So glad, too, you enjoyed the Myra programme. She was a dear woman and, as you say, warm and glowing. I loved, too, her jaunty sailor roll of a walk.

I enjoyed your Athenaeum envelope and your pleasure in using it. Quite right, too. (Too many toos, no time to rewrite.)

Forgive hurried note. I'm about to go through the papers (with their references) for the thirty candidates we interview tomorrow for Churchill Fellowships. It's been a huge task, and God give me *wisdom* in selecting the right people.

All wishes for the book.

Love,

J.G.

I've begun on volume two. Slowly . . . Too many interruptions, but from the 12th January I plan to be firm. To Leeds on the 11th for a Best-Sellers of 1977 Luncheon by the *Yorkshire Post*. After that – to work.

My dear K.M.,

Thank you for your Easter wishes. And here are mine – a little late, but as Easter is really eternal it doesn't matter – I love it for being the fulfilment of the promise – The new-every-morning certainty of God's unalterable perfection shown to us by Jesus, who left with us the Christ-idea – spiritual man, never separated from His first Cause. (The Only!) It is the sense of inseparability that I find, increasingly, so nourishing and comforting. The teaching of God as Personal has never made sense to me; it's such a *pitiful* concept and so unreliable. But God as Love, Life, Truth and all that is Good – that makes practical sense – anyway to me.

No time to write at length, because in an hour we are off to Virginia Thesiger's 'Attic' in Herts, and I must load the soups, fruits, etc., that we are providing, as well as a good deal of wool-wear against the *narsty* west winds. Where is warmth? On April 13 we go on a Swan tour taking my brother and his wife from America, and I just hope some sun will have reached the Mediterranean by then. Last time it was mild with warm middays, but we always needed a jacket, just right for excursions and climbing up ruins. But it's hard to imagine ever being truly warm after this b . . . y winter. I shouldn't complain for we have heating and warm clothes, but I am never friendly to north-east or westerly winds, are you?

All I have to report is a lot of writing being done. Volume two is growing, but slowly, and I've just decided after three weeks of it to rewrite the chapter on my time with the Pilkington Committee. It was, for me, a fascinating and eye-opening experience but as it was so long ago (1960–2), and Annan has reported since, I feel it won't interest people, except, perhaps, as a greenhorn's-eye view of such a Committee's work. I liked all our members and enjoyed the whole thing – I'll have another think.

The proofs have come of another little Christmas book, a companion piece to *George – Don't do that* which Macmillan persuaded me to produce for September. It's twelve monologues, twelve lyrics and twelve *lovely* (detailed – not rough) sketches by John Ward, and is to be called '*Stately as a Galleon*' – a quote from my Olde Tyme Dance song – so we will spend the week-end on the galleys.

What else? Saw the Courbet and Rowlandsons and the

laser beams at Burlington House, and thought Rowland-son's draughtsmanship *beautiful* even when I deplored his loathsome faces. Courbet I found heavy, peasantly, and he seems to have been unfortunate in the plainness of his lady sitters! Bulk and brawn and surliness, for the most part. We were baffled by the beams – in awe – but couldn't get to grips with the science of it at all.

John Gielgud in Julian Mitchell's *Half Life* proved to be gripping for its performances and the talk – I didn't like *any* of the characters, and yet the play fascinated us both. We dined with Janet Baker and her nice husband to meet Gerald Moore and his very attractive nice wife, and the six of us had a most delightful evening. It was very relaxed, cosy, funny, *interesting* and I thought how good it was to see two giants in their own spheres as such natural, unspoilt and appreciative beings.

I could go on though there ain't much to tell. But I must pack and load the car and lock the windows (scaffolding up for a painting job).

So glad about the book. I look forward to seeing it.

Love – in haste and illegibly,

J.G.

10 *August*   *Riverside House*

My dear J.G.,

You ought to receive a copy of my book (at last) early next month. They have been *ages* longer than they said they would in bringing it out, but I fear that is typical of the times. I am sure you don't want to read it again, but perhaps you would like to give it to someone who might be interested. Thank you again, *very* much for your help and encouragement.

I think since I last wrote I've had an eightieth birthday. That was fun – I had a party for relatives and intimate friends. My grandson set a family ode to music which was sung to the accompaniment of cello, drum, recorders and whistle. My health was drunk with home-made wine made from my own vine, which is on the front of my house (no chance of grapes ripening this year!). The present I liked best was from an old pupil – it is a second edition of John Donne's poems, 1635 – beautifully printed. It arrived by post on the right morning, and I opened it at the following poem which I don't remember ever having read before:

'Who makes the Past, a patterne for next yeare
  Turns no new leaf, but still the same things reads,
Seene things he sees again, heard things doth heare,
  And makes his life but like a paire of beads.

'A Palace, when 'tis that, which it should be,
  Leaves growing, and stands such, or else decayes:
But he which dwels there, is not so; for he
  Strives to urge upward, and his fortune raise;

'So had your body'her morning, hath her noone,
  And shall not better; her next change is night:
But her faire large guest, to whom Sun and Moone
  Are sparkes, and short liv'd, claimes another right.

'The noble Soule by age growes lustier,
  Her appetite, and her digestion mend;
We must not sterve, nor hope to pamper her
  With womens milke, and pappe, unto the end.'

I think that was a good eightieth birthday greetings – don't you? As a birthday treat I went with my daughter to the Blake exhibition. I can't imagine anything more exciting and comforting. I thought I might have missed my husband, and all my other loved companions who have gone, on such an anniversary, but I felt them with me in a way impossible to describe or understand.

This is too much about myself. I do so hope you are well and that, as usual, you are enriching and being enriched.

I am so glad 'Face the Music' has come back again, I haven't missed one yet, though I recently went to sleep during the second one. I had travelled back from Winchester by train that day, and the horse showjumping trials went on far beyond its scheduled time, which made your programme late for me, but I was determined to see it. Why does sport always take priority over everything? I *do* enjoy 'Face the Music'. I'm better than you at opera, though that's not saying much!

How is volume two of your book going?

My daughter is designing a Shakespearean Exhibition at Oxford next year. But at present she is busy producing *King Lear* with our village players. This is coming off in November and promises to be an interesting experiment. The village gasped at the idea at first, but have now got keen. She has talked to them about the play and infused them with enthusiasm. 'Kent' said to her – 'I've never read a word of Shakespeare before, nor bothered to look at him on T.V. I never thought he had anything to do with me – but he's knocked me over, he's terrific!' The 'Lear' is a very good comic actor who has taken the lead in a good many earlier village productions, and he always longed to do a serious part. I haven't been to rehearsal yet, but I've heard he's going to be good. 'Cordelia' is only fourteen – but is moving, and her youth somehow seems to convey the emotion more purely (without the distraction perhaps of personal experience it can 'come through' better – I've often been surprised how effective children are acting Shakespeare). The latest recruit is a gipsy!

My daughter and son-in-law do a lot of work with gipsies, and they are in and out of their home at all hours. One evening Jane found two waiting for her, and she thought, 'I wish I could have Araminta in the background in the storm scene,* and it would be so good to integrate her with the village.' So she told them the story of *Lear* (gipsies love stories). Then she read them the bit about Cordelia's death, and they were deeply moved – Araminta said, 'Yes – that's just how I felt when Rachel (her little girl) died – "Never, never, never, never." ' She went on to talk of her own mother's death: 'Before, I danced through life, but after my mother died there was no more butter on my bread, and no more dancing, and the sorrows of the wandering people came upon me.'

* In the end this was found to be impracticable.

You will be tired of reading this long letter, and I wonder where you are and what you are doing. May and June I spent lecturing on Chaucer and Spenser, and *with* my music lecturer on

Keats	Wordsworth	Thomson, Gray and Cowper
Schubert	Beethoven	Vivaldi, Haydn

Coleridge

Brahms   He did the music, of course.

Proceeds for Amnesty International. Then I had to do a long article for my old college's centenary magazine, which I found difficult and have done badly – so the summer, if you can call it so, has flown. I've not been away, except for short visits, but hope to have a week in Derbyshire in October.

If I've told you any of this before I apologise – I can't remember when I last wrote, but I *feel* it was long ago.

I'm reading the new life of Dr Johnson. Like most American biographies it omits nothing, but, being Dr Johnson, I don't mind. I think he was the wisest and most compassionate of men. Did you by any chance hear St Mark at the Mermaid? No time to discuss it now, but *I* thought it wonderful.

I could go on and on, but *mustn't*.

Much love and good wishes as ever,

K.M.

Writing bad, because my cat insists on being my desk and will wriggle.

15 August   *Elm Park Gardens*

My dear K.M.,

As always it was good to see your fist on the envelope and better still to read the content. Thank you. I loved hearing about the celebrations. I look foward to receiving your book. Thank you. I didn't know the Donne. It's very pleasing, isn't it? I am more and more interested in the changelessness of all that is good and true, and coming to see that the only change is the position from which we see – and understand. I love the certainty and ever fixed star of Love, for instance. Its many aspects reveal themselves as we grow a little.

The repeats of 'Face the Music' are only seen in the South of England, and only eight of them will be shown, but we are told a new series is to be made in or around April, so that's a nice thought. So glad you enjoy it. I do too.

You ask how volume two is going. Answer – creeping, but more steadily of late. I had to put it aside *so* much this spring-summer. We had a glorious two weeks Swan-touring Greece and Asia Minor on a legacy left by my Virginian grandpa, who died in 1918 and entrusted it, and eventually it matured and was distributed, and my dollop enabled us to bring my brother and his wife over from America, and take them with us. Weather poor – chilly – wet with some startlingly lovely days, and the most incredible wild flowers carpeting the land everywhere we went. Then ten days in Yorkshire-Cumbria. Then a week at Aldeburgh. Then in July ten days in Scotland doing talks to aid 'good causes' for two of my sisters-in-law, one near Stranraer and the other near Oban. Don't mention the weather . . . But the people were dear, and we liked being with them. So it is only since about mid-July that I have written, and with what I had already done earlier I am now within sight of a possible finish. It is a more difficult book to do than *Joyce Grenfell Requests the Pleasure* because, as I think I said to you earlier, there is no story-line, fewer climaxes and many less 'first times'. The last twenty-five years have been more enjoyable to me because more deeply experienced. I've become a *little* wiser – learned to discard more and relish with greater appreciation. The 'first times' are now more in the way of recognitions. And I do like that feeling. It is very confirming of my belief in eternity.

We are curiously idle about going to see exhibitions and, now, theatres, and we missed the Blake. The *Lear* production is fascinating. She has great courage, your daughter. It is a play I no longer want to go to again. I can't bear the horrors. The dialogue with Araminta, the gipsy, is altogether splendid. It should be a truly fascinating production. You must tell me about it, please, when it happens.

Your lectures with music sound good. So glad you are doing such things. The talks I did are a sort of carry on from the illustrated autobiographical pieces I produced for the English-Speaking Union dinners in America last autumn. It's a form of performing, but from behind a desk, and curiously enough it *works*. But I don't want to do too much of it. It's quite a chore preparing and then doing, and I always have to rethink it for each specific occasion and I'd rather be writing. I wonder if you have read the George Lyttelton-Rupert Hart-Davis letters (Murray)? I think you might find them interesting – the exchanges of two very literate and amusing men. They started when George was seventy-five and retired, Rupert about forty-eight (I think) and in the full spate of his life as a publisher. They were both Etonians, both cricketers, erudite and articulate. It *is* about an elite society, but none the less it is of enormous interest to read such civilised, albeit conventional, well-read outpourings. Recommended.

Did I not go to hear Alec McCowen 'do' St Mark! A revelation. It was so moving, so natural and so beautifully done. I loved the way he allowed the miracles to appear, as doubtless they did, as the *natural* outcome of all Jesus knew as the Christ. Yes, I was enormously moved and held and encouraged by the performance, and the way Alec *displayed* the whole gospel so clearly. I'd forgotten – if I ever knew – that there were two feedings of multitudes.

You apologised for your writing and your cat's interference. I have no such excuse. I just write too much, too fast, and on my knee. It was very good to hear from you. We are now here for the rest of the year, but in February Reggie is taking me on our Golden Wedding Year outing up the Nile – with Swan.

Love,

J.G.

(and, *what* a lovely October it is being!)

Dear J.G.,

I am *so* glad you approve of the look of the book. I have discovered misprints which worry me a bit, but I suppose this isn't too bad these days. *The Times* is really dreadful sometimes.

It is good news about your own book. I agree about re-writing. Yes – I am half-way through my children's book about a little chimneysweep, but it goes on by fits and starts, as I find it needs quite a lot of research, and this I find difficult to fit in nowadays. But I *do* like to have some writing always on hand. I am pleased that the long and difficult article I undertook for the centenary of my old college has met with approval.

Since I last wrote I have lost yet another old and very dear friend – an Oxford contemporary. She lived within reach, and I was with her shortly before her death – which, though it came suddenly, was not altogether unexpected. We shared many a memory and joy – a passion for the Sussex Downs, for instance, and for Dr Johnson – we were reading his new life together on my last visit. It is Dr Johnson who says: 'The friends which merit or usefulness can procure us are not able to supply the place of old acquaintance with whom the days of youth may be retraced and those images revived which gave the earliest delight.' And this is one of the inescapable truths which one has to accept. It is the 'Do you remember?' which one misses so much, but there are discovery and joys in new relationships too which go on and on. By the way, our pen friendship must reach back now to about twenty-five to thirty years?

I am glad the Churchill Fellowship job looks as though it will be rewarding and interesting and not too arduous this year.

I have devoted some energy and funds to Amnesty International for some time past, and especially this last year, when we have formed a local group and adopted two prisoners of conscience. But I am worried that headquarters have recently appointed an avowed communist member (Australian) to the important post of Research Head (which means he is responsible for choosing the prisoners to be aided). I am sure he is a good man, but I think it a pity for an avowed non-political group, whose usefulness depends on exactly this neutrality, to choose a member of any *pronounced* political party to fill a prominent public position. Amnesty International has already come under criticism for communist sympathies (unjustly, I think, but none the less these criticisms are significant). I am afraid it shows a certain lack of judgement at Headquarters. Eric Baker, a very reliable Quaker, unhappily died fairly recently. He was one of Amnesty International's founders.

My daughter is very busy with her production of *King Lear* in the village at the end of November. I could write a novel (or try to!) about it all.

No more now, and this is not meant to have an answer, but only to acknowledge yours and to thank you again *so* much for your very nice foreword to the book. I'm rather anxious about reviews, as I see too clearly my defects. Of course, use anything you like from *The Spirit of Tolerance* – I'm only too pleased.

Love,

K.M.

15 December *Riverside House*

Dear J.G.,

Thank you so much for your card and the lovely little poem, which I like so much I have copied it out on some of my Christmas cards for friends. I am so glad to hear the good news about your book. Mine has had some very good reviews – one in a paper called *The Christian Herald* (from overseas) ended, 'Here is a book worth any sacrifice to obtain'!

It is a pity (for many reasons) that all the *Times* papers are out of circulation for reviews. (I wish the B.B.C. would give the book a lift. They were enthusiastic about *Cordial Relations*, and I should have thought this was the more important.)

Our village production of *King Lear* was an enormous success – far beyond our expectations. It really was very moving and beautiful – played to full houses and brought so many together in a lovely way – learned and unlearned, rich and poor, old and young.

How lovely about your Nile trip next year. I rejoice with you for your fifty years. I had fifty years all but one month, but such joy to look back upon.

Love and *all* good wishes and always gratitude.

K.M.

One other nice bit from review: 'She never writes at the top of her voice.'

I hope I haven't sent you this Samuel Palmer before.

1979

My dear J.G.,

I can't remember when you are going abroad again, but perhaps this will just catch you. I can't lay my hand on your last letter – I have had a spate of losing things lately, but they must turn up in the end. I *do* remember, however, that you are having a special and wonderful trip up the Nile as a wedding celebration, and I send you my congratulations and good wishes for it. My book is doing pretty well in its quiet way – it misses the *Times* papers' reviews sadly but has had some very good ones elsewhere except in the *Church Times*, which was catty, but I feel better about it since I've heard that this particular reviewer is catty about everyone. I enclose a copy of one review in case it interested you. It pleased me particularly, because it is by a Catholic, and yet is so fair to the book and so well written.

I shall be very glad when this winter is over – much hardship for many.

My love always.

K.M.

I enjoyed your remarks on Heaven in 'Woman's Hour' lately. Thank you for them. How's the book going?

My dear K.M.,

What a *lovely* review – I return it with thanks. He did it beautifully. And I'm so glad it is being enjoyed, and I'm sure it will go on being enjoyed. Hooray.

The Nile was *very* interesting. When I say I don't want to do that tour again, it doesn't mean we didn't enjoy it to the *full*. It was *totally fascinating*, and the sun shone all the time except for the day it rained in Cairo and surprised *everyone*, creating mud and mess and revealing the general dirt of that unlovely city. I think it was because I found it so hard to 'relate' (U.S. term) to the ancient Egyptians, who believed such *nonsense*, and who were so cruel and elitist and super-stitious and unlovable. But the sheer scale of their temples and tombs and the feats of shifting great blocks of granite from A to B in remote places is so astonishing that you can't help being impressed – but not touched, or very rarely. Occasionally a bunch of dried-up flowers in a tomb suggests that someone once felt something . . .

The boat on which we lived for two weeks was comfort-able and quiet – no radio, telly, newspapers or the roar of aeroplanes. Just the cries of children on the banks, and the barking of their dogs disturbed the smooth passage up that great river. A yellow sandstone escarpment rose up in the middle distance to the east for most of the way, but along the very edges, sometimes as deeply as two miles, was the green lushness of irrigated silt – green as Ireland. Sailing feluccas passed – or we passed them – and we saw life being led in villages and farms and in towns as we moved silently by them. Primitive, much of it and very dirty. They use the river in every conceivable way and then drink it – and survive. It *doesn't* smell, thanks be! And often it is bright blue reflecting the cloudless skies. Cool overall weather at dawn and dusk, and hot in the middle. Lovely. We saw wonderful places in remote corners. The boat tied up to a tree and a *sort* of gangplank flung from deck to bank across which we walked to land. Early starts – 6.30 – lectures 7.15 p.m. – and in between journeys by foot, donkey, a rare camel (not me), taxi, cab with horse, dray behind a tractor, or bus. Strenuous. Bed at 9.30 after delicious meal – cooking excellent. Agreeable fellow travellers, mostly American, but all interested and interesting.

In Pleasant Places is in proof, we are hard at it. August is the time. Thank you so much for sending the lovely review.

314

I share your pleasure. I'm sorry about your sadness. Today I do an address at a thanksgiving service for Joanna Scott-Moncrieff who once edited 'Woman's Hour'. 'Death is but an horizon'. I truly *do* feel this and thank God for the feeling.

Love, dear K.M.,

J.G. (Joyce)

13 August   *Riverside House*

My dear J.G.,

It is a long time since I wrote, but I have renewed contact with you lately through the new series of 'Face the Music' – which I enjoy so very much. This evening I fell deeply in love with Gerald Moore, and as, the same evening, I was also entranced by Sir Robert Mayer I really am in a state of happy bemusement. The house is very quiet – in fact I am alone with my cat for the first time for many weeks, but I am not feeling lonely because of all the rich personalities, for beside the two named above there was yourself, Robin Ray and Paul Jennings (who has made me laugh often and often). How very lucky to live in the age of T.V. and radio when one is eighty-one and can't get about as of yore. They may be bad for the young, but they certainly are a boon for the old.

How does your book go? Is it coming out in time for Christmas?

My *She for God* continues to get nice reviews and to sell fairly steadily, and I have hopes of a paperback from it. Meanwhile I have finished my children's story about 'climbing boys', sent it off to Patrick Hardy of Kestrel children's books and am waiting in some trepidation to hear from him. Now, because I get miserable if I am not writing, I have started a mad book which I am finding amusing to write, but I don't know whether anyone will find it amusing to read, though my family are very kind about it. It is called *Mum's the Word*, and is on the theme that mothers in literature have a poor deal compared with fathers, most of them being killed off before the story starts and never

315

mentioned. I am doing a series of 'might have beens' had they lived and my present list of characters are as follows – Prospero's wife, the Duchess of Milan, Queen Lear, Mistress Polonius, Mrs Woodhouse, Little Nell, her grandmother and Mrs Copperfield's ghost. I don't know whether I can bring it off, but it is fun to do.

I've also managed some lectures this summer in aid of Amnesty.

The grandchildren are all flourishing in their various ways and are very dear, and my daughter as usual has many absorbing brave and precarious irons in the fire. My great-niece, living with me for two years (one school year more) continues to educate me in the ways of contemporary youth (she is much more representative than my grandchildren). How is *your* niece – the one who was doing work with the down and outs?

This letter has been all about myself and rather trivial things, but of course there is everything else as well. Too much to talk about and so much goodwill, but such a complication of living everywhere. Things seem to get too involved for the individual to cope with, and yet I feel that hope lies with the individual more and more, a paradox, but all life seems sometimes to be based on paradox – the marriage of Heaven and Hell. Have you read James Morris's *Farewell the Trumpets*? A really good, fair and well-written account of the decline and fall of the British Empire (covering just about the span of my life). I am also reading Hans Kung *On Being a Christian* for the second time, and Bate's splendid Life of Dr Johnson – *what* a wonderful man!

Now, in ten minutes' time lovely Mozart. My cat makes rather a wobbly and lumpy writing-desk, so I hope you can read this, and I hope you are well, dear J.G. Perhaps having a lovely holiday somewhere? I dart about for short visits here and there, and may go to Bruges (which I know), taking a niece there at the end of September. Do you know a novel by Stella Gibbons about Bruges – rather different from her other books? I can't remember the name, alas, don't possess the book.

Love always, and thanks for 'Face the Music'. K.M.

My dear K.M.,

Only yesterday I signed a copy of my new book that will be posted to you in the next day or so and comes with love and appreciation for our long pen friendship. And now your pleasing letter. Thank you so much for writing. I'm so glad you are working on the *Mum's the Word* – it's a good idea. All wishes for the sweep, too. I like picturing you writing *on* the cat.

It has been a busy year for us. I think I told you we went up the Nile in February. It was full of interest. But I am not drawn to that phase of history, and don't feel the need to go again, even though the first time was *so* rewarding. In the spring we went to Yorkshire (Rupert Hart-Davis) and on to Cumberland and back via Pembrokeshire and Reggie's newly-widowed half-sister. We went to Skomer Island and saw puffins. *Did* I write all this before? It was a good holiday – the island day was blue and calm and the place carpeted with bluebells, red and white (sea) campion and some late primroses. And puffin appeared in great numbers out of rabbit-hole nests and bobbing in the sea. The Aldeburgh Festival in June for five crowded days was lovely as usual. After that I went to five cities in six days to meet booksellers and tell them about *In Pleasant Places* for their Christmas stock. I turned into a travelling sales-person and was part of a 'show' set up by Macmillan to promote their special wares. Marina Warner, thirty-two, granddaughter of cricketing Plum, has done a book on Queen Victoria's water-colours and drawings. She had access to the archives and unearthed about fifty volumes – uncatalogued – and has made a revelationary book about them that endears one more and more to the Queen. There was also a T.V. cassette interview with Lord Mountbatten talking about his book of photographs with autobiographical text. It was hard work, but interesting, to meet so many agreeable book men. Bristol produced the most interesting and the biggest crowd. They came from as far as Truro.

I've been taping 'Face the Music' on and off all summer.

One more to do. (I'm on seven out of thirteen programmes.)
And I've had fun choosing gramophone records for six
latish night programmes for Radio 4 starting 11 September
at 10.30–11 p.m., with some chat in between about what
I've chosen. *Very* mixed bag – classics, 'jazz', speech –
serious, comedy. I also did a review of the *Letters* of Ruth
Draper (Hamish Hamilton) on Kaleidoscope last week. *Do*
read them. I thought I knew her well. She was *always* part of
my life and close to my father with whom she shared first
cousins. But they were not related. But I didn't *know her at
all*!

In Pleasant Places comes out on 30 August, and I sign at
Truslove's in Sloane Street on that day. I do hope you will
like the book. It was more difficult to write, but in a way
more enjoyable – for as everything is more precious and
deeper as one becomes more selective and brings to it more
experience and understanding.

I've got a heavy programme of luncheons and signings all
through September–October and in November we go to
Australia, and I do a lot more there. And spend Christmas
in Sydney with dear friends who live on the harbour (see the
book).

I value our correspondence. Thank you for it.

At the moment I'm trying to write a review of volume two
of the letters between George Lyttelton and Rupert Hart-
Davis. *Very* enjoyable they are too. Read them when they
come out – October I think. The review is for *Books and
Bookmen*.

This brings love and wishes,

J.G.

You ask about Sally, my niece. She spent six weeks in
Greece this summer and is now nannying to earn her keep.
(She has a child-care degree from her American college.)
She had an excess of sordidity – if there is such a word – at
the Battered Wives Centre, and two and a half years was
plenty. She doesn't know what will come next, but may
return to the United States – reluctantly. She *likes* it here.

My *dear* K.M.,

Your letter was *so* generous, and it has given me a great deal of pleasure. So have the pictures. Thank you very much for both. I can't tell you how pleased I am that the second book has given you some pleasure. I value your judgement. Thank you. And I like your looks!

I had three pleasant reviews in the daily press, and a stinker in the *Observer* on Sunday by Hilary Spurling, who it seems to me is given to bitterness, and who dismissed my book as bland . . . Nettled? Yes, because I don't consider writing out of appreciation for the good I have experienced through friends and life in general is bland. And I hoped some of the writing had 'edge'. The lady doesn't much like 'privilege' and is vindictive about those who've had it. See her notice of William Douglas-Home's book. But to be honest I am NOT really hurt by this notice, because I don't care for the values this critic holds. Had I admired her, I would mind a lot, but the general bitchiness of her criticisms does perhaps reveal lack of confidence? But I protest too much, and will shut up.

Thank you again for letting me see the photographs – herewith – but thank you even more for the letter and your comments. Made me *glow*.

We set off for Yorkshire on Tuesday where next day I do a *Yorkshire Post* Literary Lunch – my third in four years. Can I avoid repeating myself! The other speakers are high-powered historians – Elizabeth Longford and Mary Soames – and Ian Carmichael, comedian. Cleverly I have kept the notes of the last 'occasion' so I can avoid some repetition, but, as I plan to say, have only had one life.

We'll be up north for a further five days, for we move on to Loweswater, Cumberland, so I can do two informal talks with illustrations from my old repertoire in aid of, and in celebration of, the twentieth anniversary of Rosehill Theatre, Whitehaven.

Hope you enjoy the Ruth Draper letters.

At the moment I'm involved in trying to find a kind

helper to look after an eighty-eight-year-old aunt. We've already hired two and they have had to withdraw for legitimate reasons, but it is frustrating. *Otherwise all is very well*, thank you.

With love, *and* thank you.

J.G.

When you feel like it do send some of your new manuscript, and I'll love to read it. I may do it a bit slowly, because a lot is going on this and next month before we go to Australia in November.

But I *can* do it and would like to. Love,

J.G.

I like the look of your husband *so* much. And the twins. And the fiddler. And Katie, *and* you.

––––––––––––

Both my last letters to Joyce are missing. One was only a short note about the reviews of her book but, in writing the other I had a sudden impulse, after all these years, to send her two photographs of myself and my husband – together with one or two of the family. I had of course no idea whatever that she was ill, nor is there the slightest indication of this in her characteristically warm and spontaneous reply. I like to recall that almost the last words I had from her were 'All is very well, thank you.'